$27.49

D1272596

ACCOUNTING

How to Meet the Challenges of Relevance and Regulation

MODERN ACCOUNTING
PERSPECTIVES AND PRACTICE

Gary John Previts, Series Editor

ACCOUNTING

How to Meet the Challenges of Relevance and Regulation

Eugene H. Flegm

Deputy Assistant Comptroller
General Motors Corporation

Foreword by
Hector R. Anton

A RONALD PRESS PUBLICATION
JOHN WILEY & SONS
New York · Chichester · Brisbane · Toronto · Singapore

Copyright © 1984 by John Wiley & Sons, Inc.

All rights reserved. Published simultaneously in Canada.

Library of Congress Cataloging in Publication Data:

Flegm, Eugene H., 1929–
    Accounting: how to meet the challenges of relevance
and regulation.

    (Modern accounting perspectives and practices series)
    "A Ronald Press publication."
    Includes index.
    1. Accounting—Standards—United States. I. Title.
II. Series.
HF5616.U5F56   1984   657'.0218   83–12333

ISBN 0-471-09326-2

Printed in the United States of America

10 9 8 7 6 5 4 3 2

To Beatrice, my wife,
for understanding

FOREWORD

The past decade has been one of rapid development in the area of accounting and financial reporting. This development has paralleled a period of diverse and extremely exciting business activity in the United States and elsewhere. We have seen major merger booms, an energy crisis, world wide inflation and recessions, and marked changes in the financing patterns of corporations. The accounting profession itself has seen tremendous growth in size and responsibility, coupled with considerable public scrutiny and attention from congressional committees. Additionally, the decade has produced extensive litigation directed against both corporations and their auditors on matters of financial reporting and responsibility.

These factors and others have led to a formalization of accounting and financial reporting rules unprecedented in this or any other country, beginning with the attempts of the Accounting Principles Board (APB) to control the business accounting excesses of the "go-go" years—the late 1960s. The part-time APB was not equal to the task and the independent and more broadly based Financial Accounting Standards Board (FASB) resulted. The decade of the FASB has been characterized by a decided shift in emphasis in external reporting to providing data primarily for decision making by present or potential equity shareholders. This emphasis, while widely accepted, especially by practicing public accountants and academics, has had some pernicious effects. It is fair to state that at least until the late 1970s and perhaps even to the present, financial reporting has been dominated by those groups. The literature of the time—authoritative, professional, and popular—has been dominated by their views and concerns.

The corporate controller's view of accounting as primarily a discipline necessary to operate the business and to report on the management's stewardship and progress has tended to be neglected and largely untold. Beginning in early 1977, the Committee on Corporate Reporting (CCR) of the Financial Executives Institute (FEI) began to take a more active role. The impact of CCR, and the FEI more generally on accounting principles, has been strong, but perhaps even more important has been the influence of these and other business organizations as a political force. This influence has been felt in the operation of the FASB, its agenda, and its *modus operandi*. The FASB is paying more attention to non-accounting considerations such as "economic reality," "cost/benefit," and potential "legislative oversight." Whether these results were intended or not, socio-political overtones have been injected into accounting standards setting.

A strong professionally-developed and well-reasoned voice for a corporate view of modern needs for accounting and reporting standards, however, has been lacking. This book by Eugene Flegm of General Motors ably presents that view. He states the issues in a clear and forthright manner, and then develops in considerable detail the institutional and conceptual history of accounting for both management uses and for financial reporting. The background demonstrates the common roots of managerial and financial accounting and sets the stage for Flegm's espousal of alternative objectives and criteria for financial reporting standards. These are developed in a logical and consistent manner and make a powerful argument to the standards setters and all who are concerned with crucially important corporate financial reporting and its impact on the business economy.

HECTOR R. ANTON

Director, The Vincent C. Ross
Institute of Accounting Research
New York University

PREFACE

When I was asked if I would write a book about accounting, I was surprised. Although I considered myself an activist in the accounting field—serving on committees of the Financial Executives Institute, the American Institute of Certified Public Accountants, the American Accounting Association, the National Association of Accountants, and the National Advisory Forum of Beta Alpha Psi—and regularly spoke at universities, seminars, and hearings of the Financial Accounting Standards Board, I had never thought of actually writing a book.

However, as I discussed the prospect with Dick Lynch of John Wiley & Sons, citing the disturbing trends that I perceived in the accounting field, the outline of a book began to crystallize. I have been practicing accounting for over 30 years, first as a bookkeeper for a small manufacturing company, then as a principal (manager) with an international public accounting firm, and finally in my present position in charge of financial accounting and reporting for one of the largest corporations in the world. During the past few years I have noted the rapid increase in the growth of several trends that I believe could threaten the existence of accounting as a profession.

The first of these trends is the proliferation of rule-making by the standards-setters (both the FASB and the SEC) coupled with their preoccupation with uniformity in accounting at all costs. This tendency is reflected in the very education of accountants. Whereas students were once taught the subjectivity of accounting and given general concepts, today's intermediate textbook covers some 1300 pages (versus 400 of 20 years ago) and is filled with specific rules. Furthermore, these rules of the standards-setters are taught as unquestioned truths. The result is a growing specialization of accountants as interpreters of rules rather than their former role of generalists in business administration. The final disturbing development in accounting is the shift away from a cost-based measurement system to one based on a measurement of values. Many accountants appear to have developed a feeling of inferiority about their field as they seem intent on making it a branch of economics. I have also noted that much of the impetus for these trends comes from those in public accounting and academia rather than from those of us who actually practice applied accounting every day in the business world.

In my speeches given around the country, in which I have included references to the preceding trends, I have noted a broad-based feeling of concern from others who practice and teach accounting, in public and private industry. In this book then I have tried to write about the accounting field I have known and practiced for over 30 years, the hazards I believe our profession faces, and how we might resolve them.

The style of the book is the one that I am most familiar with—that of a speaker or lecturer. I have written the book as though I were addressing a graduate class in a business school that may or may not have any specific background in accounting. However, I would hope that others who use financial data prepared by accountants or who regulate the preparation of such data will also gain a better perspective of what the data represent and how they can be used from reading this book.

In writing a book of this kind, the assistance and comments of friends and associates from business, academia, and public accounting are both valued and needed. I am grateful to T. A. Murphy and R. B. Smith, who have encouraged me over the years to improve the communication between accountants and non-accountants and to seek a balance between reasonable financial reporting and excessive and needless regulation. I am also grateful for the perceptive comments of T. A. Murphy, Hector R. Anton, Duane Borst, H. Thomas Johnson, Neill Mahoney, and George W. McCagg. Finally, I want to thank Marge E. Fallon and Cammy Krist, who shared the typing of the various drafts, patiently interpreting my longhand, and Mary Jo Stockton and my wife, Beatrice, who helped in the typing and prepared the index.

E. H. FLEGM

Troy, Michigan
July 1983

CONTENTS

4   THE RISE OF STANDARDS SETTERS   61

one

THE CHALLENGES ACCOUNTING FACES

A PROFESSION IN JEOPARDY

The accounting profession* is a profession in jeopardy. It faces two major challenges. The first challenge is the impact of inflation on the traditional financial data prepared by the accounting profession and the perceived loss of relevancy of these data to the fields of economics and finance. The second challenge is government regulation of the accounting standard-setting process as well as full control of the auditing processes.

The seriousness of these challenges can best be gauged by the words of the former chairman of the Securities and Exchange Commission Harold M. Williams, in a speech given at the Accounting Research Center of Northwestern University, April 23, 1980:

> I must continue to remind the accounting profession that the credibility of financial reporting, and its effect on the depth and the efficient allocation of the Nation's capital resources, *is a matter too critical to the public welfare* [emphasis added] to be ignored or settle for halfway measures. Therefore, one should expect that *if the profession does not continue to expeditiously and adequately address the challenges before it, increased governmental intervention may well be invoked.* [emphasis added]

Although Mr. Williams's successor, Mr. John F. Shad, has adopted a less formidable stance, the respite may be brief for we must keep in mind that the adequacy of the profession's response will be judged by the regulators, that is,

---

*In using the term "profession" throughout this book, I have broadened it to include all persons with a degree in accounting, practicing accounting in industry or government, or teachers or public accountants. Those practicing public accountancy comprise the field of accounting ordinarily identified as the "profession."

the Securities and Exchange Commission (SEC) and Congress. However, the very seriousness of the challenges also means that the profession has the opportunity to expand its scope beyond the traditional financial statements by providing relevant, supplementary financial data that can be used in conjunction with the traditional data to aid in the efficient allocation of our nation's capital resources.

In this book, then, we will explore how the accounting profession has reached the critical state in which it finds itself and how the challenges before it might be met through better understanding and communication among its members and the users of the data supplied by the profession. Thus, we will be considering the roles of the members of the profession in their various fields: the preparers of the financial data in managerial accounting; the teachers of accounting in academia; the auditors of the data in internal and public auditing; and the regulators of accounting in the government and with the Financial Accounting Standards Board and the Auditing Standards Board; and the needs of the users of financial data whether they be financial analysts, creditors, investors, or business managers. Let us now turn to the recent background that led to the present state of affairs.

THE HISTORICAL CONTEXT OF THE PRESENT CRISIS

Material Wealth and Social Frustration

It is axiomatic that in the evolution of modern industrial society each generation accepts as a "natural right" the accomplishments of the preceding generation and, accordingly, raises its goals and expectations even higher. This trait has led to greater and greater progress—at least in the materialistic sense—since the Industrial Revolution began in Great Britain in the late eighteenth century. The possibility of serious limits to industrial growth has only emerged in the past decade, as the combination of the increase in population and energy needs of an industrialized society, coupled with the interdependence of the developed and the less-developed countries, has placed great stresses on the world's economy.

One of the paradoxes of the Industrial Revolution has been that with the increase in the quantitative standard of living has become a frustrating lack of improvement and even deterioration in the qualitative aspects of living. A nation that can place men on the moon should be able to develop plans that would eliminate poverty, injustice, and pain, so the thinking goes.

The Public Debate Over Corporate Social Responsibility

Against this background, the modern corporation as a value-neutral organization whose only responsibility was to earn a profit for its owners came into question. With the publication, in 1962, of Rachel Carson's *The Silent Spring*,[1] people became aware of the hazards of the unplanned use of chemicals in our society, and the consumerism movement was born. Although government had regulated corporations for many decades prior to 1962, most notably during the administrations of Theodore Roosevelt and Franklin Roosevelt, the year following *The Silent Spring* brought an almost revolutionary change in the attitude of the public as to the role of the corporation. Thus, while Milton Friedman could write, as recently as 1970, that "in a free-enterprise, private property system, a corporate executive is an employee of the owners of the business. He has direct responsibility to his employers. That responsibility is to conduct the business in accordance with their desires, which generally will be to make as much money as possible while conforming to the basic rules of the society."[2] Few managers today believe that their social responsibility does not extend further. Since 1962, we have seen such concepts as the "quality of work life," equal opportunity for minorities and women, corporate "community citizenship," environmental protection, corporate political action, and corporate morality become part of the laws and perceptions governing companies operating in the United States.

Neil H. Jacoby's book *Corporate Power and Social Responsibility*[3] contains an excellent analysis of these issues as well as a defense of the corporate structure. Another excellent book on this subject is Daniel Bell's *The Coming Post-Industrial Society*. Bell sums up the problem in this way: "The heart of the matter is the question of the nature of the corporation. Is the corporation primarily an instrument of 'owners'—legally the stockolders—or is it an autonomous enterprise which, despite its particular history, has become—or should become—an instrument for service to society in a system of pluralist powers?"[4]

THE PROFESSION ON THE DEFENSIVE

The present book, however, is not about corporate social responsibility per se but rather about the role of the accountant in a society debating these issues. Where has the accountant—public, industrial, or academic—been through all of this? Basically, trying to avoid getting caught in any crossfires. As we shall see, both the public auditing and the standard-setting sectors of the profes-

sion were almost preempted by the government in 1932, and slowly, inexo-
rably the pressure from the regulators has grown.

Then in the early 1970s, two seemingly unrelated events occurred which
led to the crisis the profession faces today—direct government regulation and
charges that accounting data lacked relevance. The two catalytic events were
the Watergate Affair and the 1973 Arab oil embargo which led to the 1500%
increase in the price of oil. Of the many consequences of Watergate, the one
which affected the accounting profession most directly was the Foreign
Corrupt Practices Act (FCPA), which grew out of the disclosures of questionable payments uncovered during the Watergate investigation. Of the
many consequences of the OPEC action of 1973 (and related moves since
then), the one that directly affected the accounting profession was the
inflationary effect. Strong inflationary pressures had already developed in the
United States following the 1965 acceleration of the Vietnam War without
any increases in income taxes. However, with the sudden increase in oil
prices, inflation became intolerable, and the relevancy of historical cost-
based accounting data was placed in serious doubt.

After Watergate and the Foreign Corrupt Practices Act

Although we will go into the FCPA in depth later in the book, let us consider
briefly the effect that the broad ramifications of this well-intentioned but
uninformed legislation have already had on the accounting profession.

One of the unexpected results of the Watergate investigation of the mid-
seventies was the revelation that many corporations had made questionable
and, in some cases, illegal payments to both United States and foreign
officials in an attempt to influence their decisions in such matters as the
awarding of contracts. The basic problem this revelation caused for the
accounting profession was that the Senators and Congressmen who drafted
and passed into law the Foreign Corrupt Practices Act of 1977 acted on the
assumption that the questionable pyaments had been facilitated by the lack
of specific legislation governing how a company should maintain its books of
account. Specifically, the report of the Securities and Exchange Commission
to the Senate Committee on Banking, Housing, and Urban Affairs analyzed
the problem of questionable payments as follows:

> The almost universal characteristic of the cases reviewed to date by the Com-
> mission has been the apparent frustration of our system of corporate account-
> ability *which has been designed* [emphasis added] to assure that there is a proper
> accounting of the use of corporate funds and that documents filed with the
> Commission and circulated to shareholders do not omit or misrepresent ma-

terial facts. Millions of dollars of funds have been inaccurately recorded in corporate books and records to facilitate the making of questionable payments.

Accordingly, the primary thrust of our actions has been to restore the efficacy of the system of corporate accountability and to encourage the boards of directors to exercise their authority to deal with the issue.[5]

The misunderstanding surrounding the FCPA, which we will explore in depth later, is typified by a statement made by Senator John Tower (R-Texas), a member of the Senate Banking committee, during the Senate debate on the bill, in which he said, "[He] would not expect this provision to establish a new accounting standard. Its purpose is to require that books and records are kept so that financial statements prepared in accordance with *generally accepted accounting principles* [emphasis added] can be derived from them."[6]

Of course, a new "standard" of accounting was established, with the result that the costs of the internal accounting operations of *all* public companies, as well as their audit fees, will almost certainly increase. In the years since the passage of the FCPA, we have had extensive in-depth evaluations of internal operations by many companies as evidenced by the seminars on this subject conducted by the Financial Executives Institute in 1979. At three such seminars (held in New York, Los Angeles, and Chicago), over 750 financial executives representing some 400 companies attended. In addition, most of the "Big Eight" public accounting firms now offer their own seminars and self-study manuals on this subject.

At the same time that the FCPA was being legislated, Congress was reviewing the effectiveness of the SEC in performing its oversight role with regard to the public accounting sector of the profession. In December 1976, the Subcommittee on Reports, Accounting, and Management of the Committee on Government Operations of the U.S. Senate published a study by its staff that was extremely critical of both the major public accounting firms and of the method by which accounting standards were established. The major recommendations of the staff included stronger federal control over the public accountant by requiring mandatory rotation of public auditors every few years, restoring the right of individuals to sue public auditors for negligence under the fraud provisions of the securities laws, quality reviews of public auditors by the government, and government establishment of standards for financial accounting, cost accounting, and auditing.[7] The subcommittee, headed by Senator Lee Metcalf (D-Montana) and later by Senator Thomas F. Eagleton (D-Missouri), held hearings in the spring of 1977 that found the public accountants on the defensive. At the same time, Congressman John Moss (D-Calif.) was preparing a House bill along the same lines as the recommendation on the Senate staff report.

As a result of this pressure, the American Institute of Certified Public Accountants (AICPA) instituted reforms creating the Division of SEC Practice Firms and a Division of Private Companies Practice Firms, as well as a Public Oversight Board. In the letter to its members that proposed the reorganization, Michael N. Chetkovich, then chairman of the board of the AICPA, said, "It appears evident that, if the profession does not take action on its own, legislation will be proposed to deal with areas where reform is perceived to be necessary—such as regulation of the profession and the setting of accounting and auditing standards."[8] The action of the AICPA forestalled any direct government action other than the FCPA, but the profession may have only bought time. In 1980, the SEC issued for comment a proposed regulation requiring a management report and an auditor's opinion on a company's internal accounting control. After receiving about 950 responses, which were overwhelmingly negative, the SEC suspended the proposal for three years pending further review and experience. The proposal was dropped from the SEC's agenda in 1982 but the SEC is maintaining an oversight role.

What will be the benefit of these changes? No one can say with any degree of certainty, but it seems doubtful that the benefits will outweigh the costs. Certainly, questionable payments of the type uncovered by the Watergate investigation should be prohibited. But legislation requiring proper accounting will not stop them. It seems almost naive to state that if a person wants to cheat, the fact that he has to falsify an accounting record will not really have much effect on his decision. So what have we accomplished with the FCPA? We have added costs for all the law-abiding companies who were already complying with the antibribery laws while failing to stop anyone who wants to make such payments. (In 1981, Senator John H. Chaffee [R-Rhode Island] made a determined effort to have the FCPA modified to eliminate its most unrealistic provisions but failed.)

The 1973 Oil Embargo and the Issue of Inflation-Adjusted Accounting

The second major event affecting the accounting profession—the 1973 OPEC oil embargo—has had a more subtle, yet penetrating, influence. For most of this century, the question of how the accounting profession should deal with the effect of changing prices (inflation) on financial data has been the subject of countless theoretical treatises and discussions, particularly by teachers and students of accounting. As far back as 1909, Henry Rand Hatfield discussed the current value concept in *Modern Accounting*.[9] Again and again after this, leading accounting theorists, such as William A. Paton, John B. Canning, Henry W. Sweeney, Kenneth MacNeal, Edgar D. Edwards, Phillip W. Bell, Maurice Moonitz, Robert T. Sprouse, and Raymond Chambers have advocated some type of measurement base other than the conventional historical cost model in order to include recognition of the effect of changing prices on financial data. However, in spite of this long history of theoretical analysis, historical cost, modified only by such concepts as the conservative "lower-of-cost-or-market" method, has remained the basic measurement base.

Origins of the Resistance to Inflation-Adjusted Accounting

Why has this reluctance to change the measurement base persisted? One factor is that modern accounting has deep roots in a pragmatic, transaction-based philosophy going back to Mesopotamia and the beginning of commerce and taxation. Clay tablets bearing notations in cuneiform and representing records of receipts and disbursements have been discovered in excavations of the ruins of the Sumerian civilization, dating from circa 3000 B.C. It seems apparent that as trade developed and flourished and as governments devised taxes on this trade, the need for keeping a record of the transactions followed.* Of course, these ancient tablets recorded the transactions of the time in monetary form. The hard, immutable logic of transactions expressed in monetary terms is the basis for the strong resistance of business to permit any change from the basic historical cost model.

Other strong factors weighing against a change to a value-based measurement model are the income tax laws coupled with the growth of the absentee-owner form of business. Although accounting is an ancient art, it was only with the Industrial Revolution and the subsequent development of capital-intensive industries and the absentee-owner corporate form of business that accounting came of age as a profession. For example, prior to the nineteenth century, the concept of "depreciation" was largely ignored and did not gain general application in the United States until a depreciation charge was specifically permitted as a deduction in computing taxable income in the first corporate federal income tax law inaugurated in 1909. This is an early example of the pragmatic link of accounting with the cash effect.

In addition to the foregoing, in the 1920s and 1930s the emphasis in accounting shifted from the balance sheet reporting to the owner-managers and creditors of "what we own" and "where we stand" to the income statement and the reporting of "what we've earned" (and, implicitly, "what we might be able to earn in the future") to absentee-owners (stockholders) and potential stockholders and creditors (investors). During this period evolved the concept of matching costs with related revenues, which finally crystallized

*For an interesting account on this historical subject, the reader should review Maurice S. Newman's *Historical Development of Early Accounting Concepts and Their Relation to Certain Economic Concepts*, vol. 1, Working Paper no. 11, Working Paper Series, The Academy of Accounting Historians, 1979.

in 1940 with the publication of *An Introduction to Corporate Accounting Standards.* [10] Although this monograph carried no formal authoritative stamp from the American Institute of Certified Public Accountants (then the American Institute of Accountants) or the Securities and Exchange Commission, who had been heavily involved in the discussion of accounting standards, the monograph's clarity, coherence, and pragmatic, sensible position led to its general acceptance by the managerial accountants. It was not until the Financial Accounting Standards Board published the Discussion Memorandum, *Conceptual Framework for Financial Accounting and Reporting: Elements of Financial Statements and Their Measurement,* in December 1976 that the matching concept based on historical cost and the income statement orientation espoused in the 1940 monograph were seriously challenged.

Why did this challenge arise? It seems apparent that something quite significant had occurred to shake the foundation upon which accounting had rested for so long. That unsettling event was the acceleration of inflation in the late 1960s as our nation tried to sustain simultaneously The Great Society and the Vietnam War without any compensating fiscal or monetary adjustments, such as increasing income taxes.

For 25 years—from 1940 to 1965—the inflation rate in the United States had averaged from 2 to 3% annually (Consumers' Price Index) except for a brief jump to 9% in 1948. Beginning in 1966, however, the inflation rate began to accelerate as our economy grew more and more unbalanced. The rate in 1972 reached a level considered at that time disturbing—6%. Then in October 1973, world politics delivered a hammer blow with which the industrialized nations, particularly the United States, have not yet learned to cope.

Our sophisticated economy had traditionally been built on cheap energy and, with the October 1973 Arab oil embargo, this era came to an end overnight, a fact we have been reluctant to accept. As world oil prices skyrocketed, the burden on our already struggling economy became too great, with the result that the inflation rate soared to above 12% in 1975. It fell off to "only" 6% in 1978 but came roaring back in 1979 to 18% and although it fell sharply in the early 1980s many consider the cost (unemployment at almost 11%) unacceptable. Furthermore, even a rate of from 4 to 6% is double that prevailing in the 1940–1965 period.

As we have found out, when inflation rises into even the low double-digit range, many traditional concepts are challenged: avoiding debt, thrift, conservatism, saving for the future—and the relevancy of the historical cost-based accounting model. All of the theories about current value, replacement cost, and general price level accounting, which were only the subject of classroom discussion for so many years, suddenly gain a new relevancy.

Questioning the Relevance of the Historical Cost Model

The SEC, led by John "Sandy" Burton, then chief accountant of the SEC, was the first to make a serious assault on the historical cost model with the publication, in 1976, of Accounting Series Release No. 190. This release required most major industrial companies in the United States to calculate the replacement cost of their productive fixed assets and inventories (unless the company had used the Last-in, First-out (LIFO) method of valuing inventories) and to publish these data in their Form 10-K as supplemental data separate from the basic financial statements.

This SEC action in 1976 was followed quickly by the FASB's publication of the Discussion Memorandum on the conceptual framework for accounting in which the primacy of the income statement and the relevancy of the historical cost model were placed in question. This discussion continues today under several different subprojects that we will explore in more depth in Chapter 7. Meanwhile, the SEC has maintained pressure on the accounting profession to improve the relevance of the financial data published by companies with particular emphasis on forward-looking data intended to improve the quality of the investment decision of the potential stockholder/creditor.

The question of the relevancy of the financial data, however, has moved beyond even the SEC and the accounting profession into the broader area of the nation's fiscal and monetary plans, particularly those regarding taxation and capital formation. Thus, one of the most crucial problems the accounting profession faces today is the question of whether the basic measurement base of accounting and financial reporting should be changed to reflect the full impact of inflation. This question brings into sharp focus the interrelationship of the three disciplines involved—economics, finance, and accounting.

Economics deals with meeting the physical needs (or perceived needs) of human beings—specifically, the system by which a group of people determines what goods and services should be produced, how they are produced, and to whom (or how) they are distributed. Finance deals with the funding of these activities and the management of the funds. Finally, accounting is the discipline by which all the preceding transactions (or proposed transactions) can be expressed in specific terms of a monetary unit of measurement and, thus, permits establishment of controls by which plans and budgets can be formulated, assets safeguarded, and performance measured. In short, accounting is the language through which the success or failure of economic and financial activities is communicated to all interested persons.

Certainly, one of the great attributes of present financial statements is that they are reasonably objective and reliable and, thus, the best basis for measuring current performance of managers by absentee-owers. In addition, it is not fair to assume that the accounting profession (and government for that matter) has failed entirely to recognize the impact of inflation on financial data. Accounting (and tax) methods, such as the LIFO method of valuing inventories and related costs of sales, the various methods of accelerated depreciation, and investment tax credits, all represent some recognition of the effect of rising prices on the ability of a company to maintain its profitability and, thus, its capital structure.

Nevertheless, double-digit inflation, coupled with the inability of manufacturing companies to price their products at a level sufficient to permit the expansion or even maintenance of their productive capacity, has placed a dramatic strain on our relatively free market system and the key role played by finance, that is, capital formation.

The problem is greatest in the capital intensive industries, of course, since for the most part service industries deal in the current cost/current price dollars of the current year and do not commit billions of today's dollars to be recovered over the next five to ten years.*

Thus, since accounting is still basically tied to the historical cost/nominal dollar base, we have the paradox of manufacturing companies reporting record stated dollar profits while profit margins plummet. We also have the situation where these "record" profits are described as "obscene" and the image of business diminishes in the public's eye.

This, then, is the problem the accounting profession has been struggling with for the past several years—should the traditional measurement base of accounting (historical cost/*nominal* dollar) be changed so that the dollars of profits today will be comparable in value to the dollars of profits earned over the years?

This debate naturally has reflected the view of the three disciplines involved. The economist has argued that the profits should be determined by measuring the discounted present value of a company's earning power while finance-oriented persons have argued for the publishing of data that would permit the prediction of future cash flows. However, many accountants, most notably those in business, joined by some teachers and public accountants, have argued against any drastic change in the basic accounting model. Generally, their position has been based on concern over the potential loss of

---

*In 1981 the government passed a major tax bill that drastically reduced the allowable depreciable lives of major capital assets, the so-called 10-5-3 bill. This bill permits buildings to be written off for federal income tax purposes in 10 years, machinery and equipment in 5 years, and cars and trucks in 3 years. The effect of this bill, coupled with the provision which permits the transfer of tax deductions between companies, will be to reduce the government's taxation of inflation-produced profits. The bill also represents a significant challenge to the useful life theory of depreciation presently applied in the accounting profession, but we will explore this in more depth later.

the objectivity the present model has, coupled with the high degree of subjectivity any value-based model would have.

The question that we will be exploring in this book then is, How can the accounting profession, which as I pointed out includes the managerial accountants who must prepare the data as well as teachers and public accountants, meet the broad, sophisticated needs of the users of accounting data, including management, investors, and creditors, as well as regulators—both consumer protection agencies and others in government who determine the nation's fiscal and monetary policies? For if the accounting profession cannot provide financial data that meets the challenges of high expectations, validity, relevancy, and objectivity, it will become an army of technicians filing detailed, specific reports with regulatory agencies pursuant to an ever rising tide of rules and regulations that will still not meet the need for objective relevant data.

REFERENCES

1. Rachel Carson, *The Silent Spring,* Houghton Mifflin, New York, 1962.
2. Milton Friedman, "The Social Responsibility of Business Is to Increase Its Profits," *N.Y. Times Magazine,* September 13, 1970.
3. Neil H. Jacoby, *Corporate Power and Social Responsibility,* Trustees of Columbia University, New York, 1973.
4. Daniel Bell, *The Coming Post-Industrial Society,* Basic Books, Inc., New York, 1973, p. 293.
5. *Report on Questionable and Illegal Corporate Payments and Practices,* Submitted by the Securities and Exchange Commission to the Senate Committee on Banking, Housing and Urban Affairs, May 12, 1976, pp. a, b.
6. *A Guide to the New Section 13(b)(2) Accounting Requirements of the Securities Exchange Act of 1934 (Section 102 of the Foreign Corrupt Practices Act of 1977),* p. 38. Copyright 1978 by the American Bar Association. All rights reserved. Reprinted with the permission of the American Bar Association and its Section on Corporation, Banking and Business Law.
7. *The Accounting Establishment,* A staff study prepared by the Subcommittee on Reports, Accounting, and Management of the Committee on Government Operations, U.S. Senate, U.S. Government Printing Office, Washington, D.C., December 1976, p. 20.
8. "Special Supplement," *The CPA Letter,* American Institute of Certified Public Accountants, New York, August, 1977.
9. Henry Rand Hatfield, *Modern Accounting,* D. Appleton & Co., New York, 1909.
10. W. A. Paton and A. C. Littleton, *An Introduction to Corporate Accounting Standards,* Monograph No. 3, American Accounting Association, Sarasota, Florida, 1940.

two

THE GROWTH OF ACCOUNTING

THE EARLY HISTORY

In seeking ways the accounting profession can deal with the challenges outlined in Chapter 1, we need to explore the origins of accounting and how its development led to the problems the profession faces today.

The Barter Economy

From its very early history, it becomes apparent that accounting is as old as civilization itself. When the Paleolithic hunter of Mesopotamia changed into the Neolithic farmer/villager about 8000 B.C., civilization began and with it occupational specialization and interdependence among the members of a community. Record keeping (the forerunner of today's accounting) was the result of an obvious need in an integrated society. Probably the first "accountants" were employed by the priests of Mesopotamia and Egypt. C. Bertil Nystromer, in his book *Four Thousand Years in the Office* portrays this need quite well:

The definition of accounting used throughout this book is "Accounting is the art of recording, classifying and summarizing in a significant manner and in terms of money, transactions and events which are, in part at least, of a financial character, and interpreting the results thereof . . . careful attention to the significant words, the art of recording, classifying and summarizing, will rule out an interpretation that no more is indicated than bookkeeping. The recording and classifying of data in account books constitute an accounting function, but so also and on a higher level do the summarizing and interpreting of such data in a significant manner, whether in reports to management, to stockholders, or to credit grantors, or in income tax returns, or in reports for renegotiation or other regulatory purposes." Accounting Terminology Bulletin No. 1 of the AICPA (August 1953).

13

Six or seven thousand years ago, when the ancient dwellers in the Nile Valley first combined to organize the artificial irrigation of their fields, a bailiff was appointed in every small village along the river to look after the irrigation canals. Each farmer had to pay him a certain quantity of grain and flax after every harvest. When the farmer had done so, a rude picture of a grain measure was drawn on the wall of his house, together with a number of lines indicating how many measures he had paid. This was the primitive form of receipt.[1]

Money and Single-Entry Bookkeeping

The early systems were, of course, very primitive—the barter system was the basic method of exchange, with cattle, silver, or gold often used as supplementary goods in the transaction. It was many centuries before state coinage of money was instituted, and money, as the normal medium of valuation and exchange, raised civilization (and accounting) to a new level of sophistication. G. E. M. De Ste. Croix writes of this in *Greek and Roman Accounting.* "The adoption of money as the normal medium of valuation and exchange made it possible for bookkeeping to rise to an entirely new level; all possessions and all transactions could at last be recorded not as so many fields, so many slaves, so many bushels of grain, or the exchange of so many casks of wine against so many pounds of silver, but in every case as so many units of a particular system of currency."[2]

What De Ste. Croix is describing is, of course, single-entry bookkeeping; that is, a simple notation of the receipt or expenditure was made with no contra entry or entries to balance the original entry and reflect the complete transaction. And so long as the transaction concerned a single unit (owner, temple, or city-state government) with no stewardship responsibilities or third parties involved, the single-entry system was quite satisfactory.

The Italian City-State and Double-Entry Bookkeeping

However, with the growth of international trade following the Crusades, particularly by the great city-states of Italy such as Venice and Genoa, trading became more complex. Joint ventures were formed with many investors joining together to sponsor a voyage for trade and profit. Accurate records of the revenues and expenses of the voyage had to be maintained in order to permit an equitable distribution of the ultimate profit (or loss) to the joint venturers.*

---

*The concept of depreciation (at best "wear and tear") was even considered as evidenced by the following quote from S. Paul Garner's *Evolution of Cost Accounting to 1925:* "As a matter of interest to indicate the care with which the accounts were kept towards the end of the 13th Century, E. H. Byrne cites a passage which shows that the 'scribes were familiar with the

With the increasing complexity of business, the demands on accounting increased. The concepts of stewardship and agency are inherent in the joint venture form of business. Of course, underlying all of these concepts are the concepts of private property and capitalism. These form the basis for the sharp break with the rudimentary single-entry record keeping that occurred in the fourteenth century. Historian Raymond de Roover writes that "the first record of a complete system of double-entry bookkeeping was found in the records of a mediaeval merchant of Genoa, Italy, originating about the year 1340. More recently, evidence has been found that double-entry preceded this date and possibly originated simultaneously in several Italian trading centers gradually over a period of time."[3]

The great popularizer of the double-entry method of accounting was Luca Pacioli, a Franciscan friar who lived in Venice. In 1494, he published a treatise on mathematics, *Summa de Arithmetica, Geometria Proportioni et Propertionalita,* which included a section on double-entry bookkeeping. While the treatise did not gain Pacioli undying fame as a mathematician, it did much to spread the double-entry method throughout Europe and gave him a permanent place in accounting history.

An interesting point about the lack of a specific originator of double-entry bookkeeping is that its obvious practicality and the need for it resulted in its "invention" by many persons, as needed. Again we see the deep roots accounting has in practical application rather than abstract theory. This is a recurring theme that we will see repeated in the development of the auditing profession later.

The need to report the success, or lack of same, of a venture to a group of hard-headed, practical investors more interested in results than alibis made the existence of a coherent, well-organized set of accounts, with documentation, an absolute must. The discipline of a system that provided for entries/contraentries that accounted for all aspects of the venture—capital, income, expenses, and profit or loss—was a necessity. As we shall see later in this book, the discipline, the rationality, the numerical logic of double-entry bookkeeping, which are its strengths, were to eventually cause harm to the accounting profession as the level of expectations of what an accounting system could provide rose beyond the level of reasonable attainment.

Up to now, we've been using bookkeeping and accounting pretty much interchangeably, principally because the simplicity of business to the time of the Middle Ages and the notational-style record keeping used until the

---

principles of depreciation and took them into account'." The University of Alabama Press, 1976, p. 4; citing E. H. Byrne, *Genoese Shipping in the Twelfth and Thirteenth Centuries,* Publication No. 5, Monograph No. 1 (Cambridge, Mass. Mediaeval Academy, 1930).

fourteenth century did not require any significant analysis and interpretation. However, with the growth of world exploration and trade in the Middle Ages, the level of sophistication of business began to increase—first through joint ventures, then joint-stock companies such as the East India Company, then, with the Industrial Revolution, the corporate form of business. During this same period of growth, the accounting "profession" also began to develop in varying forms in response to the varying needs of business and society.

The reader is reminded that the definition of the accounting profession given in Chapter 1 is far broader than the perception of the profession that the public and many in government have. The distinction is important because in attempting to establish any goals and objectives for accounting, we must understand the varying needs of the users of accounting data. That may sound like a classic example of stating the obvious but, unfortunately, in the author's opinion, the failure of all users to do just this has caused many of the problems the profession faces today.

MANAGERIAL ACCOUNTANTS LARGELY IGNORED

The narrow interpretation of the "profession" that has evolved—that it is generally limited to those CPAs practicing in the public accounting field—ignores those managerial accountants who have the basic responsibility for practicing applied accounting theory every day, interpreting and reporting results. Such an interpretation limits the "profession" to those independent auditors (public accountants) who review and attest to the reasonableness of the data prepared by the managerial accountants.

This problem is an old one, although the troubles the misconception causes are increasing as our economy and government become more and more complex. The first recognition of the distinction between public and private accountants occurred in 1919. At that time, Mr. C. B. Williams proposed the creation of a cost-accounting section of the American Institute of Accountants (the forerunner of the AICPA) at a council meeting in 1919. The council referred the question to the annual meeting and, after a general discussion, "the opinion prevailed that a separate organization would be preferable to a cost-accounting section of the Institute, and the proposal was rejected, on the ground that the *primary purpose* of the Institute was to *serve practicing public accountants*" [emphasis added].[4]

As a result, the National Association of Cost Accountants (the NAA today) was formed. The association was an immediate success, which was "due largely to the genius of its secretary, Dr. Stuart C. McLeod. . . . It was largely due to McLeod's influence (who was not an accountant but an educator) that the NACA never undertook any legislative programs, or *attempted to set technical standards,* which might have brought it into *competition with* the Institute. He insisted to the day of his death in 1944 that NACA was purely an educational organization. . . . As a consequence, the NACA and the Institute *lived happily side by side* over the years" [emphasis added].[5]

The emphasis of the NAA has changed somewhat in recent years, and while it does not attempt to set standards, it founded the Institute of Management Accounting in 1972 through which it conducts formal programs leading to the Certificate in Management Accounting (CMA). The examination for this certificate is quite comprehensive, covering economics, business finance, organization and behavior, public reporting, auditing, taxes, periodic internal and external reporting, and decision analysis, including modeling and information systems. The certificate is highly respected by academia and accountants, and about 2500 have completed the examination since its inception in 1972. And yet, it is doubtful that it will ever quite gain the universal acceptance of the CPA exam as denoting a "professional accountant." Why? Because management accounting can never be the closed club that public accounting is; that is, "membership" can never be restricted to a holder of the CMA.

THE EMERGENCE OF THE *PROFESSION* OF ACCOUNTING

The general identification of the accounting "profession" as consisting of only those persons practicing as independent public accountants is ironic since this sector of the accounting field is relatively new. As Robert L. Kane, Jr. noted,

> A. C. Littleton points out that except for the auditing of municipal and government accounts as early as the 14th Century by selected local members of the public, who could scarcely be called public accountants, there was no record of any public auditing by experts until the practice arose, probably early in the 17th Century, by the lords of the large manor estates, of employing specialists . . . to check their accounts. When the center of economic life began to shift from the agricultural manors to the towns with the beginnings of manufacturing, the earliest signs of a recognized public profession emerged. The city directory of Edinburgh, for the first time of any in the British Isles, in 1773 listed seven persons as accountants serving the public. At the beginning of the 19th Century less than fifty public accountants were recorded in the directories of all of the large cities of England and Scotland.[6]

It was not until the Joint Stock Companies Act of 1844 in the United Kingdom, which created the corporate form of business with limited liability, indefinite life, broad, shared ownership, and absentee owners who delegated the running of the business to a management group, that the practice of the public accountant (auditor) really began to grow. In 1854, the Society of Accountants was formed in Edinburgh, under a royal charter that permitted its members to use the designation *chartered accountant*.

As the Industrial Revolution gained impetus in the late nineteenth century in the United States, British capital flowed into the country, and with it came the British public accounting firms. Today, Price Waterhouse & Co.; Peat, Marwick, Mitchell & Co.; Deloitte Haskins & Sells; and Coopers and Lybrand of the so-called Big Eight public accounting firms can trace their roots back to England and Scotland (although the last two started as United States firms and later merged with British firms).

In 1850, only nineteen accountants offered their services to the public in the United States according to the major city directories of that time. By 1886, the number had grown to 363 and, in 1887, the American Association of Public Accountants—the direct predecessor of the AICPA—was formed. The growth of public accounting was in response to an obvious need, as was the growth of bookkeeping thousands of years earlier. Absentee owners needed some assurance from a qualified third party as to the stewardship of the management entrusted with the absentee owner's capital—the attestation function.

Significantly, the early auditor's opinion stressed the *correctness* of the records. Once again, we discern an emphasis on the precision and accuracy of accounting that plagues accountants even today.

THE APPEARANCE OF GOVERNMENT REGULATION

Government regulation is a natural outgrowth of the rise of society. While some may believe that we have gone too far with regulations in the United States, none would question the need for a governing body and laws to prevent the abuses and excesses unscrupulous people, left totally unrestrained, could inflict on others.

In Europe

Insofar as the accounting field is concerned, the rise of the corporation and absentee owners in the nineteenth century brought with it government regulations. The first Companies Act in the United Kingdom in 1844 required that books of account were to be kept and audited, and a full and fair balance sheet was to be prepared, sent to shareholders, and filed with the registrar of Joint Stock Companies. Although the Joint Stock Companies Act

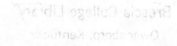

of 1856 abandoned the compulsory accounting and auditing requirements, they were reinstated in the Companies Act of 1900.[7]

In Germany, the German Companies Act of 1884 required companies to declare their profits and present balance sheets with assets valued at the lower of cost or market.

In the United States

In the United States, various regulatory agencies have been established that have had an impact on the accounting profession. Among the more significant agencies are the Interstate Commerce Commission (the first regulatory agency, formed in 1887, to exercise control over the fast-growing railroad industry), the Federal Reserve Board (1913), the Internal Revenue Service (1913), the Federal Trade Commission (1914), the Federal Communications Commission (1934), the Securities and Exchange Commission (1934), and the Federal Power Commission (1935).

Three of these agencies (the ICC, the FCC, and the FPC) deal with the regulation of privately owned public utility corporations and have not had a significant impact on the accounting profession. However, the other four have had a considerable effect. In fact, John Carey concludes that "the interest of these two bodies [the Federal Reserve Board and the Federal Trade Commission] in financial reporting and auditing led to establishment of official standards, in the absence of which independent audits by public accountants might have been widely discredited."[8]

The FTC and the Federal Reserve Board

One of the paradoxes of the growth of the need for third party attestation and, thus, the public auditing area of accounting itself, is the need for some form of enforcement power or sanction from the government if an independent, private public-auditing group is to be maintained. Of course, the need for private public-auditors has been seriously challenged by the government on at least three occasions—1916, 1932, and 1976. The relationships between the government and public auditing might be compared to having a pet bear—sometimes he can smother you, even if unintentionally. Setting the 1932 and 1976 challenges aside for later, we note the first example of the "smothering embrace" of the government, reported by John Carey:

> At the first meeting [in 1916] of the new Council [of the American Institute of Accountants], . . . an ominous letter was received from Edwin Hurley, Chairman of the Federal Trade Commission. . . . Mr. Hurley's latest letter indicated dissatisfaction, which he said was shared by the Federal Reserve Board, with financial statements certified by public accountants. Special mention was made

of the inadequacy of depreciation charges. Mr. Hurley suggested that consideration might be given to the possibility of developing a register of public accountants whose audit certificates would be acceptable to the Commission and the Board. This letter had the effect of a bombshell on the Council! The suggestion that public auditing should be regulated by the Federal Trade Commission and the Federal Reserve Board was unnerving to say the least. After some discussion, the Council's Committee on Federal Legislation [consisting of Robert H. Montgomery, George O. May and Harvey Chase] was directed to confer with the Federal Trade Commisson and with the Federal Reserve Board, advising them of the organization of this Institute, and giving them a knowledge of the plan and scope of the organization, with a view to deferring or perhaps, if possible, preventing the establishment of any governmental registration; assuring the Federal Trade Commission and the Federal Reserve Board of the willingness of the Institute to cooperate in fullest manner with them in securing proper rules and regulations regarding the certification of statements for federal or other purposes.[9]

The result of all of this was the historic Federal Reserve bulletin of 1917, first entitled, prophetically if inaccurately, "Uniform Accounting." Inaccurately because the bulletin had nothing to do with uniform systems of accounting. Instead it consisted mainly of recommended audit procedures. It was republished a year later by the Federal Reserve Board under a more descriptive title, "Approved Methods for the Preparation of Balance Sheet Statements." These Federal Reserve bulletins marked the beginning of what was to be a continuing struggle by the government to control all accounting.

Of course, the Securities and Exchange Commission (SEC) and the Internal Revenue Service (IRS) have had a major impact on the accounting field. Today probably no other agency has the continuing impact on accounting that the SEC does. However, at this time, it is enough to note that it succeeded the FTC as the designated regulator of accounting in 1934 and that the SEC will be discussed in more depth in later chapters.

The Impact of the IRS on Accounting

Some believe the Internal Revenue Service and the income tax law may have had the greatest impact on the accounting field of any of the government agencies. Although this is impossible to prove, of course, its impact has certainly been great. The taxation of personal incomes had been tried as early as 1862 while the taxation of corporate income began only in 1909 with the passage of the Corporation Excise Tax Law. Although called an excise tax, it was a tax based on "net income." "Net income" is in quotes because the calculation was to be on a cash-accounting basis. The act defined net income as "entire net income . . . ascertained by deducting from the gross amount of the income . . . from all sources, (1) expenses actually *paid,* (2) losses *actually sustained,* interest *actually paid* within the year" [emphasis added].[10] In addition, the law also required that all companies file a return annually for the year ending December 31.

This law is probably a classic case of a well-intentioned, poorly informed government establishing an impossible regulation. It was not that the accountants did not try to explain the impracticalities of the law. John L. Carey writes that "while the bill was before Congress, twelve accounting (public auditing) firms jointly signed a letter to Attorney General George W. Wickersham, with copies to every member of Congress, pointing out the impracticability of these provisions. . . . In his reply, the Attorney General plainly showed that he did not comprehend the issues: 'It may be inconvenient, but it is certainly not impossible, for any corporation which keeps *just* and *true* books [emphasis added] of account to make up a return such as that required by the proposed law [that is, as of December 31], particularly as the return requires statements of actual receipts and payments and not as you recommend in your communication, of expenses 'incurred,' interest 'accrued,' and losses 'ascertained.' The Attorney General went on to say that the bill was purposely framed to deal with receipts and disbursements, and the 'actually paid' were employed advisedly. He concluded, 'My personal acquaintance with you and a number of the other signers of the letter leads me to believe that you have underestimated your capacity.'"[11]

In reading this account, it is interesting to note such words as "just and true books" as well as the obvious confusion of cash-basis versus accrual-basis accounting, misunderstandings which are still quite common to this day.*

The Revenue Act of 1913 replaced the 1909 law. The new act established today's income tax system and also provided for the computation of taxable income on a cash basis. But it was liberally interpreted by the Treasury Department so as to follow accrual-basis accounting in general. Subsequently, Congress passed tax acts in 1916 and 1917 that moved closer to accepted accounting practice until, in the 1918 Tax Act, they recognized it in the determination of taxable income.

Departure from Good Accounting Practice

Of course, this goal has not been achieved nor even diligently sought by the Internal Revenue Service. To cite just a few major differences: Today's tax laws permit a sale to be recorded on an installment basis even though this is

---

*As a final note on the 1909 law, its administration was under the secretary of the treasury who, Carey reports (p. 66), availed himself of the advice of accountants in formulating the actual implementing regulations which, as construed by them, removed most of the difficulties that would have been encountered had the strict letter of the law been followed.

contrary to good accounting theory; the tax laws do not permit the deduction from a given year's income of estimates of future expenses related to the current year's sales, such as warranty expense, but instead limit the deduction to known warranty claims; they permit deductions for depreciation not necessarily associated with the related assets' useful life; and they permit a depreciation basis for tax purposes which is different from that used for financial reporting purposes.

Why do these deviations from good accounting exist? One of the main reasons is that tax policy is often used to further what are deemed to be desirable national goals, with little regard for the accounting theory involved. Probably the most universal example of this is the favored treatment granted homeowners. Interest on their property mortage, as well as property taxes, are allowed as deductions from income, while renters, who indirectly pay the same expenses, receive no direct allowances. Obviously, it has been deemed to be in the best interests of the nation to stimulate home ownership.

In the business field, tax incentives are often granted to stimulate private business to undertake what are deemed to be desirable national goals. As an example, tax moratoria are often granted if a new plant is constructed in a depressed economic area. Of course, the revolutionary tax bill passed in 1981 represents a major attempt by government to stimulate capital formation through tax policy. The bill not only greatly decreased the period over which an asset's cost could be recovered (e.g., as little as 10 years for buildings versus the former 30 to 50 years), but also encouraged the transfer of tax deductions and credits between companies (the so-called tax transfer leasing provision).

The various tax laws have tended to encourage consistency in accounting practice and to stimulate, if not actually guide, accounting theory. An exceptional example of this is *Eisner v. Macomber,* in which the U.S. Supreme Court's rule that a dividend on common stock was not "income" supported the accounting theory that profits can only arise when the increase in wealth is realized. The subordination of theory to tax law is also illustrated by the failure of the concept of depreciation to gain acceptance before depreciation was permitted as a deduction in the 1909 tax law.[12]

Of course, as Hendriksen points out, the effect of taxation has not always been sound accounting.

In more recent years, the income tax rules have had a considerable adverse effect on accounting theory and principles. The tendency to accept income tax provisions as accepted accounting principles and practices is unfortunate. The following are examples: (1) Any depreciation method acceptable for tax purposes is acceptable for accounting purposes also, regardless of whether or not it follows good accounting theory in the situation. (2) LIFO must be used for financial reporting purposes if it is used in the tax return. (3) Items that should be capitalized in some cases are charged to expense to obtain the earliest possible tax deduction. (4) Since the tax law does not permit it, no provision is generally made for "accruing" repair and maintenance expenses except indirectly and haphazardly through accelerated depreciation.

In summary, the effect on accounting theory of taxation of business incomes in the United States and in other countries has been considerable, but it has been primarily indirect in nature. The tax laws themselves have not pioneered in accounting thought. While the revenue acts did hasten the adoption of good accounting practices and thus brought about a more critical analysis of accepted accounting procedures and concepts, they have also been a deterrent to experimentation and the acceptance of good theory.[13]

A significant point to keep in mind in considering the effect income tax laws have had on accounting is the pragmatic, cash-orientation of business and the roots of accounting. Again and again we shall see that whenever accounting theory wanders too far from this base, confusion and controversy result.

TRADE ASSOCIATIONS IN THE ACCOUNTING PROFESSION

Thus, as the capitalistic forces of the Industrial Revolution grew more sophisticated and complex, the accounting field evolved into the broad areas outlined at the start of this book: private industry, public accounting (auditing); teaching; and government.

Today, three of the groups (government being excluded, of course) form the basis for four of the six associations that fund the Financial Accounting Foundation, the ruling organization of the Financial Accounting Standards Board. The six associations and the divisions of accounting generally included are:

1. The American Institute of Certified Public Accountants (AICPA) is made up of almost 200,000 CPAs, slightly more than half of whom are engaged in public accounting. This association is the dominant force in the accounting standards area and is strongly influenced by the so-called Big Eight international public accounting firms—Price Waterhouse & Co.; Deloitte Haskins & Sells; Arthur Andersen & Co.; Coopers & Lybrand; Arthur Young & Co.; Touche, Ross & Co.; Ernst & Whinney; and Peat, Marwick, Mitchell & Co. Membership in the AICPA is limited to those holding the CPA certificate and the public accounting segment is generally perceived as the "profession."

2. The Financial Executives Institute (FEI) is composed of over 12,000 financial executives (membership, with a few exceptions, is limited to persons

who are controllers, treasurers, vice presidents of finance, etc., at the time of their application). About 40% of its membership are CPAs. Although a small group, its membership, through its various standing national committees, carries a great deal of influence in the accounting field.

3. The American Accounting Association (AAA) is composed principally of educators although it doesn't limit its membership to just educators. Its membership of about 12,000 in all, is a prestigious one since it includes the leading accounting theoreticians and authors of accounting texts.

4. The National Association of Accountants (NAA) is the second largest association with over 90,000 members. Its only prerequisite for membership is a position in accounting or finance, be it a cost clerk or vice president or a public accountant. Although it is struggling to gain recognition and influence, thus far it has not carried the weight the first three associations have. Of course, many of the members of the first three associations are also members of the NAA.

5. and 6. The Financial Analysts Federation (FAF) and the Securities Industry Association are composed principally of nonaccountants and have not attempted to exert any influence on accounting standards-setters, even though they comprise the groups that the regulators (both the SEC and the FASB) seem most concerned with satisfying.

It is the difference among the preparers of financial data (represented before the FASB by the FEI and the NAA), the auditors of such data (represented by the public accounting sector of the AICPA), the teachers (represented by the AAA), and the investors/creditors (represented by the FAF and the Securities Industry Association), each with a differing view of the purpose and use of such data, that has led to the confusion in accounting (and auditing) and the subsequent reaction of government to press for more and more regulation.

With the preceding as a basis for recognizing the wide variety of practitioners of accounting, let us move to a review of the greatest misconception in accounting—*Generally Accepted Accounting Principles.*

REFERENCES

1. C. Bertil Nystromer, *Four Thousand Years in the Office,* National Office, Management Association, Stockholm, Sweden, 1940. Reprinted in the *World of Business,* vol. 1, Harvard Business School, Simon & Schuster, New York, 1962, p. 62.

2. G. E. M. De Ste. Croix, "Greek and Roman Accounting," in A. C. Littleton and B. C. Yamey, eds., *Studies in the History of Accounting,* Richard D. Irwin, Inc., Homewood, Ill.,

1956. Reprinted in the *World of Business,* vol. 3, Harvard Business School, Simon & Schuster, New York, 1962, pp. 74–77.

3. "The Development of Accounting Prior to Luca Pacioli According to the Account Books of Mediaeval Merchants" in A. C. Littleton and B. S. Yamey, eds., *Studies in the History of Accounting,* Richard D. Irwin, Inc., Homewood, Ill., 1956, p. 115.

4. Carey, *The Rise of the Accounting Profession,* vol. 1, p. 311.

5. Ibid., p. 312.

6. *CPA Handbook,* vol. 1, Robert L. Kane, Jr., ed., Copyright American Institute of Certified Public Accountants, New York, 1952 and 1956, p. 2.

7. George J. Benston, *Corporate Financial Disclosure in the U.K. and the U.S.A.,* Saxton House, Hampshire, England, 1978, p. 2.

8. John L. Carey, *The Rise of the Accounting Profession,* vol. 1, Copyright AICPA, New York, 1969, p. 62.

9. Ibid., p. 129.

10. Ibid., p. 64.

11. Ibid., p. 64.

12. Eldon S. Hendriksen, *Accounting Theory,* 3d ed., Richard D. Irwin, Inc., Homewood, Ill., 1977, pp. 48–49.

13. Ibid., p. 49.

three

GENERALLY ACCEPTED ACCOUNTING PRINCIPLES: THE GREAT MISCONCEPTION

NO COMPREHENSIVE SET OF PRINCIPLES EXISTS

First of all, it is important that before we explore the origin of the phrase, "generally accepted accounting principles," we understand that no formal, comprehensive, basic set of generally accepted accounting principles exists. At present, we have 51 Accounting Research Bulletins published by the AICPA's Committee on Accounting Procedure (CAP) from 1939 to 1959, we have 32 Opinions of the Accounting Principles Board (APB) published from 1959 to 1972, and 72 Statements of Financial Accounting Standards of the FASB (still publishing), as well as numerous interpretations and technical bulletins of the FASB and nearly 300 Accounting Series Releases of the SEC and 32 Statements of Position of the AICPA.

In addition to these myriad rules and regulations, which are a *part* of what is called GAAP, we have had several attempts to describe a basic underlying "grand theory" of accounting, the most significant attempt being *An Introduction to Corporate Accounting Standards* by W. A. Paton and A. C. Littleton.[1] This monograph has been reprinted 16 times and over 60,000 copies have been sold. However, in spite of its significance and impact, this monograph carries no formal or official weight in the profession.

The second major attempt of significance was a white paper published by the Accounting Principles Board in 1970 as Statement No. 4, *Basic Concepts and Accounting Principles Underlying Financial Statements of Business Enterprises.*[2] However, this document also did not have any official professional endorsement, nor did it achieve its goal of establishing GAAP.

In the words of Elden S. Hendriksen, "In summary, Statement No. 4 is not a theory of current accounting practice *nor a clear statement of generally accepted accounting principles*"[3] [emphasis added]. Thus we still do not have a basic, comprehensive, formal set of generally accepted accounting principles. It is not because the profession has not tried. As we shall see, it has been trying for over 80 years with some degree of success, albeit at an unbelievably slow pace.

Basic Schism Between Managerial and Public Accounting

The reason for this painfully slow evolution can be traced to the basic schism between managerial accounting and public reporting discussed earlier and the confusion this split has caused between the reporting of financial results and accounting principles as applied in practice.

As pointed out in Chapter 2, the portion of the accounting field called the "profession" is really only the public auditing section of a far broader profession. Furthermore, it is a relatively new field—getting its start in the nineteenth century with the growth of the absentee-owner and publicly held company. Prior to the growth of public accounting we had a far larger group of accountants practicing what is termed "managerial accounting," which continues to this day.

Reporting Standards Versus Accounting Principles

The significance of the growth of public accounting is that when people speak of generally accepted accounting principles, they are really speaking of selected public *reporting* standards as opposed to managerial reporting and accounting concepts, although internal reporting may reflect some of the public reporting standards.

Let us explore the development of the phrase *Generally Accepted Accounting Principles* and of accounting concepts so that we can better understand how the profession, in its broadest sense, can still be searching for GAAP and a conceptual framework over 100 years after the advent of the corporate form of business in the United States.[4]

EARLY THEORY BASED ON MANAGER'S NEEDS

As discussed in Chapter 2, accounting is an ancient art, which developed from a basic need for a disciplined system of record-keeping and analysis of transactions and *not* as an offshoot of the economist's search for a definition of intrinsic wealth and value. It is important to keep this genesis in mind as we move through the study of the search for accounting principles, the relationship of the effect of inflation on accounting data, the search for a conceptual framework, and the ever present threat of government regulation of accounting.

Accounting evolved essentially as managerial accounting. The owner or partners of a business needed to keep account of how much money had been put into the business, what had been spent, what had been sold, and how much was left. Until the Industrial Revolution and the growth of manufacturing, the bulk of business was that of the merchant. Thus, initially, mercantile rather than cost accounting was the dominant form of accounting. As business grew into complex manufacturing organizations, cost accounting, that is, accounting for direct labor, raw materials, and indirect costs (overhead), became a major sector of managerial accounting.

Before the Industrial Revolution then, accounting was firmly based on transaction-oriented data. Accountants concerned themselves with the recording of cash receipts and expenditures. In addition, as the concept of the extension of credit grew, record keeping too became more sophisticated. It became necessary to record receivables and payables, but these too were based on firm transactions that were expected to be settled in cash.

Underlying all of this was the concept of a society and a form of government that honored the right of a citizen to hold property. This right to private property, which most of us take for granted, is more critical in today's highly industrialized society than it was 500 years ago. For implicit in the right to private property is the right of citizens to join together and invest in private ventures, which led to the development of the modern corporation and the accumulation of the vast amounts of capital needed to realize the potential of the Industrial Revolution.

The "Italian Method"

It was the increasing complexity of the multiowner ventures that led to the great expansion of the use of double-entry bookkeeping and the discipline it provides. Hendriksen lists four characteristics of the accounting theory underlying the "Italian Method" developed in the fourteenth and fifteenth centuries:

The first was the need to provide information to the owner(s), a means for reporting on stewardship and a basis for granting of credit. It is particularly significant to note that "as a result of this, the accounts were held in secrecy and there was no *external* [emphasis added] pressure for accuracy or uniform standards of reporting."[5] This desire for secrecy, for the right of privacy of one's affairs, persists to this day and is part of the communication problem among those managing the business, those who have invested in the business, and those who are interested in the business for political and social reasons.

The second characteristic of the Italian Method was the idea that a business was an entity separate and distinct from its owner(s). This idea, of course, reached its ultimate expression in the corporations that have come into operation in the past 150 years in England, the United States, and the free world.

The third, and most significant, characteristic of the Italian Method was the *lack* of a "going-concern" concept. In Italy in the sixteenth century, the great city-states, such as Venice, Genoa, and Florence, were heavily engaged in trading ventures that, for the most part, had a limited "life." Without the going-concern concept, there was no need to calculate a periodic profit or loss and, thus, no need to be concerned with the allocation of revenues and costs to an interim period through the application of an accrual method of accounting. Generally, fixed assets were not a major factor in trading activities; hence, the concept of depreciation was not widely needed or used. It was necessary to keep account of amounts owed to (receivables) and by (payables) the entity as well as its inventories, but this record-keeping was more a matter of being able to prepare a final reckoning than determine a periodic profit or loss.

The effect of the limited life of commercial activities was that calculating the profit or loss of an entity was far simpler 500 years ago. The books of account were based on firm transactions, and the work of the bookkeeper was the recording of facts. Accounting, as a profession requiring analysis and interpretation, was just beginning in the Middle Ages. As we shall see later in this chapter, the growth of complex manufacturing companies and the absentee-owner led to the sophistication of accounting theory as it became essential that periodic reports of progress be prepared both for management and for the absentee-owners.

It is also significant to note that bookkeeping has retained its precision throughout the development of sophisticated allocation theories of accounting. For given the analysis and interpretation of what the allocation method should be (e.g., the useful life and depreciation method of an asset), the recording of that decision is as precise as an entry made in the sixteenth century.*

The final characteristic of the Italian Method was the need for detailed descriptions of every entry because of the lack of a single stable monetary

---

*This paradox of estimates and precision leads many nonaccountants mistakenly to believe in the exactness of a given profit figure. Such belief is a contributing factor in the misunderstandings present in attempts to regulate accounting, as will be seen in the discussion of the Foreign Corrupt Practices Act later.

unit. Thus, "not only was the name of the buyer or seller recorded, as well as the description of the goods with its weight, size or measurement, and price, but the terms of payment were also shown" and "wherever cash was received or disbursed, the record would show the kind of currency and its converted value. . . ."[6]

Of the four elements of the Italian Method—need for reliable data, separate entity, *lack* of continuity, and *lack* of a stable monetary unit—the first two have survived to this day and can still be considered basic. The fourth element was changed from no stable monetary unit to the assumption of one.

Change to Perpetual Business Form Altered Accounting

However, the change from enterprises that *lack* continuity to today's corporations that have perpetual existence has proven to be the source of a great deal of debate and disagreement. For if the accountants could wait until the end of the life of a business venture before reporting the net results of the undertaking, their job would be quite simple since the net cash available for final distribution would be the final "net profit." Thus so long as proper controls were exercised over the receipts and expenditures during the course of the venture, little argument as to the amount of the final result would ensue. Matters today are not so simple. Some acrimony might develop among the venturers if the results were less than expected, but, controls being adequate, the amount wouldn't be in question, just the explanation. The partners might be unhappy with the effect of inflation on the purchasing power of the final cash distribution but that would not change the amount.

An important point to keep in mind as we consider the development of accounting principles, economic values, and the nonaccountant's understanding of accounting, although it is rarely stated quite so simply, is that all accountants are trying to do in their recording and reporting is to allocate to a given period the net cash the entity can reasonably expect to realize as the result of the transactions undertaken during that same period of time. It is the growth of the need to make relatively arbitrary determinations of the net cash which could be realized at given points of time in an entity's "life" that has been both a blessing and a curse to the accountant.

It is a blessing in that the art of analyzing and interpreting transactions and their possible future consequences has created the profession of accounting, which evolved from the ancient art of bookkeeping. It is a curse because of the failure of the accounting profession to make clear the differences between the precisions of bookkeeping and the subjectivity of accounting; thus it made itself vulnerable to government regulation, with its accompanying inefficiencies.

Professor A. C. Littleton expressed this concept thus:

The central problem of accounting is to bring into association, in the present, the revenues identified with the present and their related costs, and to bring into association, in the future, the revenues identified with the future and their related costs. In solving this problem those who use accounting are, in effect, matching enterprise efforts and accomplishments. Some efforts are effective in the present; they are measured by the costs (effort) currently deductible from revenue (accomplishment); they are the revenue costs of the present. Other efforts are expected to be effective in the future; they are measured by the costs that are deferred as being revenue costs of the future (assets). Some efforts prove ineffective in the present and are judged unlikely to be effective in the future; they are measured by the costs that must be currently deducted from revenue as recognized losses. The *fundamental problem of accounting* [emphasis added] therefore is to cut through a continuing stream of costs and correctly assign portions to the present and to the future. . . .[7]

This problem of assignment of costs and, to a lesser degree, revenues to an arbitrary period, coupled with the need to report operating results periodically, has grown to dominate the entire accounting profession.

BASIC THEORETICAL CONCEPTS IN MANAGERIAL ACCOUNTING

Before we explore the problem of periodic reporting, let us review the basic theoretical concepts used by the managerial accountant in analyzing and classifying the financial data dealt with each day. Although the various parts of the following concepts are regularly included in accounting textbooks and reference books, they are not formalized as a part of the official GAAP, although their inclusion in Statement No. 4 of the Accounting Principles Board might be considered by some to be close to this status. The concepts are as follows, although not in any order of importance:

1 Separate entity
2 Going concern
3 Right to private property
4 Reliability of data
5 Monetary expression
6 Cost basis
7 Realization
8 Conservatism

9 Matching of costs and revenues
10 Consistency
11 Materiality
12 Timeliness and estimates
13 Capital/income distinction
14 Impartiality
15 Dual effects—double entry
16 Form and substance

The remainder of this chapter will be devoted to a discussion of these 16 general concepts, which I have selected from accounting literature as being the foundation of accounting theory.

Separate Entity

Under this concept the business, be it a proprietorship, a partnership, or a corporation, owns assets, owes debts (including "owing" the owners the equity capital they have invested) and produces or supplies a product and/or service. In short, it has a legal existence separate from the owners. This concept of separateness is the keystone of the double-entry system of accounting. The concept of the business "owing" the investors for their capital contribution permitted the development of double-entry accounting, which, as we have seen, greatly enhanced the discipline and analysis of business transactions.

Going Concern

The concept of a "going concern," that is, the indefinite life of a business, is closely related to that of a separate entity and indeed develops naturally from it. The concept is relatively new in the business world, stemming, for the most part, from the development of the corporate form of business and the complex economic activities of the Industrial Revolution.

The going-concern concept has proved to be of great significance because it implies a need for determining "net income" and "financial position" at arbitrary points in time so that absentee-owners can evaluate their investments and, also, so that new investors might be persuaded to furnish the capital needed from time to time to regenerate and make possible the continuation or expansion of the business.

As an example of the controversy this concept has caused, consider the possible appreciation of fixed assets owned by a manufacturing firm. From a going-concern basis, the liquidation value of those assets is of little interest to the owners: if the company is successful, the management (and owners) intend to continue the operations of the firm, not to sell the assets. Yet a potential creditor would be quite interested in the liquidation value of the assets since it would probably form the collateral for a loan. Of course, the economist would argue that the increase in value of the fixed assets is "income" to the firm regardless of the reality of turning that increase in value into cash.

Right to Private Property

Obviously, the "separate entity" concept of ownership can only exist in a society that acknowledges the right of a citizen to own anything. The economics of the free world have, for the most part, been allowed to develop under private citizen control—the "free enterprise system." This right of private ownership has always been subject to the caveat that its use should not interfere with the rights of others or be contrary to the public interest. Gradually, as our society has become more industrialized, urbanized, and interdependent, the balance between free enterprise and the public interest has become more and more critical. Thus, the role of the corporation in a modern society, as well as the role of government regulation, has become a major economic issue in today's business environment.

Reliability of Data

Any functioning business-information system implies that the information it gathers can be relied on to be valid and reasonable. This reliability depends in part on developing and maintaining a system of controls that safeguards the assets of the business from theft or other form of loss.

Monetary Expression

Business transactions and activity can be measured in physical quantities or service hours. In fact, many of the general indicators of the nation's economic health are expressed in such terms. Examples would include the number of freight car loadings, units of cars and trucks produced, tons of steel manufactured, and so on, and such measurements have the definite advantage of not being affected by changing price levels.

Of course it is simply not possible to add, subtract, multiply or divide units of cars and trucks and tons of steel and have any meaningful data. Money, the medium of exchange, permits mathematical comparisons among different items. However, over time, the rather substantial changes in the purchasing power of money due to inflation limit the usefulness of financial data covering several years if these data are based on historical cost. The problem is compounded further when transactions are considered between companies in different countries with different currencies. In later chapters, we will explore this problem in more depth, but for now we recognize the need for some monetary basis for accounting.

Cost Basis

Earlier we considered accounting's roots in "hard" transactions based on objective, independent exchange prices. As Professor Philip E. Meyer puts it, "The cost basis of accounting is probably the most distinctive feature of accounting as it has been practiced throughout its history. Accordingly, it has been the most impregnable of all the elements comprising generally accepted accounting principles. In its own way, the historical cost principle has exemplified the plight and indeed the perseverance of accounting itself—both as a profession and a discipline."[8]

The objectivity of actual transactions based on independently determined prices as a basis for accounting cannot be overemphasized. Take the controversy over the accounting for oil and gas reserves, for example. Such reserves are reported at their cost value in a company's balance sheet. Most oil and gas companies have steadily resisted any effort to record the estimated value of such reserves, including the proposal by the SEC in 1979 (since rescinded).[9] The opposition was not because the companies did not think the reserves had a value far greater than their original (historical) cost; rather it was because of the expense involved in obtaining an estimate for each reporting period from a qualified engineer, which would still be highly subjective *and* which could result in the reporting of "income" long before any cash might be received or dividends paid.

Realization

"Realization" also exemplifies the hard-headed pragmatism of accountants. Earlier we reviewed accounting's enduring practice of dealing with economic events that have occurred, originally, the cash receipts and disbursements of ancient times. As society grew more complex and sophisticated, so did the type of economic events with which accountants had to deal, and the analysis and interpretation of these events became more difficult as many lost their direct cash receipt/disbursement orientation, that is, lost the quality of being clearly "realized."

Nevertheless, the basic concept of a realized event remains. Unless an event has occurred which, in the short term, will *ultimately* be settled in cash or its equivalent, the accountant will be reluctant to record the event. This concept represents the sharpest difference between accounting and economics. In economics a change in value of an asset is a "profit" or a "loss" even though no event (transaction) involving the asset has taken place or is even likely to occur.

The great defender of the transaction basis for accounting, Professor A. C. Littleton, put it thus: "At the heart of accounting is the nature of the exchange-priced transactions of business enterprises. Such events have several significant characteristics; because of these, accounting is what we know it to be: (1) the facts are realistic and actual because of the independence of the initiating parties, (2) the events are made quantitative by a price agreeable to the parties involved, (3) both the event and the agreed price have legal status, and (4) the transaction expresses managerial decisions initiated by separate parties and, thus, provides, in summary with other transactions, a basis for reviewing the results of such managerial actions."[10]

Some of the most controversial positions taken by the APB and the FASB have been controversial because they tended to ignore or even contradict the concept of realization. For example, APB Opinion No. 11, "Accounting for Income Taxes," which required the application of interperiod allocation of income taxes (i.e., the normalization of income taxes between reporting periods) has been a continuing problem for both business and the FASB because the deferred charge or credit created under the opinion is not a true receivable or a liability and, thus, of questionable validity in the balance sheet.*

Of course, the total disregard for the realization concept implicit in the most controversial statement—Statement No. 8, *Accounting for the Translation of Foreign Currency Transactions and Foreign Currency Financial Statements*—is the primary reason for its unpopular status with the business community, as will be discussed later.

However, accountants must and do make valuation adjustments, notably the adjustments applied to inventories and marketable securities to bring them to the lower-of-cost-or-market. Although this adjustment may appear to contradict the concept of accounting for transactions rather than changes in value, it really represents a judgment of the utimate cash expected to be realized from the assets. It is significant to note that such adjustments are usually only applied to current assets since noncurrent assets are usually a permanent part of a firm's operations rather than part of the inventory-receivable-cash and securities operating cycle. Such adjustments also repre-

---

*As an aside, the principle expressed in the opinion represents probably the ultimate application of the desired matching of costs and revenue concept discussed later in this chapter.

sent the application of the next basic concept that further illustrates the *nature* of accountants and accounting.

Conservatism

There is a maxim often quoted by accountants, whose author is lost in antiquity, to the effect that accountants "should provide for all possible losses but not anticipate any gains." This concept, which is often quite irritating to the more optimistic managers of a business, is actually quite realistic and in accord with basic human nature. Few of us, if we were expecting to receive $5000 from the sale of our used car, are very much upset if we receive $5500. However, if we lay our plans and make commitments based on the anticipated receipt of $6000, then we are not only upset but perhaps even economically embarrassed if we receive less. To put it more formally, we should minimize our maximum losses; we can adjust to maximum gains quite easily.

The use of the historical cost basis is the classic example of conservatism in accounting. Thus, accountants in the United States no longer record upward revaluations of land and buildings. This was done by American accountants until the 1920s and is still quite common in many foreign countries, particularly in those nations experiencing hyperinflation, such as Brazil. Accountants will, however, write current assets down if the current value is *less* than the historical cost. As mentioned earlier, this is not a departure from transaction-based accounting; it is simply an adjustment to the amount of cash that can be expected from a completed transaction.

The concept of conservatism has been applied quite rigorously by accountants, including the standard-setting bodies. In the early part of this century, accountants were criticized for being too conservative.* In a major speech at the 1930 national convention of the AI(CP)A, J. M. B. Hoxsey spelled out seven major criticisms of accounting practice at that time, one of which was overconservatism: "The emphasis upon providing information to creditors and to management-owners fully familiar with all of the details of the business [a questionable premise in a business of any size] *provided some justification* for making profits and ownership equities *appear smaller* than they really were. The techniques for doing this included *excessive depreciation* charges, the *charging* of *new plant to operating expenses,* the *setting up* of *abnormal contingency reserves,* and the *undervaluation of inventories* [emphasis added]. When no outside investors relied upon this information,

---

*Accountants were also accused of being too liberal in the definition of income—but more of the latter under the concept of "Capital versus Income."

no one was actually deceived to his detriment, but the management-owners were deliberately fooling themselves."[11]

The charging of new plant directly to operating expenses was probably never widely practiced and possibly was only mentioned by Hoxsey to dramatize his comments on overconservatism.*

The valuation of inventories is still a judgment call, although today the concurrence of an independent public accountant is required for virtually all public companies. Of course, the widespread use of the last-in, first-out (LIFO) method of valuing inventories has resulted in inventory values generally being significantly understated in the balance sheet.

The standard-setters have used this concept of conservatism also, a prime example of this being Statement No. 2, *Accounting for Research and Development Costs.* Although a company would presumably not spend funds on research and development unless it thought the projects had some future benefit, Statement No. 2 requires that *all* such expenditures be charged to expense as made, regardless of the company management's opinion as to the

---

*The validity of Hoxsey's comments and the general acceptance of the practice of overconservatism is amply illustrated in a 1916 textbook by R. J. Bennett: "The terms 'hidden reserves' and 'hidden assets' are practically synonymous with 'secret reserves.' The latter term is familiar to accountants as representing the excess of actual net worth of a concern over and above the amount indicated on its balance sheet. For some reason, the directors may not wish to disclose in a financial statement the true status of the company's condition, and they act accordingly in understating the true facts. This may be done in the spirit of conservatism which is, no doubt, permissible in case no one is injured thereby. . . . Following are various acts or omissions which result in the creation of secret reserves: 1) Intentionally or inadvertently omitting assets which should be included. 2) Undervaluing assets, intentionally or otherwise. 3) *Writing off too much depreciation* [emphasis added]. 4) Charging additions and improvements to Repairs or Maintenance instead of to Plant Account. 5) Creating reserves for bad debts in excess of the amount required. 6) Charging production costs intentionally or otherwise, to general expense instead of to the manufactured article, thus undervaluing the cost (and inventory). 7) Including *fictitious* [emphasis added] liabilities in the accounts or overstating actual liabilities. 8) Making additions or improvements and charging the cost to Surplus account, thereby hiding their value. 9) *Neglecting* to take into consideration in the accounts *natural increases in value* of real or other property [emphasis added—shades of current-value accounting!]. 10) *Understating values* in good years and increasing them in lean years as a means of keeping the dividends uniform from year to year [emphasis added—more current-value accounting].

"The hidden reserve is a *commendable creation* [emphasis added] in case it is not carried to excess and provided it is not detrimental to interested persons. The spirit of conservatism, to a reasonable extent, is to be commended by the accountant rather than criticized. If, however, stockholders are kept in ignorance of secret reserves of a considerable amount, the auditor should draw attention to this fact in his report".[12]

[It is interesting to note that Hoxsey thought such practices might be justified so long as everyone with an interest in the business knew of the extreme conservatism. Even today, when an investment analyst speaks of a "high quality of earnings," he is referring to the nearness of income to realization in cash and the basic conservatism of the accounting practices applied by the company being valued.]

future benefit of a research project. Under the matching concept, the current costs of such research should be deferred as an asset and matched with the revenue subsequently produced, or written off if it becomes clear that no revenue will be realized. The FASB overruled such arguments on the basis of the uncertainty of the future benefits, that is, because of conservatism.

Matching of Costs and Revenues

As we saw in Chapter 2, and will explore in more depth in Chapter 4, the first third of this century was a period of dramatic growth for the accounting field, which very nearly culminated in government regulation of the public auditing sector of the profession. The confusion in accounting practices during the same period led to the formulation of the matching concept for the determination of net income. The development of this concept gave recognition to the shift in emphasis from *reporting* results from the balance sheet in the first quarter of this century to the income statement. The growth of the corporation as the concrete expression of the separate entity, going-concern concepts, along with the development of scientific business management and sophisticated cost-accounting concepts, and the advent of income taxation, all gave great impetus to the growth of the "net income" view.

As we shall see, managerial accountants and engineers actually developed the principle of matching through their efforts to measure and control costs of operations. However, the specific concept was first spelled out in "A Tentative Statement of Accounting Principles Affecting Corporate Reports" published in 1936. This statement defines historical cost principles as the fundamental axioms of accounting. It points out that "accounting is thus not essentially a process of valuation, but the allocation of historical costs and revenues to the current and succeeding fiscal periods."[13]

The 1940 Paton and Littleton monograph expands on this concept. They note that "It was pointed out earlier that accounting for costs involves three stages: (1) ascertaining and recording costs as incurred, appropriately classified; (2) tracing and reclassifying costs in terms of operating activity; (3) assigning costs to revenues. The third state is crucial from the standpoint of periodic income measurement; it likewise comprehends most of the difficult problems of accounting analysis. Matching costs and revenues requires more than careful procedure and accurate compilation. . . . recording the outflow of costs embodied in revenue is essentially a matter of judgment and interpretation."[14]

It is important to keep in mind that the matching concept does not aid in the *definition* of revenue and costs; it simply requires that, once properly defined, a matching of the two will yield the net income assignable to the sum of the activity for a given period.

Accrual-basis accounting is implicit in this concept. A proper matching is not likely to occur if cash-basis accounting only is used. As Professor Meyer states it, "The inherent weakness of cash-basis accounting is that it matches cash-in and cash-out rather than focusing on the more substantive issue of relating benefits and costs to each other."[15]

Briefly, this means that if I sell a widget for $100 that cost me $75 to make, and offer a full one-year warranty, then my profit is $25 before income taxes *only* if the warranty experience on my widgets is so excellent that although I have made and sold 1000 of them, none has ever failed under warranty. If, on the other hand, my failure rate is expected to be 10% and my average cost of repair is $15, then I should accrue an estimated warranty liability of $1.50 for each widget I make (10% failure rate times the $15 repair cost) and, thus, report a profit of $23.50 per unit before income taxes. This handling of warranty stems from the practical, cash-oriented concept of accounting. It is one that bears no relationship to the economist's view of "profits," and it is a concept that accounting theorists have struggled with to this day, as we shall see in the discussion of inflation and its effect on accounting.

As Professor Yuji Ijuri pointed out, the Paton-Littleton monograph, in which matching is formulated, is a true classic of accounting literature.[16] And, as Reed Storey noted in his address to the American Accounting Association at Boston in 1980, this monograph is the only publication of the American Accounting Association to gain widespread acceptance. Why is this so? Its success resulted from the fact that the matching concept articulated and legitimatized the ad hoc theory that the managerial accountants had developed over the 75 years preceding the monograph.

Consistency

There is an old accountant's story to the effect that it doesn't matter so much whether or not an error is made in a given period so long as the error is made consistently from period to period! Now accountants are not quite that naive, even though they are concerned with a consistent application of the accounting theory. But that bit of hyperbole does illustrate the concern for this concept.

The consistency concept is sometimes confused with the user objective of uniformity and comparability *among different enterprises.* However, it really is based on the rather obvious need for a single enterprise to select and apply accounting practices uniformly and consistently over time so that management can compare results from period to period and make decisions based on analyses of variances between periods. Thus, for example, if one year's income statement reflects a cost of sales based on the First-in, First-out (FIFO) method of costing the usage of inventory in production while the next year's income statement reflects a change to the LIFO method of costing the usage of inventory in production, it is obvious that reasonable conclusions as to the change in the net results from year to year cannot be made without giving recognition to the effect of the accounting change.

In reviewing the evolution of the consistency concept, it is interesting to note that it is a very recent development in accounting theory, having been formalized only about 50 years ago in the correspondence between the AI(CP)A and the New York Stock Exchange concerning deficiencies in financial reporting and auditing.

This correspondence (which we will discuss in more detail later in Chapter 4) culminated in the publication by the AI(CP)A in 1934 of "Audits of Corporate Accounts," which included a discussion of the need for consistency in the application of accounting theory from period to period.

Although the consistency concept is eminently logical from both a management and public user/analyst point of view, as applied to a single enterprise, the insistence by the public user/analyst that it be applied among enterprises is one of the most controversial issues with which the FASB and the SEC have had to deal. For in order for there to be consistency in application of accounting methods among several enterprises (so as to enhance apparent comparability and analysis) there must not be any alternative methods (e.g., FIFO versus LIFO) of accounting for the same type of transactions among firms.

The issue of consistency (uniformity) (i.e., elimination of alternative methods) and hence comparability is one that we will explore later. For the time being, however, we will just note that there is disagreement on the desirability or the need for consistency in methods among enterprises. Paul Grady included "Diversity in Accounting Among Independent Entities" (i.e., alternative accounting methods) as one of the 10 basic concepts underlying accounting principles.[17] Initially, the majority of the accounting profession acknowledged the reasonableness of this position. As Grady puts it, "It is evident . . . that the joint undertaking for improvement in financial reporting (in 1932) between the Institute (AICPA) and the New York Stock Exchange, which as previously noted created the concept of consistency in accounting between periods for the same entity, recognized and *deliberately did not change the previously existing concept that there is diversity in accounting as among separate independent entities*"[18] [emphasis added]. However, the concept of diversity is now under severe pressure.

Materiality

Another basic concept of accounting that seems quite simple and logical at first but that is, in reality, quite ambiguous when applied, is that of materiality. From the very beginning of the formalization of GAAP, the concept of materiality has been acknowledged. Thus, the very first Accounting Research Bulletin, *General Introduction and Rules Formerly Adopted*, states that "The committee contemplates that its pronouncements will have application only to items large enough to be material and significant in the relative circumstances. It considers that items of little or no consequence may be dealt with as expediency may suggest."[19]

The significance of this statement is that the Committee of Accounting Procedure of the AICPA intended it to apply to published financial statements audited by independent certified public accountants. It is really doubtful that they gave any thought to its application in internal accounting and reporting. This is a key point that must be continually kept in mind as we consider the interrelationship of the public user, government, and internal management. As I said earlier, a better description of the published ARBs, APB Opinions, and the SFASs would be GARP—Generally Accepted *Reporting* Principles—rather than GAAP.

The independent certified public accountant who is performing an audit of a company does not care if the internal financial reports to management reflect the standard-setters' rules or not. For example, the internal reports to management may ignore the capitalization of interest required by Statement No. 34, as long as the financial statements prepared for publication and bearing the auditor's attestation do recognize the requirements of SFAS No. 34. Thus many companies will ignore SFAS No. 34 internally and only make the necessary adjustments by what accountants term *overnight entries* in the summary books of account from which the published financial statements are prepared.

On the other hand, managerial accountants approach the concept of materiality somewhat differently. Entries involving cash, for example, are never waived on the basis of materiality, whereas other types of entries are waived on just this basis. For example, a question may arise as to the need to accrue an estimate of the future warranty cost applicable to a product that has been sold. An estimate, based on experience if possible, will be made but if the total exposure is insignificant in relation to the company's assets and liabilities and earnings, the accrual may be waived. (Of course, it may be necessary later to convince the independent auditor that the waiver is reasonable on the basis of immateriality.)

This concept is one of the most baffling paradoxes of accounting to nonaccountants (and sometimes even to accountants), inasmuch as it juxtaposes the precision of bookkeeping with the subjective flexibility of accounting. Many observers cannot understand how an estimate, rounded to the nearest million dollars, can be made which then may have to be allocated to periods and units with such apparent precision that the entries in the books of account balance to the penny!

In the author's opinion, it is this *apparent* precision of accounting that has led many users and legislators to misunderstand the nature of accounting and to place too much reliance on the ultimate accuracy of the results or records. Of course, many accountants perpetuate this misconception by such references as "true cost" or by comments such as "about $101,732.17."

Obviously, while the concept of materiality is quite logical, its application can be very subjective. Many lawsuits have hinged on the reasonableness of such a subjective decision. The principle usually applied in cases of litigation is that of the "prudent man." Paul Grady defines this test thus: "A statement, fact, or item is material, if giving full consideration to the surrounding circumstances, as they exist at the time, it is of such a nature that its disclosure, or the method of treating it, would be likely to influence or to 'make a difference' in the judgment and conduct of a reasonable person. The same tests apply to such words as significant, consequential, or important."[20]

In the Statement of Financial Accounting Concept No. 2, *Qualitative Characteristics of Accounting Information,* about 11 pages are devoted to a discussion of materiality,[21] but they do not give much more guidance than Paul Grady's definition.

Timeliness and Estimates

It was mentioned earlier that if accountants could wait until the completion of the life cycle of the entity to report the results of its operations, the accountant's job would be easy and a profession would be unnecessary. But the concept of timeliness does illustrate the goal of accrual-basis accounting—to allocate estimates of the net realizable cash to arbitrary interim periods in the entity's life cycle.

Again, this concept of timeliness also illustrates the paradox of accounting and bookkeeping. Estimates of future cash payments that will probably result from current sales of products or services, such as warranty claims, must be made and the estimated liability accrued so that the estimated profit from the sale will not be overstated. However, once the estimate of the cost is recorded, the workings of the bookkeeping function with its *inherent discipline* will result in a profit being calculated with an apparent precision that is illusory. As Paton put it so well, "Impressed by the neatly ruled lines and the array of equal footings exhibited by the typical system of accounts and financial statements, the layman is likely to conclude that accounting deals with certainties, with data capable of exact and precise statement; that *accounts are either accurate or inaccurate* [emphasis added]; that the principles and procedures of double entry, if applied without *clerical* error, will *always lead to correct conclusions* [emphasis added]. Indeed, the accountant at times may be found slipping, somewhat unconsciously, into the same misapprehension. . . .

"As a matter of fact, the accountant is being constantly faced with the necessity for judgments. The accountant, as has been said many times, must be an analyst; he must be able to analyze and pass judgment. Accounting is full of estimate(s) (and assumption[s])."[22]

Those words were first written by Professor Paton in 1921 but could not be more true today. Unfortunately, they have proved to be almost prophetic in the sense that the lack of understanding of the true nature of accounting has led to many of the problems challenging the profession today.

Capital/Income Distinction

Although the distinction between capital and income is not included as a basic concept in the various attempts at formulating a summary of GAAP during the past twenty years, it is implicit in the determination of net income based on the matching of costs and revenues. And although the distinction between capital and income is now taken for granted, this was not always the case. As Hendriksen reports:

> During the early period of the railroad industry in the United States (Nineteenth Century), it was not uncommon for promoters to pay huge dividends out of capital during the early life of the firm. Investors, believing this to be the true income of the firm, paid high prices for the stock only to find later that the ability to pay dividends in the future was being eroded because of these huge early dividends. Equity (fairness) requires that both buyers and sellers of common stock have adequate information to make expectations regarding the current and future dividends of the firm.

> With the separation of ownership and control in most large corporations, accounting also has the responsibility to report on the stewardship of the management group entrusted with the proper use of the invested capital. A proper distinction between income and changes in capital is one of the means of determining the extent to which management has carried out the function of operating the enterprise for the benefit of the owners.[23]

The problem of the lack of a clear legal distinction between capital and income in the 1920s and the difficulties this caused the accounting profession may well have been a strong contributing factor to the boom and bust economy of that decade. There is no doubt that the problem was the basic reason for the attempt to formalize a set of generally accepted principles. For example, both John L. Carey in his *The Rise of the Accounting Profession* and Gary John Previts and Barbara Dubis Merino in their *A History of Accounting in America* report the abuses and deficiencies in accounting and financial reporting and auditing during this period that led to the historic correspondence between the Special Committee on Cooperation with Stock

Exchanges of the American Institute of (Certified Public) Accountants and the Committee on Stock List of the New York Stock Exchange from 1932 to 1934. This correspondence, published in 1934 by the AI(CP)A in a pamphlet, *Audits of Corporate Accounts* resulted in a listing of five basic "principles" of accounting in which the acceptable methods of accounting were discussed.* Finally, the New York Stock Exchange adopted the recommendation that the form of the auditor's opinion be changed so that the auditor would specifically report that the proper accounting had been followed.

The correspondence contained in *Audits of Corporate Accounts* represents a milestone in accounting. As Previts and Merino put it, "These basic views indicate that accountants had recognized the validity of the argument that the inability, or perhaps unwillingness, of the profession to properly aggregate capital and income had been one of the major reasons for unsatisfactory reporting in the previous decade (1920s)."[24]

This correspondence was also the origin of the phrase "accepted accounting principles" to which the word *generally* was added in 1939 when the auditor's standard short-form report was revised by the AICPA.[25]

The apparent failure of the accounting profession to more clearly distinguish between capital and income should be shared at least by the legal profession. Previts and Merino report that accountants vetoed the use of no-par stock to increase the equity account without differentiation. Previts and Merino go on to cite Robert Montgomery, of Lybrand, Ross Bros. and Montgomery, who explained (in 1927) the "dilemma of accountants in the proper treatment of surplus. First, there had been the problem of appreciation. He noted that when accountants first began writing up fixed assets, there was almost 'unanimous agreement' that unrealized appreciation should be credited to a separate account. Then came no-par value stock, stated capital, paid-in capital, initial and capital surplus complications coupled with formidable legal opinions that accountants should mind their own business and *not* use such terms as earned surplus. He concluded that legal pressure had forced accountants to use a single surplus account."†[26]

The issue of the relationship of capital and income is where accounting and economics meet and disagree. In 1973, the Trueblood report commented that "economists generally agree that income is the change in well-being or 'better-offness' that occurs in specific time periods. But economists' measures of these changes in well-being or better-offness are not well defined in terms

*The "principles," which were more in the nature of rules forbidding poor or improper accounting practices, will be reviewed in Chapter 4.
†It is interesting to note the reference by Montgomery to the write-up of fixed assets. The bad experience of the profession with such write-ups and "watered" stock in the 1920s lingers to this day and influences many accountants when the subject of a value-based measurement system is raised.

of the operational aspects of an enterprise. Accounting income or earnings should measure operations and represent the period-by-period progress of an enterprise toward its overall goals. Accounting measurements of earnings (income) should recognize the notion of economic better-offness, but should be directed specifically to the enterprise's success in using cash to generate maximum cash."[27]

However, as E. S. Hendriksen points out, this is a contradictory statement: "The former [goal] is the concept of capital maintenance and the latter [goal] is another form of the profit maximization concept or measurement of efficiency."[28] Since the goal of capital maintenance is difficult, if not impossible to measure, the pragmatic accountant stays with the goal of profit maximization and its cash orientation.

Nevertheless, since the fiascos of the 1920s, accountants have been careful to draw a distinction between capital and income. The definition of these terms is the subject of the largest, most expensive research project ever undertaken by the accounting profession—the FASB's Conceptual Framework for Financial Accounting and Reporting, which will be reviewed in depth later. However, for now the working definition of capital being applied by practicing accountants is cash or other assets acquired by an entity without the performance of any reciprocal action by the entity at the time of receipt, that is, no service or product was given to the contributor. Of course, implicit in the action by the contributor is the expectation that the managers of the entity will utilize that capital to generate future cash flows to the contributor. Income, then, is the result of the utilization of capital to generate cash flows through the performance of a service or delivery of products.

It is important to note that the definition refers to the generation of cash flows. To practicing managerial accountants, this cash orientation is critical. Managerial accountants (and their bosses) are not interested in the hypothetical exit values of assets they do not intend to sell but only the cash that can be ultimately realized from using those capital assets.*

Impartiality

Implicit in any profession is the concept of fairness. Hendriksen notes that "D. R. Scott suggested that the basis for the determination of accounting practice reaches back to the principles underlying social organizations. His basic concepts were: (1) accounting procedures *must* provide *equitable* treatment to all interested parties; (2) financial reports should present a *true*

---

*The distance from cash realization of the translation gains and losses was one of the major objections to SFAS No. 8—*Accounting for the Translation of Foreign Currency Transactions and Foreign Currency Statements.*

and *accurate* statement without misrepresentation; (3) accounting data should be *fair, unbiased* and *impartial* without serving special interests."[29]

In practice, managerial accountants continually strive to "call them as they see them" since it is essential that top management have faith that the comparative analyses of actual results with budget and forecast data are as impartial and free from bias as is humanly possible. The reason for this objectivity seems obvious since any other course would have the effect of influencing and perhaps misleading the decisions of management. Of course, public accountants too are striving for this same objectivity.

Dual Effects—The Double-Entry Principle

In Chapter 2, we discussed the significance of the development of the double-entry bookkeeping system and the discipline that it affords to business transactions. Its logic and discipline are so strong that it quickly replaced the single-entry and variations of dual-entry systems that had served the accountant for thousands of years. The following is a summarization of this basic concept.*

Implicit in every transaction is its duality. Thus, if I give someone cash, other than as an outright gift, it is usually in exchange for some good, either an asset or service, or for future repayment with interest (a loan). This duality is expressed by accountants in the equation: assets (something of future benefit) equal liabilities (future claims against the entity) plus owner's equity, the owner(s) claims against the entity, composed of capital stock and undistributed earnings or losses.

The addition of the owner's equity concept by the Italians in the fourteenth and fifteenth centuries was the key point in the development of modern double-entry bookkeeping. As Professor Littleton notes, "This consciousness of the proprietorship is much more fundamental than equality of debit or credit."[30] The significance of this distinction was that the difference between capital and income could now be accounted for (the "net income") and therefore the return on capital calculated for specified periods. This is accomplished by analyzing a transaction or event as to the effect it has on the owner's capital or equity position. Thus, if a loan is obtained from a

---

*For an in-depth analysis of the concept, I would urge the reader to read Littleton's "Characteristics of Double Entry," a collection of excerpts from various articles written by Professor Littleton in the 1920s and 1930s and published in 1961 by the University of Illinois in *Essays on Accountancy*, pp. 22–54; also William A. Paton's 1917 article from the January issue of the *Journal of Accountancy*, "Theory of the Double-Entry System," published in 1964 by the University of Michigan as a part of *Paton on Accounting*, pp. 3–18: and James Ole Winjum's *The Role of Accounting in the Economic Development of England: 1500–1750*, University of Illinois, 1972.

bank, cash as well as liabilities increase. There is no effect on "net income" because the owner's equity was neither increased or decreased, although the owner's relative debt-to-equity position was changed; that is, the owner increased his assets (cash) by giving others (the bank) a claim on the assets that carries precedent over his own claim.

Some users of financial data are confused by the use of the terms *debit* and *credit* by accountants, particularly since a debit entry can not only increase an asset, which is favorable, but can also, in an expense account, increase the expense, which is unfavorable. The same confusion is present as well in credit entries. A credit entry to a liability increases the liability, which is unfavorable, while a credit entry to a sales account also increases it, which is favorable.

The basic point to keep in mind is that, obviously, debit or credit entries by themselves are neither favorable or unfavorable. Conceptually, accountants are only dealing with assets, liabilities and owner's equity. The sales and expense accounts (termed *operating accounts*) are simply subaccounts of owner's equity. Thus, these accounts are increased or decreased by the same type entries that increase or decrease owner's equity. The accountant then must analyze every transaction and decide first of all, is it a capital or income transaction? Once that has been decided, the transaction can be recorded if it meets the other tests of realization, conservatism, substance over form, and so forth.

Under the Italian theory of accounts, the equation of assets, liabilities and equity was viewed as ownership and proprietorship, whereas under the English theory, the influence of the feudal system in medieval England gave rise to the concept of agency and stewardship. Today, both concepts are intermingled in our accounting theory. It really does not affect the practice so much as it affects the theoretical basis for the practice.

Form and Substance

This concept is the last of the major concepts underlying accounting practice and it is, in the author's opinon, by far the most significant.

The accountant, with a natural affinity for structure and logical order, must be particularly careful in analyzing a given transaction in order to determine the appropriate accounting. The reason for the need for caution is the unfortunate fact that some people will carefully prepare formal legal documents in support of a purported transaction that has no economic substance. For example, in the 1960s and 1970s, it was common practice for some real estate developers to buy acreage, subdivide it into residential lots, and then sell the still undeveloped lots to retail customers at the price of a developed lot with a promise to complete the development (paved streets, sewers, etc.) at a later date. Such sales were usually made through a land contract with only a nominal down payment and easy terms over several years. Thus, with a small cash outlay, the buyer could speculate on the appreciation of his lot over a period of time. Meanwhile, the real estate developer would record the full sales price as an immediate sale, estimate the costs of finishing the development and thus record a profit on the "sale" at once. This practice had the effect of "front-end loading" the real estate developer's reported earnings, which, in turn, tended to drive the price of the developer's stock up; hence, the early stockholders realized a profit on the market appreciation of their stock.

Now the legal documents covering this type of transaction were usually in good order. There was no doubt that two executory contracts had been signed—one by the buyer and another by the developer. Initially, many accountants followed the legal *form* and recorded the price of the fully developed lot as a sale, accrued the estimated cost of completing the development, and reported a profit on the "sale." Since practically no cash had been received from the buyer and since a great deal of cash remained to be spent, it should not have been surprising that many of these transactions failed as buyers changed their minds and reneged. The practice was finally stopped, not by the application by accountants of the concepts of form versus substance or realization, but by the publication of rules by the AICPA that spelled out the conditions under which a sale could be recorded and, thus, extricated the accountants, both public and managerial, from their difficult position.[31]

A similar problem occurred, with even more sensational results, in the franchising business in the late sixties. Promoters sold franchises in fast-food businesses, nursing homes, movie houses, and so forth, and front-end loaded their income statements by reporting currently the total franchise fee paid by the franchisee as income when the contract was signed even though a considerable portion of the fee had yet to be earned.

In applying the concept of form versus substance, the accountant must look through the form of the transaction and try to determine what the true intent of management was as well as the substance of what actually happened, and account for the transaction accordingly. In many cases it may take courage to do this. Courage to explain to management (or the client) why a particular transaction is more properly recorded in a manner not to the management's or the client's liking. It is the combination of courage, tact, and judgment, as well as technical skill, that makes accounting a profession.

The preceding 16 concepts were selected by the author from the various sources indicated. Professor George Staubus found 93 "broad operating principles" in APB Statement No. 4,[32] whereas the FASB's Statement of Financial Accounting Concepts No. 2, *Qualitative Characteristics of Ac-*

counting Information, lists only 11, and 2 of those (predictive value and feedback value) are questionable as accounting concepts since they deal with some of the functions of accounting. Of course, this variety in the list of basic concepts only illustrates again the subjective nature of accounting and the lack of a precise catalog of GAAP.

The most interesting and overlooked aspect of the development of accounting concepts is that they were developed by practicing managerial accountants and businessmen to meet their own obvious operating needs. The reader will have noticed that the 16 concepts discussed so far do not spring from a great breakthrough in accounting thought. They have evolved over the last few centuries from the pragmatic need for system, logic, and order in the increasingly complex business world of an industrialized society.

Nowhere is this evolution better illustrated than in the career of Pierre Samuel duPont. Of all the men who forged the great American industrial system at the turn of this century, he alone has the distinction of heading two of the largest companies during their transition into the major classic corporate form—the DuPont Company and General Motors Corporation. He was treasurer, vice-president, and president of DuPont from 1904 to 1920, as well as chairman of the board of General Motors from 1916 through 1927. This fascinating story of American business is told by Alfred D. Chandler, Jr. and Stephen Salsbury.[33] The authors note, "At both DuPont and General Motors, Pierre viewed his job as Chairman of the Board as involving two tasks: one was to review and give a final approval to dividends, capital appropriations, and other financial policies, the other was to make sure that the professional executives managing both companies were of the highest caliber."[34]

As treasurer of DuPont, Pierre du Pont set out to develop an accounting system that would permit the calculation of the "return on investment figure on the monies expended for the production of each type of goods produced. He, John Jacob Raskob, and their assistants would continue to refine this analysis until the return on investment data became the company's single most important analytic tool."[35] In Chapter 6 of the du Pont book the authors tell of Pierre du Pont's efforts to develop a system that would give him and the Executive Committee a firmer financial grasp of the company. Costing and pricing policies were particularly significant. In 1904, Pierre took charge of the development of a uniform cost accounting system and he "continued for many months to devise methods to assure that cost of materials, labor and general overhead were allocated in each mill the same way."[36]

The story of DuPont is repeated throughout American business history. The basic accounting concepts enumerated earlier had their origin in the need of management to obtain the financial data that would permit them to allocate properly their resources, weeding out or improving unprofitable product lines, increasing their investment in their "winners" and, at the same time, maintaining a satisfactory cash position—in short, planning the successful operation of a business.

Cost Accounting Concepts Often Overlooked

In his excellent chapter, on "The Historical Development of Cost Accounting," Professor David Solomons notes that "an adequate account of the evolution of record keeping into a tool of industrial management has yet to be written."[37] Professor Solomons goes on to point out that the early accounting texts ignored manufacturing (cost) accounting even though it was developing during the same period: "Reference has already been made to the fact that neither Paciolo nor his successors for two centuries attempted to apply their record-keeping technique to industrial problems [rather than merchants or traders], nor, as deRoover points out, did they refer to the use of subsidiary books. It is clear, therefore, from the Medici records [sixteenth century] that at this time *practice was well ahead of theory* [emphasis added]. The record-keeping system of the Medici, writes deRoover, was not yet a cost-finding system, but it came very close to being one."[38]

Professor S. Paul Garner writes of the very practical need for cost accounting, accounting controls, and reliable data. He cites some major problems facing the nineteenth-century manufacturer, which will strike a familiar note for today's manager:

1 An adequate supply of raw materials and the records pertaining thereto would be wanted by the managers of the foundry, as it was recognized that too much inventory might be kept on hand.
2 The large payments made to employees required a system which would tend to diminish payroll frauds or errors.
3 The problem of depreciation became more important in view of the more expensive equipment used and the obsolescence factor.
4 In view of the keen competition which began to prevail, it was essential that the managers know to what extent prices could be cut in dull seasons and yet cover "prime costs" (direct labor and material); in other words, a knowledge of variable and fixed costs was required. [The] latter brought up the whole problem of overhead.
5 The transfer of product from process to process needed to be watched carefully and costs compared from period to period.

Professor Garner then notes that "it is a striking fact that cost literature of this period is very scarce. *The persons who worked on the problems seemed to have been very practical, busy men who had no time to write concerning their problems and how they met them in practice"* [emphasis added].[39]

However, Professor Garner later comments on what I believe is the principal reason for the lack of cost literature. He states, "On the other hand, it should be noted that perhaps another reason why so little was written on cost accounting before 1885 was the traditional attitude of business men towards divulging any comparative advantages in manufacturing techniques to possible competitors."[40]

Industrial Engineering Involved

Another strong factor in the development of cost accounting is that many of the techniques, such as the machine-hour burden absorption rate and standard costing, were developed by industrial engineers, such as Frederick W. Taylor, working with the managerial accountants. Professor Garner writes, "In fact, it may be safely stated that the profession of cost accounting developed out of the attention which was shown the subject by early industrial engineers, if that term is used to refer to the group of engineers who showed interest not only in the technical engineering problems of industry, but also in the more skillful management of manufacturing enterprises."[41] And Professor Solomons supports this statement, noting that "it is impossible to take any discussion of the origins of standard costing far without acknowledging its close connection with the 'scientific management' movement in America generally, for standard costs mean little without standard processes and standard operating times, such as F. W. Taylor and his followers developed. No one can read Taylor's famous paper on 'Shop Management' of 1903 without seeing that many of the essential elements of standard costing are there, including what is perhaps the first reference to 'management by exception.' "[42]

One of the paradoxes of accounting is that the goals for financial data the businessman seeks within his company—reliability, objectivity, realization, proper matching of costs and revenues, consistency, distinction between capital and income, impartiality, and substance over form—are the same goals the potential investor seeks. Yet when the attempt is made to develop uniformity in standards so that comparability between companies will be improved, the standard-setters and business managers clash.

This conflict is due, to a great degree, to the difficulty in finding separate companies with operations and management so similar that uniformity could even be appropriate. Thus, genuine differences in operations and goals, coupled with the inherently subjective nature of many accounting decisions, result in business's objecting to broad generalized standards that will not fit all companies.

The significance of the preceding is that while managerial accountants utilize the basic accounting concepts discussed at the beginning of this chapter to make fundamental operating decisions, the accounting principles published by the regulators won't be of much help since they are basically reporting principles designed to assist the would-be investor to make an investment decision rather than to help the manager make the decisions necessary to produce a product or a service.

BASIC DICHOTOMY BETWEEN FINANCIAL DISCIPLINE AND POTENTIAL VALUE

This basic dichotomy between how managerial accountants view the role of accounting (i.e., to provide the financial discipline and data that management can use to earn the highest return on the owner's investment compatible with the acceptable degree of risk) and how the regulators, both governmental and private, view the role (i.e., to "provide information that is useful to present and potential investors and creditors and other uses in making rational investment, credit, and similar decisions")[43] is the heart of the debate about the key issues in the profession. These debates, which become quite heated from time to time, concern, among other subjects, inflation and accounting, the conceptual framework of accounting, the uniformity/comparability of accounting principles issue, and the unpopular statements of the FASB, such as Statement No. 8 on the translation of foreign currency statements. The basic issue seems to be the need to have either the income statement or the balance sheet predominate.

Dispute Centers on Income Statement Versus Balance Sheet

There is no doubt in the mind of the managerial accountant of the primacy of the need to make as reasonable a determination of operating income for a given period as good judgment will permit. The company's liquidity position is vital too, of course, as is the debt-to-equity ratio and its effect on bond rating. Nevertheless, the balance sheet is basically a collection of unallocated costs and expenses and estimates of future costs and expenses.

The distinction between the balance sheet and the income statement is best illustrated by their internal use. In all companies familiar to the author, the top management regularly scrutinizes various analyses of the income statement as part of their review of past results and future prospects. On the other hand, few bother reviewing a full balance sheet, dealing instead with only the working capital, debt position and requirements, and the capital budget.

However, as we mentioned in the discussion of the double-entry concept, the primary theoretical base of accounting is the balance sheet, with its relationship of assets equal to liabilities plus owner's equity, and with the profit and loss accounts as extensions of changes in owner's equity. Thus, the early theoreticians considered the balance sheet as the primary financial statement. A. C. Littleton observes in writing of this controversy, "Put in a slightly different way, the balance sheet was visualized as the statement of resources and liabilities or the statement of property and claims which shows the solvency of the business. The balance sheet shows the status of the real accounts at the end of the year. It gives a summary view of the situation at a definite moment of time."[44] Of course, this was the goal of the lender. And the annual reports of the first two decades of this century reflected this view. The balance sheet was featured with a full income statement usually omitted; and in its place, a movement of the retained earnings from year to year was displayed. Of course, the statement of changes in financial position—the funds statement—was omitted since it was not required as a basic financial statement until 1971.

Here again, in this controversy we see how the development of cost accounting by industrial engineers and managerial accountants diverges from the development of financial reporting. Previts and Merino discuss this schism in accounting thought: "One finds little discussion [in the writings of the theoreticians of the early twentieth century] of the need for income determination, and although the concept of realization was addressed, it was not fundamental to the development of most early theory. Implicit in the early debate was the enduring belief that accountants must view either the income statement or balance sheet as fundamental, and the other residual. It was during this period that the perplexing enigma of double entry was recognized. If financial statements were to articulate, one had to choose up sides by opting for a proper income statement or a proper balance sheet, the belief being that you could not have relevant values in both."[45]

Entity Theory

Previts and Merino go on to cite the activities of the cost accountants led by Clinton Scovell of Scovell and Wellington. Scovell was evidently a proponent of Paton's entity theory, which ignores the distinction between owner's equity and liabilities, viewing them both as sources of capital upon which a satisfactory rate of return had to be earned by the company. Thus, imputed interest on owner's capital and undistributed earnings should be accrued or charged against income as a cost of production.* Thus Scovell "insisted that profits accrued only after all factors of production received payment for their factor shares, including payment for the use of capital. . . . Minutes of the [American] Institute [of Certified Public Accountants], 1912–1919, and issues

---

*This theory reappears from time to time, most recently during the FASB's considerations leading to Statement No. 34, *Capitalization of Interest Costs,* in 1979.

of the *Journal of Accountancy* during those same years show that the debate was indeed heated. Cost accountants, who took an entity view, claimed it was immaterial to management whether investors or creditors provided funds. . . . Had the debate continued it might have been effective in raising some pertinent questions . . . but it was rendered moot by the appearance of *Uniform Accounting* [published by the Federal Trade Commission in 1917 and which dealt with auditing and reporting standards not 'uniform accounting'] which specifically precluded interest on capital as a cost of production. Scovell, addressing Robert Montgomery [of Lybrand, Ross Brothers & Montgomery], who had been one of his steadfast opponents, asked what this meant. Montgomery told him that as a member of the AI(CP)A he was prohibited from including such charges in audited financial statements. Scovell became enraged and indicated that he just might ignore such a prohibition which, in fact, many practitioners did."[46]

Cost Accounting Ignored

Perhaps even more significant than the preceding exchange are the Previts and Merino comments that "Montgomery's attitude towards cost accounting was enough to make many cost accountants bristle. He told Scovell, 'I not only will say I know nothing about cost accounting, I claim it.' In 1919, when the National Association of Cost Accountants (now NAA) was being promoted, Montgomery refused to see it as a challenge telling the Council that, 'I think the Institute, as an Institute for *professional* [emphasis added] accountants, need fear no specialized, technical organization, no matter how large and powerful it may be.' "[47] It is interesting to note that today the FASB also does not concern itself with cost accounting per se.

Probably the most significant aspect of accounting in the early years of this century was that whereas well-run companies, such as DuPont, had developed effective internal managerial accounting systems, many companies did not, and the public reporting of financial results was distorted to say the least. Hendriksen notes that in a survey done in 1915–1916, the Federal Trade Commission found that of 60,000 successful corporations doing business in excess of $100,000 per year, fully one-half did not include a depreciation provision in their statements or accounts.[48]

Early Emphasis on Credit Favored Balance Sheet

We have already commented on the overconservatism of that era. Hendriksen summarizes "that its special conservatism was acceptable to bankers appears to have been the main factor responsible for the popularity of the balance sheet audit. Its popularity was very important to the development of accounting theory because it temporarily counteracted those forces which normally would have shifted the emphasis from the balance sheet to the income statement much sooner. The development and growth of the large corporation, the rapid development of cost accounting, and the income tax laws all tended to emphasize the profit and loss viewpoint."[49] However, as we shall see, the abuses of the 1920s cited earlier were to bring the world of regulation down upon the profession and business as the nation looked for the reasons for the Crash of 1929 and the ensuing Great Depression.

John Carey notes that as early as 1922 the New York Stock Exchange showed some concern about the prevalent financial practices, such as those mentioned in the earlier quotation of Hoxsey's.[50] These practices were certainly cause for concern. However, it is important to remember that well-managed companies did not abuse their responsibilities and, instead, followed sounder accounting concepts.

DRIVE FOR SPECIFIC RULES

The problem of poor practices was two-fold—the unscrupulous businessman and the vacillating auditor who rationalized rather than stood his ground. A good share of the blame for regulation must be borne by those who sought a third party to whom they could point as the reason for an unpopular position. It is always easier for the independent auditor* to cite a third party's "rule" that "ties the auditor's hands" when a client suggests a less conservative, less substantive, though entirely legal, accounting approach than it is for the auditor to state simply that the transaction lacks substance and the form should not be followed in the accounting.

The independent auditor's desire for specific rules which ease the burden, coupled with the analyst's desire for comparability among companies, is still the driving force behind the regulation of accounting that they were in the 1920s when it all started.

As we will explore in more depth later, speculators in the investment field are always seeking the "sleeper" investment. This tendency, coupled with the exaggerated emphasis on earnings per share, price/earnings ratios, and bond ratings, means that less conservative accounting practices tend to emerge. Although well-run companies that last for the long run generally follow more conservative accounting practices, the abuses of the speculators, both in business and in investing, create the conditions that can lead to regulation, as we will see.

---

*I must express some degree of sympathy for the independent auditor's position. There is no doubt that the field of accounting has its own "Gresham's Law"—poor financial reporting practices do tend to drive out the good practices—at least in the short run.

This problem was articulated by Charles G. Steele, managing partner of Deloitte Haskins & Sells, in an interview with Donald J. Kirk, chairman of the FASB, and Oscar S. Gellein, a former member of the FASB and retired senior partner of Deloitte Haskins & Sells. In response to a question about specific rulemaking versus broad standards, Mr. Steele replied, "I wish we were living in a world where we didn't have to have standards that became so specific they became rules. In today's competitive conditions, if we don't have fairly specific rules or standards, *we will find companies shopping for what they want and we will have firms that will bend their interpretations to permit those companies to have what they want* [emphasis added]. I would like for us to be able to operate in an atmosphere of broad standards interpreted by intelligent, reasonable individuals. However, I'm afraid that's not the world we're living in. Although I abhor the idea of going toward a detailed rule book, I'm afraid that's where we're headed."[51]

To sum up, although there is no formal set of generally accepted accounting principles that is immutable or complete, there are well-understood broad concepts that are used daily by all accountants. The abuses of these concepts by a relative few, however, coupled with the lack of understanding of the subjectivity of accounting, has resulted in a steady drive toward uniformity, rule-making, and regulation. In the next two chapters, we will review in depth this drive toward regulation.

REFERENCES

1. Paton and Littleton, *An Introduction to Corporate Accounting Standards.*

2. *Basic Concepts and Accounting Principles Underlying Financial Statements of Business Enterprises,* Statement No. 4, AICPA, New York, 1970.

3. Hendriksen, *Accounting Theory,* p. 84.

4. Much of the background of this chapter came from 11 books, which will be quoted from time to time: Carey, *The Rise of the Accounting Profession;* Kathryn Current Buckner, *Littleton's Contribution to the Theory of Accountancy,* Research Monograph No. 62, School of Business Administration, Georgia State University, Atlanta, 1975; *The Academy of Accounting Historians—Working Paper Series,* vol. 1 and 2, Edward N. Coffman, ed., The Academy of Accounting Historians, 1979; Sidney Davidson and Roman L. Weil, eds., *Handbook of Cost Accounting,* McGraw-Hill Book Company, New York, 1978, reproduced with permission; Paul Grady, *Inventory of Generally Accepted Accounting Principles,* Accounting Research Study No. 7, AICPA, New York, 1965; Hendriksen, *Accounting Theory;* Homer Kripke, reprinted with permission from *The SEC and Corporate Disclosure: Regulation in Search Of a Purpose,* Copyright © 1979 by Law & Business, Inc., Harcourt Brace Jovanovich, New York, all rights reserved; Philip E. Meyer, *Applied Accounting Theory,* Richard D. Irwin, Inc., Homewood, Ill., 1980; W. A. Paton, *Paton on Accounting,* Herbert F. Taggart, University of Michigan, ed., Ann Arbor, Michigan, 1964; C. D. Pound, ed., *The Development of Accounting Principles—A Study of Diversity,* A. F. M. Exploratory Series No. 6, Dept. of Accounting and Financial Management, University of New England,

Armidale, Australia, 1979; Gary John Previts and Barbara Dubis Merino, *A History of Accounting in America*, Ronald Press—Wiley, New York, 1979.

5. Hendriksen, *Accounting Theory*, p. 36.

6. Ibid., p. 37.

7. Buckner, *Littleton's Contribution*, p. 78.

8. Meyer, *Applied Accounting Theory*, p. 46.

9. Accounting Series Release No. 300, SEC. October 8, 1981.

10. A.C. Littleton, "Integrity," *The Illinois CPA*, vol. 26, No. 3, spring, 1964, and Buckner, *Littleton's Contribution*, p. 146.

11. Hendriksen, *Accounting Theory*, p. 60.

12. R. J. Bennett, *Corporation Accounting*, Ronald Press, New York, 1916, pp. 325–326.

13. "A Tentative Statement of Accounting Principles Affecting Corporate Reports," Paton and Littleton, *The Accounting Review*, 1936.

14. Paton and Littleton, *An Introduction to Corporate Accounting Standards*, p. 69.

15. Meyer, *Applied Accounting Theory*, p. 48.

16. *The Accounting Review*, March 1980, p. 620.

17. Grady, *Inventory of Generally Accepted Accounting Principles*.

18. Ibid., p. 33.

19. Accounting Research Bulletin (ARB) No. 1, Committee on Accounting Procedure, AICPA, New York, September 1939, p. 3.

20. Grady, *Inventory of Generally Accepted Accounting Principles*, p. 40.

21. *Qualitative Characteristics of Accounting Information*, Statement of Financial Accounting Concept No. 2, pp. 50–54, plus Appendix C of the Statement, FASB, May 1980.

22. Paton, *Paton on Accounting*, p. 123.

23. Hendriksen, *Accounting Theory*, p. 145.

24. Previts and Merino, *A History of Accounting in America*, p. 238.

25. Grady, *Inventory of Generally Accepted Accounting Principles*, p. 50.

26. Previts and Merino, *A History of Accounting in America*, pp. 231–232.

27. *The Report of the Study Group on the Objectives of Financial Statements*, Robert M. Trueblood, chairman, AICPA, 1973, p. 22.

28. Hendriksen, *Accounting Theory*, p. 144.

29. D. R. Scott, "The Basis for Accounting Principles," *Accounting Review*, December 1941, pp. 341–49. Reprinted in Hendricksen, *Accounting Theory*, p. 17.

30. A. C. Littleton, *Accounting Evolution to 1900* (New York; American Institute Publishing Co., Inc., 1933), p. 159, as quoted by James Ole Winjum, *The Role of Accounting in the Economic Development of England, (1500–1750), University of Illinois, 1972, p. 28.*

31. *Statement of Position*, No. 78-4, "Application of the Deposit, Installment and Cost Recovery Methods in Accounting for Sales of Real Estates," New York, June 30, 1978.

32. George Staubus, "An Analysis of APB Statement No. 4," *Journal of Accountancy*, February 1972, p. 37.

33. Specified excerpt from *Pierre S. duPont and The Making of the Modern Corporation*, by Alfred D. Chandler, Jr. and Stephen Salisbury. Copyright © 1971 by Alfred D. Chandler, Jr. and Stephen Salisbury. Reprinted by permission of Harper and Row, New York.

34. Ibid., p. 572.

35. Ibid., p. 147.

36. Ibid., p. 151.

37. Davidson and Weil, *Handbook of Cost Accounting*, p. 2.

38. Ibid., p. 3.

39. S. Paul Garner, *Evolution of Cost Accounting to 1925*, The University of Alabama Press, 1954, pp. 28–29.

40. Ibid., p. 30.

41. Ibid., p. 346.

42. Davidson and Weil, *Handbook of Cost Accounting*, p. 22.

43. Statement of Financial Accounting Concepts No. 1, Financial Accounting Standards Board, 1978, p. 16.

44. Buckner, *Littleton's Contribution*, p. 41.

45. Previts and Merino, *A History of Accounting in America*, pp. 183–184.

46. Ibid., p. 184.

47. Ibid., p. 196.

48. Hendriksen, *Accounting Theory*, p. 60.

49. Ibid., pp. 58–59.

50. Carey, *The Rise of the Accounting Profession*, vol. 1, p. 160.

51. Interview with Donald J. Kirk, Oscar S. Gellin and Charles G. Steele. *The Week in Review*. Deloitte Haskins & Sells, June 19 and 26, 1981.

four

THE RISE OF STANDARDS SETTERS

SHIFT TO INVESTOR ORIENTATION

The pursuit of *Generally Accepted Accounting Principles* began in earnest in the 1920s and 1930s. Keep in mind, however, that the goal then, as now, was not *accounting* principles so much as *reporting* principles. Hendriksen comments that "the most important shift in basic accounting thought coming out of the writings and discussions of the late 1920s and early 1930s was the change in the objective of accounting from that of presenting information to management and creditors to that of providing financial information for investors and stockholders. The pressure for this change in objective came from the financial sectors and stock exchanges rather than from accountants."[1]

From the standpoint of the investor, the stock exchanges, the independent public accountants, and even the academician, this comment appears to be true. However, no such "shift in basic accounting thought" took place in managerial accounting. The concepts typified by Pierre S. duPont and other leaders of well-managed companies discussed in Chapter 3 remained unchanged. Furthermore, it is my opinion that management does not have different goals from the *long-term* investor or creditor. In virtually all companies the management are also stockholders. All stockholders want the maximum return of cash from their investment commensurate with the degree of risk. Certainly this goal is not always, or even often, achieved, and yet companies continue to operate. Although this may appear to be contradictory to the basic goal, it is not. The management, stockholders, and creditors of losing operations still want to maximize their return. The fact that they cannot but still keep trying (as, for example, in the case of Chrysler Corporation in the early 1980s) simply means that so much capital has been invested that they are unable to "cash out"; that is, no one will pay the investors enough for them to recoup, and, thus, they must keep trying to make the investment pay off (i.e., they are "locked in").

Long-Term Investor Versus Short-Term Speculator

The significance of the *long-term* investor cannot be overemphasized. The basic conflict between regulators and managerial accountants comes from the need for the regulators to curb the abuses of accounting by the managerial *speculator* and the misconception on the part of regulators that they should serve the needs of the short-term investor, that is, the investing speculator.

John Maynard Keynes wrote of the distortions in the financial markets caused by the speculator.[2] After discussing how the level of investment is dependent on the rate of interest and the relationship between the supply-price of a capital asset and its prospective yield, he expands on the factors involved in estimating the prospective yield of the asset. These factors, which Keynes terms "the state of long-term expectations," include an estimate of the future tastes of the consumer for the product or service the asset will produce, the strength of the demand, and so forth. He then writes of the use of a "convention" by which this concept is applied by the stock markets: "The essence of this convention—though it does not, of course, work out quite so simply—lies in assuming that the existing state of affairs will continue indefinitely, except in so far as we have specific reasons to expect a change."[3] Of course, he explains, everyone knows this is most unlikely but the "convention" does provide a basis for planning. He notes, "it is its precariousness which creates no small part of our contemporary problem of securing sufficient investment."[4]

Lord Keynes then goes on to cite some of the factors which accentuate the precariousness of the convention. The first is "the gradual increase in the proportion of the equity . . . which is owned by persons who do not manage and have no special knowledge of the circumstances, either actual or prospective, of the business in question. . . ." The second factor is that "day-to-day fluctuations in the profits of existing investments, which are obviously of an ephemeral and nonsignificant character, tend to have an altogether excessive, and even absurd, influence on the market." The third factor is that "a conventional valuation which is established as the outcome of the mass psychology of a large number of ignorant individuals is liable to change violently as the result of a sudden fluctuation of opinion due to factors which do not really make much difference in the prospective yield, since there will be no strong roots of conviction to hold it steady."[5]

As relevant as these observations still are today, however, it is the fourth and final factor that is the most pertinent to our consideration of the question of accounting and reporting standards.

Lord Keynes continues with the fourth factor: "But there is one feature in particular which deserves our attention. It might have been supposed that competition between expert professionals, possessing judgment and knowledge beyond that of the average private investors, would correct the vagaries of the ignorant individual left to himself. It happens, however, that the energies and skill of the professional investor and speculator are mainly occupied otherwise. *For most of these persons are, in fact, largely concerned, not with making superior long-term forecasts of the probable yield of an investment over its whole life,* but with foreseeing changes in the conventional basis of valuations *a short time ahead of the public* [emphasis added]. They are concerned, not with what an investment is really worth to a man who buys it 'for keeps,' but with what the market will value it at, *under the influence* of mass psychology, three months or a year hence"[6] [emphasis added]. Anyone who doubts the timeliness of these observations has only to recall the effect on the New York stock market of the Granville phone calls in January 1981 and the London and Tokyo exchanges in September 1981.*

EXCESSIVE SPECULATION IN 1920s

This emphasis on short-term speculation began with a vengeance in the 1920s. In *The Great Crash*,[7] Professor John Kenneth Galbraith recounts a fascinating history and analysis of the speculative period preceding the Great Crash of 1929—the Florida land boom (and bust) of 1925–1926, the era of "boundless hope and optimism," the investment trusts, the incredible frauds of Charles Ponzi, Ivar Krueger (the "match king"), Samuel Insull, and other excesses of the period. But above all, the orgy of speculation. As Professor Galbraith puts it, "Far more important than rate of interest and the supply of credit is the mood. Speculation on a large scale requires a pervasive sense of confidence and optimism and conviction that ordinary people were meant to be rich."[8] He then goes on to cite five major weaknesses of the economy that not only contributed to the crash but caused it to worsen into the Great Depression:

1 The bad distribution of income. . . . it seems certain that the 5% of the population with the highest incomes in that year received approximately

---

*This emphasis on the short term has now become the "whipping boy" as the reason why the United States has fallen behind the Japanese in management, productivity, and economic success. However, there seems little doubt that the capital markets themselves have fostered the short-term view.

one-third of all personal income. . . . [This] meant that the economy was dependent on a high level of investment or a high level of luxury consumer spending, or both.

2   The bad corporate structure. . . . The most important . . . was inherent in the vast new structure of holding companies and investment trusts. . . . Here . . . was the constant danger of devastation by reverse leverage. In particular, dividends from the operating companies paid the interest on the bonds of upstream holding companies. The interruption of the dividends meant default on the bonds, bankruptcy, and the collapse of the structure. Under these circumstances, the temptation to curtail investment in operating plant in order to continue dividends was obviously strong. This added to deflationary pressures. The latter, in turn, curtailed earnings and helped bring down the corporate pyramids.

3   The bad banking structure. . . . The weakness was implicit in the large numbers of independent units. When one bank failed, the assets of the others were frozen while depositors elsewhere had a pregnant warning to go and ask for their money. Thus one failure led to another . . . with a domino effect. . . . it would be hard to imagine a better arrangement for magnifying the effects of fear.

4   The dubious state of the foreign trade balance. [The U.S. was a net exporter and followed a high-tariff policy that further restricted imports. During the twenties, we built up receivables from foreign countries for our exports and war debts.] This meant that they had either to increase their exports to the U.S. or reduce their imports or default. [Our high tariffs prevented the first so they defaulted, which reduced our production through lost exports.]

5   The poor state of economic intelligence.[9]

Against this background of economic instability, managerial accountants of well-managed companies were going about their business, analyzing and recording transactions, preparing budgets and forecasts, comparing actual results to the budgets and forecasts, assisting the treasurer in cash flow and liquidity analyses, analyzing the costs of products, controlling inventories, and generally assisting management in the day-to-day operations of their company.

Great Diversity in Application of Accounting Concepts in 1920s

However, there was a great diversity in the competence of accountants, both in industry and in public auditing. As a result, to cite two prime examples, the concept of depreciation was inconsistently applied, and as discussed in Chapter 3 there often was not a clear distinction made between capital and income or a reasonable application of the realization concept. But the major problem of accounting and financial reporting was the poor application of the concept of substance over form. This last situation is still a major problem today and always will be until rules can be written that specify how good sense, judgment, and courage are to be applied—an impossible goal.

The lack of any specific accounting standards, principles, or rules enforced by a regulatory unit with "teeth," coupled with the American tradition of the "wheeler-dealer" led to such questionable accounting practices in the 1920s as the writing up of asset values without any verifiable basis for such valuations, the formation of ostensibly new companies and new stock issues based on unsupported valuations, which created "watered stock," and the payment of dividends out of capital without clearly designating that the dividend was a return of capital to the stockholder, not income. On the other side, we have already cited the extensive use of "hidden reserves," which resulted in far too conservative a presentation of a company's financial position.

The Federal Reserve Bulletin of 1917 titled *Uniform Accounting* was the first major attempt to come to grips with the excesses in financial reporting. A second attempt was made when the bank credit officers, represented by the Robert Morris Associates, called a meeting with the AI(CP)A in 1921 to discuss what they perceived to be a decline in integrity of the independent auditors' opinions. In his memoirs, George O. May, then managing partner of Price Waterhouse & Co., gives an interesting insight into the problem of communication. Although some of the criticism of the auditors was warranted, Mr. May recalls, "In reply I offered some criticisms of attitudes of bank toward auditors, pointing out that some banks when requested to confirm balances refrained from mentioning other material facts bearing on the financial position of the corporation. I also explained the work of the Institute [of CPAs] in promoting better accounting practices and handed out the copies of the [firm's] letter on [the subject of onerous] commitments [as an example]."[10]

Mr. May's observations might well have been written today since they point up the essential problems of generally accepted accounting principles, uniformity, and regulation of accounting, which are still unresolved.

Well-managed auditing firms follow sound auditing practices and maintain a high level of integrity in their practice. By the same token, the management of companies such as DuPont apply sound accounting practices and also maintain a high level of integrity in the reporting of their stewardship to their stockholders. But, as we noted earlier, Mr. Steele (of Deloitte Haskins & Sells) pointed out as recently as June 1981,* practice will *tend* to sink to the lowest level of competence. Thus, even though the majority of auditors and managerial accountants are practicing at a sound, competent level, the exceptions cause problems for everyone.

This was certainly true in the "Roaring Twenties." Although as early as

*The Week in Review, Deloitte Haskins & Sells, New York, June 19, 26, 1981.

1922, the New York Stock Exchange president, Seymour L. Cromwell, had expressed the uneasiness of the Exchange with the financial practices of that time, nothing of any consequence was done to improve them and to dispel the feeling of concern. Times were good, World War I had been won, and the world was safe from war forever; a new middle-class was rising, Henry Ford had put the country on wheels, and everyone was going to be rich! Or so it seemed at the time.

Criticism of Diversity and Excesses

There were critics, of course, notably Professor William Z. Ripley of Harvard, insofar as finance and accounting were concerned. Ripley "wrote with zest of the 'docility of corporate shareholders permitting themselves to be honeyfugled'; and about 'the hoodwinking of the shareholders' in the field of public utilities. 'The accountants', he wrote, 'are enabled to play ball with figures to an astounding degree.' "[11]

As mentioned earlier, responsible members of the auditing field shared Professor Ripley's concern, though perhaps not his hyperbole. Notable among them was George O. May who, in 1926 relinquished his administrative duties as managing partner of Price Waterhouse & Co. to "consider a broader field of activity."[12] At the same time, the New York Stock Exchange instituted a fundamental change in its attitude toward listed companies due, in some part, to the Ripley articles,* and J.M.B. Hoxsey was appointed as executive assistant to the Exchange's Committee on Stock List. Since Hoxsey was concerned with the same problems that troubled May, they soon met and began an informal cooperation on accounting matters. May reports that "in the ensuing years, conferences between Mr. Hoxsey and myself were frequent and many important issues were discussed, including such questions as the scope of audits, greater uniformity in accounting principles, etc. At one time, the suggestion was made that the Exchange should establish some standards and have a list of approved accountants. I told Mr. Hoxsey that if the latter suggestion were adopted, my firm would not apply to be put on the list since it would not accept any nongovernmental jurisdiction other than that of a professional character. This idea was dropped."[13]

Although it is pure speculation, it is probable that barring any catastrophe, the Exchange and the AI(CP)A would have eventually worked out some reasonable standards for the reporting, as well as the auditing, of financial data. However, a catastrophe did occur—the Great Crash in 1929,

---

*Professor Ripley wrote of the poor accounting practices throughout the 1920s in such periodicals as *The Atlantic*. In 1927, a collection of these articles was published in book form entitled, *Main Street and Wall Street*. (Little, Brown and Company, Boston, Mass.)

which was followed hard by the Great Depression—and the auditing profession and the Stock Exchange no longer had any time left. As John Carey puts it, "The Stock Exchange suddenly showed an eager interest in reform and a desire to cooperate with the [Accountants] Institute in improving financial reporting."[14]

FIRST ATTEMPT AT STANDARDS SETTING

Mr. Hoxsey was sent to the institute's 1930 annual meeting at which he gave his famous speech, "Accounting for Investors" (quoted in Chapter 3), and a special committee on cooperation with stock exchanges was formed. May was named chairman. The committee struggled for four years, and in 1934 published the first formal attempt at setting Generally Accepted Accounting Principles in *Audits of Corporate Accounts* (mentioned in Chapter 3). Briefly, the five "principles" formalized may be summarized as follows:

1   Unrealized profit should not be credited to income either directly or indirectly.
2   Capital surplus should not be used to avoid charges that should be made against income
3   Earned surplus of a subsidiary earned prior to acquisition by another should not be added to that of its new parent company.
4   While in some cases, treasury stock may be shown as an asset, dividends on such stock should not be treated as income.
5   Notes or accounts receivable due from officers, employees, or affiliates should be shown separately on the balance sheet.

A sixth "principle" was added at the AI(CP)A meeting in 1934 as the result of an SEC decision dealing with donated stock.[15]

6   If capital stock is issued nominally for the acquisition of property and at about the same time some or all of the stock is donated to the company, the par value of the stock cannot be used as the cost basis of the property.

Looking at those "principles" today, it is hard to imagine that anyone would consider them to be the first principles of accounting. Moreover, it is doubtful that they had the slightest effect on any well-managed company of the time, although they undoubtedly curtailed some of the excesses of more than a few "wheeler-dealer" firms. As Carman Blough put it, the five principles "forbade some of the worst common practices."[16] That, of course, is precisely why they were published. The development of GAAP up to 1934 and for the nearly 50 years thereafter has been a history of reaction to a problem caused by the excesses of "wheeler-dealers" seeking to take advantage of the people and their gambling, "get-rich-quick" instinct. Some of these speculators, such as Samuel Insull, Ivar Kreuger, McKesson-Robbins, Billy Sol Estes, or the people involved in Equity Funding, committed outright frauds, while others were just opportunists who used strictly legal, though perhaps ethically questionable, tactics to utilize the magic of leverage and form over substance to amass fortunes created by market appreciation of their stock holdings. Examples of the latter would be the real estate development companies of the late 1950s and early 1960s and the "pooling of interests" craze of the 1960s.

Use of "Principles" Misled Many

It is unfortuante that the word *principles* was finally selected to describe what were obviously intended to be just sensible practices. In his memoirs, George May comments on the selection of the word.[17] He explains how *conventions, practices,* and *principles* were used in various correspondence of his committee. It appears that the New York Stock Exchange might have preferred *principles,* possibly because of the connotation of sound theory rather than *practices,* which sounds as though no one had really attempted to develop a logical theoretical basis. Of course, although some noted theoreticians, such as Hatfield, Paton, and Littleton, had written on basic theory at that time, the primary source for the preferred practices cited by the May committee were deduced from their experience of the practices followed by the companies that were the most successful in the long run.*

Nevertheless, the term *principles* was adopted and, as a result, an aura of precision, logic, and finality was formally and inappropriately applied to accounting. Over the ensuing years this would prove to be a continual source of embarrassment as events proved again and again that not only was there no such broad, all-encompassing set of GAAP but even that the application of the few Generally Accepted Accounting Principles that did exist could be quite subjective.

In reviewing the history of GAAP, it is important to keep in mind that the independent auditor was "under the gun" in the early 1930s. Indeed, it may well be that the auditor has never quite gotten out from that precarious

---

*It is interesting to note that the Controllers Institute of America (later changed to the Financial Executive Institute) reviewed the report and expressed their concurrence, taking only mild exception to the fifth "principle" on the grounds of cost/benefit. (See *Audits of Corporate Accounts,* AIA and NYSE, 1932–1934, pp. 29–30.)

position. The Great Depression changed the entire history of the world and one of the changes was the unequivocal end of laissez-faire in our economy. While the 1929 crash alone might not have brought about radical changes in our government's economic policies, the basic flaws in our economy that resulted in the depression ensured the drastic changes that followed during the early Roosevelt years.

MAJOR FRAUDS OF 1920s LED TO GOVERNMENT INTERVENTION

Samuel Eliot Morison gives us a brilliant perspective from which to judge what was to happen in the 1930s. Describing the 1920s as "the greatest orgy of speculation and over-optimism since the South Sea Bubble," he goes on to say,

> There was a great deal wrong, besides overspeculation, with the national economy and the laws regulating it. Corporations, which as early as 1919 employed 86.5% of all wage earners in industry, were proliferating under practically no control. Certain states, such as Delaware and New Jersey, allowed anyone paying a registration fee to incorporate a company, leaving its directors free to issue new stock, and with no obligation to make an annual report or accounting. The number of Delaware incorporations with authorized capital stock of $20 million or more, rose from 55 in 1925 to 619 in 1929. One characteristic device was to form a holding company comprising a large number of electric light and other power corporations, the "utilities" as these were called. Holding companies were often so rigged that an outsider who bought stock knew nothing of what was going on . . . [presumably because of the lack of reporting of consolidated results or subsidiaries' activities].
>
> Stock pools burgeoned and blossomed. A group of men would get together, buy a sizeable block of no matter what, then trade shares back and forth, hiking the price and pulling in outsiders who hoped to get in on the profits. When the stock reached an agreed [by the insiders] point, members of the pool dumped it on the market, took their profits and retired, leaving the suckers to take the rap. The reverse was a "bear raid" on a stock already doing well. Rumors would be circulated that the company was being badly managed or overcapitalized, by operators who sold short, drove down the stock, and bought it back at a very attractive price.
>
> The boom was world-wide and the two promoters who were most successful in fleecing the American lambs were foreigners—Samuel E. Insull, originally from London, and Ivar Krueger, the Swedish match king. . . . Insull, who emigrated young to Chicago, became chairman of 65 company directorates which operated in the utilities field in 23 different states. He was no common crook, but a public-spirited magnate who saved the city of Chicago from bankruptcy, built a palatial opera house, and started a natural-gas pipeline

from the Texas panhandle to Lake Michigan. Regarding the depression as temporary, he continued to overextend in 1930, and his elaborate edifice crashed in April 1932 with a loss to American investors of $700 million. Insull found a pleasant asylum in Greece; extradited he was acquitted of breaking the law. Not so nice was the career of Ivar Kreuger, who even counterfeited Italian government bonds to deceive auditors. "Uncle Ivar" looked so virtuous . . . that he was able to buy American companies like Diamond Match "on a shoe-string.". . . Investors as well as speculators . . . bought about $250 million of his worthless securities.[18]

Krueger had built the largest "pyramid club" in history and when it collapsed he killed himself in March 1932.

These massive frauds, coupled with the depression into which the nation had fallen and the election of a dynamic new president triggered an investigation in 1933 into the field of investment banking by the Senate Committee on Banking and Currency under the direction of their counsel, Ferdinand Pecora. In his inaugural address, President Roosevelt struck the tone: "Yes, the money changers have fled from their high seats in the temple of our civilization. We may now restore that temple to the ancient truths. The measure of the restoration lies in the extent to which we apply social values more noble than mere monetary profit."[19]

1933–1934 Securities and Exchange Acts

The Pecora investigation led to the Truth-In-Securities Act of 1933 followed by the Securities Exchange Act of 1934 and the Public Utility Holding Company Act of 1935. The first legislation covered sales of new securities while the second regulated the stock exchanges and existing corporations and also established the Securities and Exchange Commision which took over administration of the 1933 act from the Federal Trade Commission as well as the 1934 and 1935 acts.

Berle's Book Highlighted Perceived Needs

Another major contributing factor to the passage of these acts was the publication in 1932 of *The Modern Corporation and Private Property*[20] by Adolph A. Berle, Jr., a Columbia University law professor, who became a part of Roosevelt's "brain trust" group, and Gardiner C. Means, an economist who also ended up in the Roosevelt administration.

This landmark book highlighted the concentration of industrial wealth in a relatively few major corporations from which the stockholders had effectively been "divorced" from control. The book, which was concerned primarily with the economic consequences of the concentration of industrial wealth and power included a slap at accountants: "The directors . . . have a large measure of control over the company's income acount. *So long as accounting standards are not hardened* [emphasis added] and the law does not impose any specific canons, directors and their accountants may frame their figures, within limits, much as they choose."[21] The book goes on to cite the poor practices of the era that we mentioned earlier and then states, "One of the reasons why the power of the directors in this regard is so wide lies in *the fact that accountants themselves have as yet failed to work out a series of standard rules* [emphasis added]. The reason may be that in the nature of things, strict rules are out of the question. A residual rule that there must be a good faith attempt to approximate the facts as the directors and their accountants believe them to be is perhaps as close as either accountants or lawyers can now come."[22]

Later in their chapter on "Flotation and Bankers' Disclosure" Berle and Means again hammer at the need for accounting standards. "Accountancy plays a great part . . . in the market career of the security. It is customary for bankers to rely in making up their statements on (independent) accountant's reports, and the integrity of the accountant and the soundness of his method are the greatest single safeguard to the public investors and to the market in general. But rules of accounting are not as yet fully recognized rules of law in this field; though it is obvious that the development of the law of corporation finance makes almost mandatory the legal sanction of good accounting practice. In fact, the failure of the law to recognize accounting standards is probably due to the lack of agreement among accountants; but year by year certain tenets are forged out, finding their way into the body of standard accounting practice and ultimately into the law. In general the problem revolves around securing a method of accounting which will give an approximately accurate picture of the situation."[23]

New York Stock Exchanges Specified an Independent Audit

Meanwhile, in January 1933, the New York Stock Exchange adopted a policy requiring that the financial statements accompanying a listing application bear the certificate (opinion) of auditors "qualified under the laws of some state or country."[24]

Morison indicates that had the New York Stock Exchange acted swiftly enough after the passage of the 1933 Securities Act, the 1934 Exchange Act might have been avoided.[25] This comment seems a little strong in view of the temper of the time. However, regardless of how it came about, the SEC was created. Morison goes on, "President Roosevelt, to the consternation of many, appointed as Chairman of the Commission Joseph P. Kennedy, one of the leading plungers before the crash. But as one who knew all the 'angles' of the market, and was convinced of the need of reform, Kennedy was the man to do it. Supported by some of the more liberal and penitent moguls of finance such as James V. Forrestal [Roosevelt's Secretary of Navy in WW II], Robert Lovett, and W. Averell Harriman, the SEC formulated rules to prevent future skulduggery, stepped up the margin for stock trading from 10% to 45%, and also worked hard to obtain new financing [issues]."[26]

Accountants Dismayed by Government Action

The accountants were at almost a complete loss to know how to respond to the dramatic change. First of all, the basic problem was one of a relatively small group of speculators, not accounting practices per se. Galbraith estimated that "the number of active speculators (borrowing to buy or buying on a small margin) was less—and probably much less—than a million."[27] The member firms of 29 exchanges in 1929 reported accounts with 1,548,707 customers, 1,371,920 of which were with members of the New York Stock Exchange. This was out of a population of about 120 million people. "The striking thing about the stock market speculation of 1929 was not the massiveness of the participation. Rather it was the way it became central to the culture."[28]

Second, the accounting practices of a great many well-run companies were ignored as everyone concentrated on the excesses. Managerial accountants were all "tarred with the same brush" even though most were only observers of what they too thought were bad practices.

Third, the managerial accountants, although they had organizations such as the NAA and the Controllers Institutes (FEI), were effectively being represented by the independent auditors, although the auditors generally did not have experience with or responsibility for the financial management of a company.

Difference Between Auditing and Accounting Not Clear

It becomes clear in reading about this period that there was a great deal of confusion as to the difference between accounting and auditing, a problem that exists to this day. Many of the objectionable practices of accounting could have been prevented by stricter auditing standards specifying the circumstances under which an auditor could give an unqualified (clean) opinion as to the fairness of the presentation of the financial statements.

Finally, to add to the already chaotic conditions in the financial world, the auditors were even fighting among themselves. Carman Blough commented, "Two organizations, the American Institute of Accountants and the American Society of Certified Public Accountants, divided the profession. Almost equal in membership, with some people belonging to both, they were not too inclined to cooperate. Indeed, there was a considerable amount of belligerent ill will by some . . . towards the other."[29] After much infighting and dissent, the two groups merged into the AICPA in 1936.

It is no wonder in 1932 that the president of the AI(CP)A, Charles B. Couchman, would write almost plaintively,

> A constant problem of the accounting profession lies in the development of procedures to keep pace with changing economic conditions. It must be remembered that the fundamentals of accountancy were built up during a period when commercial transactions were simple and direct. Within the past few decades the whole status of business organizations has changed. Transactions have become complicated beyond the conception of the businessmen of the 19th century. These complexities were not scientifically planned in advance; they grew step by step as expediency dictated.
>
> The accountant called upon to record these operations has had to adapt the established rules to the particular cases. As complexities grew, this adaptation of simple rules has become increasingly difficult and complicated. In the 20 years from 1910 to 1930 there was never a pause sufficient to allow a careful scientific devising of methods adequate to meet the changing conditions. Any attempt at this found that before such rules could be established business had already devised new complications. . . .
>
> Small wonder that accountants trying to record the results of these transactions should have been extremely puzzled to find a logical solution. . . . The accountant has faced a more difficult task throughout these years. The laws which he attempts to interpret as to their application to specific transactions have not even been enacted in any set form. He has been compelled to apply the variable laws of economics and the fundamental bases of accountancy rules to transactions which were beyond the contemplation of the businessman or the economist of a decade before.[30]

But no one in power was interested in explanations, much less in alibis. The old system had failed, and anyone involved had better shape up and fast! Still the profession hesitated to take action of its own, partly because of internal dissension among the public accountants, partly because the managerial accountants (represented by the NAA and the FEI) were too poorly organized to respond, and partly because many had difficulty perceiving how accounting could correct the excesses of speculation. Finally, a committee on the development of accounting principles was formed in 1932 by the American Institute of Accountants with the ubiquitous George O. May as chairman.

As mentioned earlier, in January 1933 the New York Stock Exchange took two important steps. First, it required financial statements audited by an independent accountant to be filed with listing applications and to be published annually thereafter. Second, the Exchange also asked listed companies to furnish a statement from an independent accountant describing the scope of their audit, the fairness of the presentation of the financial statements, the consistency of application of the accounting practices, and whether or not these practices were not inconsistent with the five principles that had been spelled out in a 1932 letter to the Exchange by the institute's committee on cooperation and later published by the AICPA.

Government Control Proposed by Berle

However, such progress was still deemed too slow by some. A paper prepared by Professor Adolph A. Berle, Jr. for the 1933 annual meeting of the AI(CP)A gave the members another shock. The paper stressed the growing importance of accounting, raised the same questions about poor practices, and then stressed the desirability of comparisons of the results of one company with others in the same industry. He went on to ask for the consistent development of principles of accounting and suggested that the first approach should be by the accountants themselves. However, he questioned whether accountants could do the job alone, and "whether individual accountants [auditors] could maintain completely impartial minds when under the instructions of a client." He then predicted that a bureau would be set up ". . . to standardize accounting practices of various industries."[31]

Audits of Corporate Accounts mentioned earlier was published in 1934, the same year that the SEC was set up. However, it came too late to affect the passage of the 1934 Exchange Act, assuming, as Professor Morison indicated, there was a chance of forestalling the 1934 legislation.*

It is quite doubtful that either the New York Stock Exchange or the American Institute of Accountants had any thought of influencing legislation, however. Carey notes that in spite of all that had been going on, the introduction of the Truth-In-Securities Act in May 1933 came as a surprise to the profession. The institute did not appear formally at the hearings. As Carey puts it, "After all, the profession's record in developing standards of financial reporting was not impressive. Even the basic philosophy outlined in

---

*In addition to the five principles listed earlier, the *Audits of Corporate Accounts* included an example of what was to become the independent accountant's standard unqualified opinion. The accounting requirements of the New York Stock Exchange, spelled out in the *Audits of Corporate Accounts,* were almost irrelevant since in the initial drafts of the 1933 Securities Act there was no provision for audits by independent accountants. Presumably, Congress either intended that government auditors perform any necessary audits or else overlooked the point entirely. In either event, the testimony of the managing partner of Haskins & Sells, Colonel Arthur H. Carter, covered in Chapter 5, saved the day for the independent accountant by convincing Congress that it would be more efficient to make use of the independent accountants and require audits by them.[32]

the Stock Exchange correspondence was not yet available for public reference. If official representatives of the Institute had testified at the hearings, they might have been subjected to hostile questioning. This could have resulted in further adverse publicity and possibly even more punitive legislation than that proposed."[33] In short, the institute did not feel qualified to explain the art of accounting nor the difference between accounting and auditing, nor the lack of definitive rules on both! (As noted on page 74, Colonel Carter was not so reticent.)

Securities and Exchange Commission Formed

The securities and exchanges acts gave the SEC broad powers to prescribe rules and regulations covering the data to be furnished to investors, including the authority to establish rules and regulations governing the reporting and accounting of all companies listed on a national stock exchange.* The auditing profession still equivocated. For the next three years nothing was accomplished beyond the publication of the five principles and the merger of the two competing associations mentioned earlier. In fact, the institute's committee on reporting recommended to the SEC that the regulations should not require disclosure of sales and cost of sales on the grounds of competitive disadvantage.† Of course, the SEC was not in a mood to agree to the institute's proposal, and the requirement for the disclosure of sales and cost of sales was put into effect.

Public Accountants Fear Liability

The great fear of the independent public accountants was the broad expansion of their liability under the two acts. This fear virtually precluded any

---

*It is almost humorous in light of what happened in 1933 and 1934 to read of the attitude of management one hundred years ago. Weldon Powell, a partner of Haskins & Sells and first chairman of the Accounting Principles Board, said, "Modern financial accounting is a relatively new development—one that has come about largely within the lifetime of a number of accountants who are in active practice today. As recently as the 1890s, the amount provided for depreciation by a number of large corporations was considered to be a function of profits. The first modern published report of a major industrial corporation that I know of—that of United States Steel Corporation for the year 1902—was issued in 1903. Only about twenty-five years before that time a stockholder of a large railroad company who requested information concerning the company had been told that it had issued no statements for at least five years and had no intention of making its *financial affairs known to the public.*" (From a speech on the historical perspective of financial accounting given at a symposium held in 1965 at Duke University.)[34]
†Up to that time, the preeminence of the balance sheet, coupled with the fuzziness as to the nature of capital and income had resulted in most companies only disclosing a change in equity rather than what we know today as the all-inclusive-income statement.

initiative on their part. In speaking to the New York Society of CPAs in 1933, the future chairman of the SEC, James M. Landis (who succeeded Kennedy in 1935) made a significant observation: "Accountancy, as distinguished from law, has generally been portrayed as an *exact science* [emphasis added] and its representations have been proffered to the unlearned as representations of fact and not of opinion. If it insists upon such fact representations, it is, of course, fair that it should be burdened with the responsibility attendant upon such a portrayal of its results."[35] (We really have not made much progress in correcting this impression in the nearly 50 years since it was made, as evidenced by the legislation covering the Foreign Corrupt Practices Act.)

Finally, Landis, then SEC chairman, became so perturbed by the attitude of the public auditing sector of the accounting profession that in a speech to the Investment Bankers of America on December 4, 1936, he said, "The impact of almost daily tilts with [public] accountants, some of them called leaders in their profession, often leaves little doubt that their loyalties to management are stronger than their sense of reponsibility to the investors."[36]

It is important to keep in mind that Landis's quarrel was with the independent public accounting (auditing) sector of the accounting field. When he referred to "accountants" he meant the public accountants. Then, as now, this sector of accounting was, and is, generally thought of as the "accounting profession," in spite of the fact that today nearly half of the members of the AICPA are not in the practice of public accounting.

Managerial Accountants Ignored Issues

Where were the managerial accountants during all the fuss over accounting in the 1930s? Generally minding their own business. The situation was analogous to that of a number of drivers on a busy highway with the SEC acting as a traffic coordinator and the public accountants as somewhat reluctant enforcement officers. While most of the drivers (managerial accountants) obey the traffic laws a few reckless drivers do not and command the attention of the enforcement group, the SEC and the public accountants.

In the 1930s the rules that the SEC, the public accountants, and the New York Stock Exchange were establishing (such as the first five principles) had no effect on most of the practitioners of managerial accounting (the good drivers) and, thus, created little stir except in the enforcement group. This condition continued for nearly 30 years. It was not until such standards as Opinion No. 8, "Accounting for the Cost of Pension Plans" (issued in 1966), that everyone began to feel the constraint of broad, uniform rules. As we shall see, not until then did the managerial accountants, through such organizations as the NAA and the FEI, begin to take an active part in the activities of the enforcement group.

Academicians Attempt Standards Setting

However, if the independent accountants were hesitant about and the managerial accountants uninterested in uniform standards in the 1930s, the third major sector of the accounting profession—the academician—was neither hesitant nor uninterested. Professor Herbert F. Taggart tells of W. A. Paton's activities in this area: "Early in 1936 he [Paton] was appointed the first research director of the [American Accounting Association] and in June, 1936, the *Review* carried the first product of the new research activity. This was modestly entitled, 'A Tentative Statement of Accounting Principles Affecting Corporate Reports,' and there are those who think that its appearance stimulated the AI(CP)A to organize the Committee on Accounting Procedure (CAP) in an endeavor to make sure that the upstart academicians did not monopolize the business of formulating accounting principles."[37]

The "Tentative Statement" led to the Paton and Littleton classic, *An Introduction to Corporate Accounting Standards,* published in 1940. This monograph legitimatized many of the concepts employed by managerial accountants, including the concept of the matching of costs and revenues.*

However, Paton and Littleton were writing of applied managerial accounting, not auditing, that is, independent verification, and the Securities and Exchange Commission was concerned with uniform reporting. With this last goal in mind, the commission created the Office of the Chief Accountant, and in December 1935 Carman G. Blough, who was assistant director of the Registration Division at the SEC, was appointed as the first chief accountant. Mr. Blough, a CPA, was an extremely fortunate choice. He not only had several years of governmental staff work, professional experience, and teaching, he also had a rare combination of common sense and good judgment.

Government Presses Public Accountants

In his essay on this era, Mr. Blough discusses whether or not the Commission should exercise the clear authority given it to issue comprehensive rules designed to eliminate the larger number of differences in accounting practices that existed. He and a majority of the Commission "recognized the dangers of arbitrary governmental fiat in this field without extended research and a thorough knowledge of the business activities and the reasons back of each controversial practice."[38]

*Interestingly, the monograph uses the word *standards* rather than *principles*. As Paton and Littleton put it, "The term 'standards' is used advisedly. 'Principles' would generally suggest a universality and degree of permanence which cannot exist in a human-service institution such as accounting." (p. 4)

However, the public accounting (auditing) sector of the profession was not moving fast enough to suit the SEC. In spite of the work being done by the AAA, it was the auditors that had to respond to the SEC, for the auditors were obviously the "lever" through which the SEC could enforce the consistency and uniformity in reporting that they sought.

The unique position of the independent public accountant (auditor) results in an interesting paradox. The public accountant today recognizes the diversity and subjectivity of accounting and, yet, because of his potential legal liability and his desire to avoid confrontations with a client, the public accountant often finds it easier to seek specific rules that can be cited as the reason for the required action.

In 1937, Mr. Blough lost his patience with the AICPA and in a tough speech to the New York Society of CPAs, he "stressed the vital need for reducing . . . areas of differences (and) stated that the Commission would prefer to have the profession itself take the necessary steps to reduce these differences, but if the profession did not do so, the Commission had the authority and would."[39] This was a clear warning that could not be ignored. Mr. Blough reports that following this, "steps were taken at the very next meeting of the Council of the Institute, which resulted in the creation of the Committee on Accounting Procedure (CAP) with authority to issue opinions on accounting matters."[40]

SEC Delegates Standards-Setting to AICPA

This authority was delegated to the AICPA by the SEC through Accounting Series Release No. 4, which was issued April 25, 1938 by a 3-to-2 vote of the Commission.* It was a close call but the accounting profession—public ac-

---

*In a report of an in-depth interview of Carman C. Blough, Professor William Cooper tells of the intensity of the internal discussions at the SEC leading up to the final vote. "Of particular importance to me was Accounting Series Release No. 4, issued April 25, 1938. In that release, the Securities and Exchange Commission (SEC) stated that the Commission would not dictate accounting policy but would accept accounting principles that were widely followed in the accounting profession, a concept defined as 'substantial authoritative support.' Blough was a key figure in formulating this release, for many in the Commission strongly advocated establishing a rigid set of accounting principles. The most notable commissioner who advocated such a step was William O. Douglas, later a member of the Supreme Court. During the winter of 1936 and all of 1937, the SEC must have been an interesting place to have worked because two giants of the legal and accounting profession were locked in a deep philosophical debate that would directly affect a federal commission and an entire profession. Blough argued that the theoretical concepts supporting the accounting profession would become stagnant if the government dictated accounting procedures; moreover, he felt that no one in government could effectively draft a regulation that would contain all the informational requirements of the reader. Blough's logic won the day for the Commission, in a 3 to 2 vote, decided against establishing accounting rules and procedures as favored by Douglas." (*The Accounting Historians Notebook,* Fall, 1981, The Academy of Accounting Historians, Atlanta, Georgia.)

countants, managerial accountants, and academicians alike—had escaped full government control of their profession. However, the power is still vested with the SEC, and from time to time it has exercised that power and overruled the CAP and its successors, the Accounting Principles Board and the Financial Accounting Standards Board (FASB) (e.g., all-inclusive income concept, 1947; investment tax credit, 1964; and oil and gas accounting, 1978). Even today, this delegation by the SEC is not viewed as desirable by some critics. New York University Chester Rohrlich Professor of Corporate Law Homer Kripke comments, "It is clear that without Congressional authorization to do so the SEC delegated its statutory control of accounting to the industry itself."[41]

Public Accountants Play Unique Role for SEC

It is worthwhile to expand a little on how the power to determine accounting principles is exercised by the SEC since it is an indirect route and not well understood. The Securities and Exchange Act of 1934, which created the SEC, gave it the authority to regulate the stock exchanges and, by transferring the administration of the 1933 Securities Act from the FTC to the SEC, gave it the authority to generally regulate the sale of securities to the public. Thus, if a company is either listed on a stock exchange or wishes to sell securities publicly, it generally must comply with the SEC's rules, including any accounting rules it might establish.

The SEC, however, does not have a large audit staff of its own through which to ascertain that its rules are being followed. Instead, it utilizes the independent public accountant. The SEC specifies the reporting requirements for documents filed under various registration rules of the agency. One of these rules is that the financial statements will be in accordance with GAAP. The AICPA ethics Rule 203 requires that its members must ascertain that the financial statements being audited conform to the opinions and statements issued by the CAP, the APB, and the FASB (i.e., GAAP); if they do not, the auditor must qualify his opinion. The SEC, in turn, will not accept a report containing an auditor's opinion qualified for failure to conform to GAAP. Thus, this Catch-22 situation means that if a company were to insist that it would not conform to Statement No. 34, for example, which requires the capitalization of interest, and the amount involved were deemed material, the qualification of the auditor's opinion would result in a deficiency notice by the SEC and, ultimately, if unresolved, result in the delisting of the company's stock and the suspension of trading in that stock.

Once this roundabout enforcement procedure is understood, the actions of the FASB become more clear. Prior to 1979, the FASB had no sanction power other than Rule 203 of the AICPA which tied their pronouncements to the SEC. Thus, until Statement No. 33, covering reporting the effects of inflation on financial data, was issued in 1979, the FASB sought to bring all of their requirements under the audit "blanket," that is, Rule 203.

However, Statement No. 33 was a major breakthrough by the regulators in the financial reporting area because it was the first time that the FASB required supplemental unaudited data outside of the financial statements and footnotes. The necessary sanction power to ensure full compliance was put in place by the AICPA through Statement No. 27 on auditing standards. This standard is distinguished by the fact that it requires a qualification of the auditor's opinion (which would be unacceptable to the SEC) if the client company fails to report the unaudited data required by SFAS No. 33.

As a result of this complex enforcement procedure, the SEC effectively delegated the principles- and standards-setting process to the independent public accountants while retaining an overriding review. Thus, the independent public accountants, somewhat against their will, became the "enforcers." As time went on, the auditors discovered that there are some desirable features to this relationship. It is always easier for an auditor to claim that while he tended to agree with the client on the appropriate accounting for a transaction, even if he really didn't, an SEC rule prevented him from acting differently in a given case.

It is this sanction power that really was the deciding factor in determining who would set GAAP. The academicians could theorize and publish, but they had no means by which to impose or require the use of a "principle."*

AICPA BECOMES PRINCIPLES SETTER

In 1938, then, the institute formally authorized its Committee on Accounting Procedure to issue pronouncements on matters of accounting principles and procedures. The membership was enlarged to 22, including the president of the AICPA as chairman. George O. May, however, served as the executive head. The membership was dominated by the AICPA with 18 accountants from public accounting firms. Only Carman Blough (SEC) and three outstanding academicians, A. C. Littleton (Illinois), W. A. Paton (Michigan), and Roy B. Kester (Columbia), were from outside the public accounting field. Notably absent was anyone from managerial accounting.

The CAP functioned until 1959, publishing 51 Accounting Research Bulletins (ARBs). Although it did not even attempt to develop any conceptual basis for accounting or GAAP, it did accomplish a great deal. During its

---

*This same condition exists today with the IASC—International Accounting Standards Committee. This committee, composed principally of international public accounting firms, drafts and publishes International Statements of Accounting Principles. But they can be ignored with impunity by anyone who chooses because there is no international "SEC." What happens in practice is that the standards usually closely follow the U.S. statements and, thus, are followed at least in the U.S. by coincidence.

existence, the terrible abuses and excesses of the 1920s were eliminated. The basic problems that remained—frauds and lack of uniformity (comparability) between companies—were far more difficult to deal with and still are.

The basic approach of the CAP, and to a lesser degree, its successors, the APB and the FASB, was to deal with specific problems on a case-by-case basis. None of their pronouncements specifically deals with the 16 basic concepts discussed in Chapter 3.

Early Standards Formalized Good Managerial Practices

Although many of the ARBs dealt with a specific problem in reporting several were broad-ranging in establishing uniformity in reporting, for instance: ARB No. 6 (1940) "suggested"* the use of comparative financial statements; ARB No. 30 (1947) specified the display of working capital; ARB No. 40 (1950) formally endorsed the concept of "pooling of interests," the rock upon which the Accounting Principles Board would founder in the late 1960s, and ARB No. 51 (1959) ratified the concept of consolidated financial statements.†

ARB No. 51 illustrates the comment made earlier about the effect the early standards had on managerial accounting. Generally, the CAP was just formalizing sound accounting practices that had been applied for years by the managerial accountants of well-run companies who were interested in furnishing their management relevant, reliable financial data, such as those operating under the management concepts of Pierre du Pont. Previts and Merino commented on the same development: "As the trust and holding companies gained headway [late nineteenth century] popular writers and prominent authorities predicted that such businesses would fail. Their belief was founded upon the view that no one person or board of directors could successfully master such large organizations in a competitive environment. But accounting administrative control systems being developed during this period provided the information and means of direction to place at the disposal of management factors relevant to operations. Steel companies, rubber companies, munitions works and transportation, sugar and [oil] refining companies provide examples of the success of such internal man-

*The specific sanction power of Rule 203 wasn't enacted until 1964; prior to then it was implicit rather than explicit.
†This ratification occurred nearly sixty years after Arthur Lowes Dickinson, managing partner of Price Waterhouse, and W. J. Filbert, controller of U.S. Steel, decided that the newly formed U.S. Steel Corporation should include financial statements which reflect the substance (one entity) rather than the form (parent company with investments in separate legal companies) of the operations in their annual report for 1902! Previts & Merino, *A History of Accounting in America*, p. 177.

agement accounting system operations during this period for such large scale enterprises."[42]

However, the independent public accountants have always been very reluctant to have the managerial accountant become involved in the establishment of GAAP. As noted, the original CAP included three academicians but no one from business, even though logic would seem to indicate that those who faced the subjective choices of various day-by-day transactions would be particularly well-suited to deal with the problem of establishing reasonable principles.

Pressure for Uniformity Continues

The Committee on Accounting Procedure (CAP) lasted for about 20 years as the SEC's surrogate standard-setter primarily because most of the standards set in that period did not change the accounting of well-run companies. However, the uniformity/comparability issue plagued the CAP and eventually led to its downfall.

John Carey wrote of the "Pressure for Comparability of Earnings" during the 1940s and 1950s.[43] He observed the rapid growth of stockholders that began in the 1920s, slowed during the Great Depression, and then soared following World War II. As a result, private investment decisions became a matter of national concern. The regulatory agencies of the government, notably the SEC and the FTC, vigorously pursued policies aimed at protecting the general investor. One of the basic themes underlying their efforts was uniformity of accounting principles and application so that companies could be compared with each other on what appeared to be the same basis. In addition, the usage of "earnings per share" as the most significant measure of performance began. As is so often the case in our era of superficial analysis, the phrase Generally Accepted Accounting Principles was widely used and misunderstood, and the myth of precision and uniformity in accounting and financial reporting was reinforced and exaggerated. The result "was increasingly heavy pressure on the accounting profession*—specifically the AICPAs—to eliminate alternative methods of accounting for similar transactions. . . . This mounting pressure came principally from five sources: the SEC [the regulator], the American Accounting Association [the academicians], the financial analysts [later represented on the Financial Accounting Foundation by the Financial Analysts Federation], the financial press, and elements within the AICPA itself. However, powerful countervailing pressures also developed among some corporate managements and

---

*Mr. Carey defined the profession as just independent public accountants.

organizations representing them, such as the National Association of Manufacturers, and the Financial Executives Institute."[44]

Carey goes on to report how the pressure on the Committee on Accounting Practice was crystalized in 1956 by a speech made by Leonard Spacek, then managing partner of Arthur Andersen & Co. and long an outspoken critic of the profession. After advocating an inflation-adjusted depreciation policy, he blasted the public accountants for hiding behind GAAP when they gave unqualified opinions on income statements prepared on the traditional historical cost basis. "There are many people in the accounting profession who feel that their obligation is fulfilled by reporting the figures and amounts taken from the records of the company. . . . You may have heard the assertion that income statements prepared in this manner [without reflecting the effect of inflation on depreciation] conform to the 'generally accepted accounting principles' currently prevailing as the policy of the American Institute of [Certified Public] Accountants. Let me assure you that it has not become heresy to raise the question, *'What are generally accepted accounting principles?* [emphasis added] . . . Nor, in my view, can an accountant excuse himself or his actions by seeking cover in the shadow of a *phrase which cannot stand re-examination* in the light of day"[45] [emphasis added]. Mr. Spacek went on to give several more such speeches and to advocate an accounting court that would set principles and eliminate accounting alternatives.

Carey notes in all fairness that "it was not that managements were against comparability [uniformity]. They simply were against relinquishing their right to present *their* [emphasis added] financial statements which had stood the test of time and, as they saw it, were best suited to the peculiar nature of their businesses. . . . After all, the SEC had stated officially that management had primary responsibility for its financial statements. What authority did auditors have to dictate to management the accounting methods it must follow?"[46] There has been little change in the attitudes of all concerned since Carey wrote those words in 1970.

Nevertheless, the pressures on the CAP became too great and at the AICPA's 1957 annual meeting, President Alvin R. Jennings responded by calling for an increased emphasis on research as the key to the development of sound accounting principles.

Now it is important to keep in mind that while first the SEC, then the AICPA, and finally the FASB speak of the need to "develop accounting principles" or a "conceptual framework" of accounting, they really mean uniformity and the elimination of alternatives in accounting. As we have seen, accounting was practiced for centuries by management accountants based on the concepts discussed in Chapter 3. Today, as the FASB struggles to formulate a conceptual framework, thousands of management accountants are applying these concepts and are having no problem using accounting to manage, analyze, and control their businesses.

AICPA Forms Committee to Study Rules-Setting (1958)

However, the search for rules went on. In 1958, Jennings appointed a blue-ribbon committee to study how the practice of accounting could be better organized. The committee consisted of:

Weldon Powell, partner, Haskins & Sells

Andrew Barr, chief accountant, SEC

Carman Blough, former chief accountant of the SEC, then (1958) director of research for AICPA

Dudley E. Browne, controller of Lockheed, representing the Controllers' Institute of America (now the Financial Executives Institute)

Arthur Cannon, professor, University of Washington

Paul Grady, partner, Price Waterhouse & Co.

Leonard Spacek, partner, Arthur Andersen & Co.

William W. Werntz, partner, Touche Ross and a former chief accountant of the SEC

Robert K. Mautz, professor, University of Illinois

It is interesting to note that only Dudley E. Browne on the committee was from the managerial accounting field.

ACCOUNTING PRINCIPLES BOARD FORMED (1959)

This committee's work resulted in the formation of the Accounting Principles Board (APB) in 1959. This board consisted, at first, of 18 volunteer members and, later, 21. Again, the group was heavily dominated by representatives of public accounting although industry representation was now allowed.

Accounting Research Formalized by APB

The board's functions were essentially the same as the CAP although a new wrinkle was added—the Accounting Research Studies. During the 1960s, 15 in-depth research monographs were prepared by distinguished academicians and partners of major public accounting firms. These studies represented a determined effort by the AICPA to set GAAP once and for all as the following listing of the titles illustrates:

ARS No. 1, *The Basic Postulates of Accounting* by Maurice Moonitz.

No. 2, *Cash Flow Analysis and the Funds Statement* by Perry Mason.

No. 3, *A Tentative Set of Broad Accounting Principles for Business Enterprises* by Robert T. Sprouse and Maurice Moonitz.

No. 4, *Reporting of Leases in Financial Statements* by John H. Myers.

No. 5, *A Critical Study of Accounting for Business Combinations* by Arthur R. Wyatt.

No. 6, *Reporting the Financial Effects of Price-Level Changes* by the staff of the Accounting Research Division.

No. 7, *Inventory of Generally Accepted Accounting Principles for Business Enterprises* by Paul Grady.

No. 8, *Accounting for the Cost of Pensions Plans* by Ernest L. Hicks.

No. 9, *Interperiod Allocation of Corporate Income Taxes* by Homer A. Black.

No. 10, *Accounting for Goodwill* by George R. Catlett and Norman O. Olson.

No. 11, *Financial Reporting in the Extractive Industries* by Robert E. Field.

No. 12, *Reporting Foreign Operations of U.S. Companies in U.S. Dollars* by Leonard Lorensen.

No. 13, *The Accounting Basis of Inventories* by Horace G. Barden.

No. 14, *Accounting for Research and Development Expenditures* by Oscar S. Gellein and Maurice S. Newman.

No. 15, *Stockholders' Equity* by Beatrice Melcher.

Research Effort a Disappointment

However, although several of the studies formed the basis for landmark opinions by the APB,* overall the research approach was a disappointment. Several studies represented such a radical departure from existing practice that they were ignored or rejected outright.

The most notable examples of outright rejection by the APB were Research Studies No. 1 (basic postulates) and No. 3 (a tentative set of principles). With these two studies, the public accountants and academicians made

---

*Notably: APB Opinion No. 3 which established the funds statement (Research Study No. 2); APB Opinions Nos. 5 and 7 covering leases (Research Study No. 4); APB Opinion No. 8 covering pension costs (Research Study No. 8); APB Opinion No. 11 covering interperiod allocation of income taxes (Research Study No. 11); APB Opinions Nos. 16 and 17 covering business combinations and intangible assets (Research Studies Nos. 5 and 10). In addition, ARS No. 12 became the basis for Statement No. 8, covering foreign currency translations, issued by the FASB in 1976.

another attempt at spelling out the general conceptual framework of accounting. However, the studies, done in 1961 and 1962 by Professors Maurice Moonitz of the University of California at Berkeley and Robert Sprouse of Stanford (Sprouse moved to the FASB in 1973), represented a more specific bias and again raised the issue of inflation-adjusted accounting. The reaction against the studies was so strong that the APB issued what amounted to a disclaimer: "The Board is therefore treating these two studies . . . as conscientious attempts by the accounting research staff to resolve major accounting issues which, however, contain inferences and recommendations in part of a speculative and tentative nature. . . . The Board believes, however, that while these studies are a valuable contribution to accounting thinking, they are too radically different from present generally accepted accounting principles for acceptance at this time."[47]

1962 Investment Tax Credit Trips APB

The APB itself did not meet with any better fate. At the very beginning of its existence, it ran afoul of accounting for the investment tax credit. Carey describes this brouhaha as "one of the most heated controversies ever to take place within the accounting profession, and the most widespread public criticism of the profession since the McKesson case broke in 1938."[48] The Revenue Act of 1962 provided for this entirely new capital spending incentive for business. The struggle the APB had in trying to decide how the credit should be accounted for is a classic illustration of the subjective nature of accounting. It also illustrates how the problem could have been resolved if the board had only kept in mind the basic cash/transaction orientation of accrual-based accounting.

The basic questions concerning the investment tax credit (ITC) were: Is the credit a government subsidy and, thus, a contribution to capital (no one really pushed for this)? Was it a reduction in the cost of the related asset and, thus, amortizable over the useful life of the asset (the deferral method favored by the theoreticians)? Or was the credit a direct reduction in income tax expense in the year claimed in the tax return (the flow-through method favored by most companies, some theoreticians, and the chief accountant of the SEC, Andrew Barr)?

SEC Overruled APB

The APB voted by the minimum required two-thirds vote (14 to 7) to issue Opinion No. 2, which specified the deferral method as the *only* GAAP. Various members of the board then met with the SEC and tried to sell this view to the SEC. However, in January 1963, the SEC issued Accounting

Series Release No. 96, *Accounting for the Investment Credit*, in which they permitted a company to adopt either the deferral or flow-through method. More significantly, the SEC stated that they would accept financial statements in which the auditor had qualified this opinion as the result of the use of the flow-through method (which would be contrary to Opinion No. 2). Thus, the AICPA had its teeth pulled and "most corporations chose to ignore . . . Opinion No. 2. . . ."[49] Accordingly, the APB issued Opinion No. 4 in 1964 in which it was concluded that, "Opinion No. 2 had not attained the degree of acceptability necessary to be effective" and, thus, either the flow-through or the deferral method was acceptable. Carey reports that the press had a field day, *"The New York Times, The Wall Street Journal, Forbes, Barron's, Fortune,* and many other publications had their say. The 'flexibility' of accounting principles was harshly criticized; the difficulty of comparing earnings of one company with those of another was mentioned frequently; the question whether auditors were truly independent of management was raised more than once."[50]

1963-1964 Congressional Hearings on GAAP

All this commotion* led to Congressional hearings in 1963 and 1964 on the subject of investor protection. Congressman Harley O. Staggers questioned SEC Commissioner Carey on the subject of uniformity, comparability, GAAP, and alternative accounting principles at some length. In closing, Mr. Staggers asked Commissioner Carey to "file . . . a statement setting forth . . . the areas of accounting where alternative practices could produce materially different results [than] under GAAP."[51] Subsequently, the SEC did file a statement listing the following such areas (their resolutions are noted in parentheses):

1 Valuation of inventories (FIFO versus LIFO, still an option today)
2 Depreciation and depletion (tax versus book "useful lives," a major option today)
3 Income tax allocation (later resolved by APB Opinion No. 11)
4 Pensions (later resolved, at least for a time, by APB Opinion No. 8)
5 Research and development costs (subsequently resolved rather arbitrarily by FASB Statement No. 2)
6 Goodwill (later resolved by APB Opinion No. 17)

---

*In spite of all this furor and embarrassment, the public accountants did not learn much, as evidenced by a repeat of the fiasco when the 1971 investment tax credit was passed (as we shall see later).

7   Time of realization of income (still an open area today)

8   All-inclusive versus an operating concept income statement (a major issue today as the result of Statement No. 52 covering translation of foreign currency financial statements)

9   Intercorporate investments (still a question today)

10 Long-term leases (basically resolved by FASB Statement No. 13)

11 Principles of consolidation (although ARB No. 51 generally covers this area, there are still some open issues today)

12 Business combinations (later resolved in part by APB Opinions Nos. 16 and 17)

13 Income measurement in finance companies (later resolved by APB Opinion No. 13)

14 Intangible costs in the oil and gas industries (still an issue today)

Rule 203 Adopted

All this unwanted attention led the AICPA executive committee in 1964 to seek means by which it would be possible "(1) to give greater authority to Opinions of the APB; (2) to define more clearly the role of the profession in providing leadership in the development of accounting principles; (3) to strengthen and give meaning to the concept of generally accepted accounting principles, and to aid in eliminating undesirable and unnecessary differences in accounting practice."[52]

The means by which the executive committee sought to accomplish these goals was a resolution of council which in 1973 would be formally made a part of the AICPA Code of Ethics as Rule 203. As mentioned earlier, this rule, in effect, makes explicit the compulsory nature of at least the formalized, published GAAP. Carey describes the debate over this resolution as "the most heated, and the most extended which had ever occurred at a meeting of the Institute's Council."[53] In an unusually perceptive statement a spokesman (not identified by Carey) for the executive committee majority view noted that " 'generally accepted accounting principles' sound like something definite. Actually it means substantial authoritative support. This in turn indicates not only Institute bulletins [Accounting Research Bulletins] and SEC releases, but also practices of the business community, textbooks and authoritative precedent. We cannot provide a satisfactory answer to the question, generally accepted by whom—the Institute; the corporations which are being audited; the textbook writers?"[54] These remarks were made in 1962; after 20 years the profession, business, and government are still seeking the answer. However, the Council resolution was approved, and the authority vested in public accounting by the SEC in 1937 was made more explicit.

Emphasis on Uniformity Increased

But the emphasis on uniformity kept increasing. The feeling, expressed by Commissioner Byron D. Woodside in 1965, seemed to be that the business world was more sophisticated and that while comparability between companies had not been the primary objective in the 1930s, it now appeared that investors' needs required this to be the goal.[55]

Although the shift in the 1930s in the objective of public accounting from presenting data to management and creditors to providing data to investors and stockholders was not really as drastic a change as it might seem (since in both cases the stewardship concept was the basis for the reporting), the shift to uniformity/comparability in the 1950s and 1960s was a dramatic shift. Such an approach required a rules-setting approach to accounting whereby an outside authority would dictate the accounting method to be used by all companies to the exclusion of all other alternatives, regardless of their merits. The shift to total uniformity represented a severe encroachment by the regulators (both the APB and the SEC) into areas of judgment where their expertise was certainly no better and, in many cases, not as good as the managerial accountants who were intimately familiar with the intricacies of their individual companies' operations. The result of this new thrust by those outside management was one of conflict which continues to this day.

Court of Accounting Appeals Proposed

The last seven years of the APB were filled with dissent, both from within the auditing profession as well as from business and Congress. As was mentioned earlier, Mr. Spacek proposed the creation of a United States Court of Accounting Appeals.[56] Under this proposal, a court consisting of five members appointed by the president of the United States would have jurisdiction over the accounting rules of the five federal agencies primarily concerned with accounting: the Securities and Exchange Commission, the Federal Power Commission, the Interstate Commerce Commission, the Civil Aeronautics Board, and the Federal Communications Commission. (Evidently Mr. Spacek did not think that the Internal Revenue Service was concerned with accounting.) The full judicial process of petitions for redress (of an accounting rule), oral arguments, briefs, and so on, would be used to resolve the disputes that arose. Although this proposal never really got off the ground, it typifies the tumult that surrounded the APB. For the 1960s were chaotic times in finance and accounting as well as in the society in general. It was the era of the formation of conglomerates, of leverage, of soaring stock prices tied to an ever-growing earnings trendline and price-earnings ratios, and lawsuits against public accountants as frustrated investors searched for someone to blame.

Through all this period, the APB struggled to satisfy simultaneously the SEC, investors, and business. But this was becoming harder and harder to do. The expectation level of a public grown used to problem-solving had risen faster than the accounting profession's ability to respond in a business world growing even more sophisticated and complex.

The pressure for uniformity that had resulted in the formation of the APB forced the APB, which was dominated by public accountants, to issue opinions that tried to eliminate the element of judgment from accounting. In addition, contrary to the bulletins of the APB's predecessor, the CAP, several of these opinions tended to "fix things that were not broken" and to impinge on the accounting practices of *all* companies, whether or not any abuses of accounting theory were occurring.

Standards Become More Theoretical

Another development that began in earnest during the era of the APB was the marked departure of many of the opinions (and statements of FASB) from the traditional cash-transaction orientation of accounting.*

As a result of these two trends—elimination of alternatives and a movement away from a cash orientation—the standards being set by the APB began to lose their relevance to managerial accounting and, even worse, to impinge on the day-to-day accounting for transactions by managerial accountants and affect the ways of actually doing business. Alarmed by these trends, managerial accountants, through such organizations as the FEI, began to take a more active part in standards setting.

MAJOR APB OPINIONS

Let us turn now to a review of some specific examples of major opinions issued by the APB that illustrate these trends (as well as the current status of these issues):

No. 5 "Reporting of Leases in Financial Statements of Lessee" (1964)

No. 7 "Accounting for Leases in Financial Statements of Lessors" (1966)

---

*Oddly enough, although the APB's work marked a basic departure from cash-orientation, they also published Opinion No. 3, "The Statement of Sources and Application of Funds," which established this new statement as a primary statement ranking with the balance sheet and income statement. This opinion represented formal recognition of the relationship between cash and accrual-based accounting even though its emphasis on working capital rather than cash proved to lessen its impact on the readers of financial data.

No. 8   "Accounting for the Cost of Pension Plans" (1966)

No. 11   "Accounting for Income Taxes" (1968)

No. 16   "Business Combinations" (1970)

No. 17   "Intangible Assets" (1970)

APB Opinions Nos. 5 and 7, "Covering Leasing Transactions"

One of the major sources of capital for a company is borrowings, particularly long-term debt. Since creditors make wide use of various ratios, such as the debt-to-equity ratio, in their analysis of the financial strength of a company, the desire by financial managers to design what is called "off-balance-sheet" financing transactions is quite strong. The most popular of this form of financing to evolve in the 1940s was the lease.

Rather than buy a building and incur a mortgage, a company would lease the building. This approach avoided any down payment and kept mortgage debt off the balance sheet while gaining the use of the building. (Of course, the building would not appear as an asset in their balance sheet either.)

As this type of transaction began to evolve, many accountants were troubled by the issue of form versus substance. For example, in a long-term lease with a transfer of title at a nominal value at the end of the lease, the substance of the transaction was that of a purchase. In 1949, then, the Committee on Accounting Procedure issued ARB No. 38 which basically required the disclosure, in a footnote to the balance sheet, of this type of transaction. The bulletin also stated "where it is clearly evident that the transaction involved is in substance a purchase, the leased property should be included among the assets of the lessee with suitable accounting for the corresponding liabilities. . . ."[57]

This bulletin served the profession until the 1960s. However, its vagueness left too much to the judgment of the managerial accountant and the public accountant to suit many people. Thus, in 1964, the APB moved to tighten up the conditions under which a lessee had to capitalize a lease with APB No. 5. Two years later, APB No. 7, covering the lessor, attempted to do the same thing for the lessor.

These two opinions, with two amendments, continued in effect until 1976 when the FASB (the successor to the APB) made another attempt at drawing up specific conditions covering the capitalization of leases with Statement No. 13. This last statement has been modified, interpreted, refined, and revised by so many subsequent statements and interpretations (13 in all) that the FASB found it necessary to publish a compendium of all the rules.

The saga of leasing is a classic illustration of the futility of attempting to write rules to fit a subjective, complex field such as accounting. It would have been far more reasonable to have placed the reporting emphasis on disclosure (as the CAP did in 1949 in this case) than on attempting to write specific rules to cover the myriad of transactions entered into daily in business, which is the approach adopted by the APB and the FASB as well as the SEC. The Research Report of the FASB on leasing, insofar as lessees are affected, illustrates this point. In addition, it also illustrates the emptiness of the fears expressed by the business community since it concludes that all the machinations of the FASB concerning leases had, "(a) no significant changes in average risk-adjusted returns were associated with the changes in the accounting for leases, . . . and (b) there was no conclusive evidence of association between changes in market-based measures of risk and capitalization of leases [p. 127]. Finally, we found no evidence of significant association between bondrating changes for sample companies . . . " (p. 163) (*The Economic Effects on Lessees of FASB Statement No. 13, Accounting for Leases,* by A. Rashad Abdel-khalik, principal researcher, FASB, Stamford, Conn., 1981).

APB Opinion No. 8, "Accounting for the Cost of Pension Plans"

This landmark opinion was one of the better efforts of the APB. The concept of pensions, virtually unheard of 80 years ago, arose in the 1930s as our nation became more industrialized and people left the farm (where they had been independent and relatively self-sufficient). Initially accountants adhered to a cash basis in the accounting for pension costs. As the pension plans became more complex and broad, however, it became apparent that the simple expensing of cash payments, either to a trustee or to retirees, was not achieving the appropriate matching of the long-term pension cost of an employee with the term over which his efforts produced revenue.

In 1956 the CAP attempted to deal with this problem in ARB No. 47. The wording of the bulletin, however, proved to be too vague and, although it specified a preference for the accrual of the estimated long-term costs, the practice of cash-basis accounting persisted. In 1966 the APB tightened up the wording of ARB No. 47 and spelled out the requirement that the annual expense be based on an acceptable actuarial method for the determination of the long-term pension cost per employee. In addition the opinion required the amortization of the estimated cost of benefits granted for prior years' service according to a specific formula.

Although Opinion No. 8 greatly improved the accounting for pension costs it does allow for considerable judgment through the various actuarial methods that can be used to estimate the expense.* This flexibility, however, was

---

*Even the classification of actuarial cost methods is quite subjective, depending on the characteristic being described. The FASB defined five broad approaches in their Discussion Memo-

inconsistent with the general goal of uniformity adopted by the FASB, and in 1980 a Discussion Memorandum on pension costs was issued and hearings were held the following year. One of the basic themes of the hearings was the FASB's obvious concern with the justification for the continuation of several different actuarial methods for determining the annual expense. (In 1983 this issue along with the overall accounting for unfunded pension costs, actuarial gains and losses, post-employment costs, over-funded pension plans and other related questions concerning employee benefit programs, became a major topic of discussion in the accounting field. The discussion was initiated by the publication by the FASB, in December 1982, of "preliminary views" on such matters which proposed the recording of the unfunded pension costs as a liability with an intangible asset also being recorded as well as what was termed a "measurement valuation account" and the use of a single method of amortizing such costs and assets. The "preliminary views" clearly reflected the FASB's emphasis on the balance sheet as well as its drive towards uniformity.)

APB Opinion No. 11, "Accounting for Income Taxes"

This opinion, which required interperiod allocations (i.e., normalization) of income taxes, represented the highwater mark in the application of the matching concept of accounting but, at the same time, was a major departure from the traditional basic cash/transaction orientation of accounting. Business was firmly opposed to this opinion, probably because it resulted in the accrual of contingent liabilities to provide for the possible future payment of income taxes and, of course, adversely affected earnings, significantly in some cases.*

Briefly, Opinion No. 11 required the normalization of income tax expenses regardless of the amounts actually paid based on the various tax returns. As noted earlier, the U.S. income tax laws generally do not require that treatment of an expense on a company's books conform to the handling of the

---

randum of February 19, 1981: accumulated benefits; benefit/years-of-service; benefit/compensation; cost/years-of-service; and cost/compensation; and then expanded the definition to the specific application; e.g., cost/compensation involves the calculation of the entry age normal cost, the projected benefit cost, the frozen initial liability, and the aggregate cost. FASB Discussion Memorandum, *Employers' Accounting for Pensions and Other Postemployment Benefits,* February 19, 1981, p. 69 and p. 191.

*Although this was typically the result, not all companies were in such a position. The auto companies actually had to set up contingent "receivables" because charges on their books for depreciation and tool amortization were greater than the charges currently allowed for tax return purposes. However, since these charges would eventually be allowable for tax purposes, the current book charge would eventually reduce future income taxes—hence, a contingent "receivable" was created.

same expense on the tax return. (The LIFO method of costing inventories is the notable exception to this rule.) As a result a company could depreciate property as fast as the tax laws permitted and get the cash benefit of paying lower income taxes while reporting higher net book income than shown on the tax return because of two factors. First, the depreciation rate used for the books would generally be lower and more in line with the useful life of the asset.* Second, prior to Opinion No. 11, the book tax expense was generally based on the amount paid as reported in the tax return. Thus, if a fast write-off were used, the tax expense would be reduced and actually be much lower in relation to book income than the statutory rate.

Opinion No. 11 stopped the second situation by requiring the booking of a tax expense at the statutory rate based on *book* income with the difference between taxes paid and book tax expense (called "timing differences") being recorded as deferred credits (contingent liabilities) or deferred charges (contingent assets). To repeat, this opinion represented the ultimate in the matching of costs and revenues. However, it moved too far from the realization concept and, as a result, today accountants are struggling with the large deferred credits/debits that have arisen in companies' balance sheets.

APB Opinions Nos. 16 and 17, "Business Combinations and Intangible Assets"

Other even more controversial opinions were to follow from the APB. As noted earlier, the 1960s were, to say the least, a turbulent era in American history. There was an apparent dynamism reminiscent of the 1920s, the feeling was that most of us had solved the mundane problems of just living, and the time had come to solve the problems for everyone by establishing the Great Society.

A new crop of entrepreneurs discovered the magic of an old accounting concept—the pooling of interests. It was abuse of this device, coupled with the frantic search by speculators for the stock that could appreciate the fastest and poor judgment and resolve by public accountants, that led to the brief era of instant earnings through poolings.

It should be clear that the author does not share the view of many critics of business that all business people cannot be trusted. The spirit of the entrepreneurs, such as the du Ponts, Andrew Carnegie, or Thomas Watson, is the lifeblood of our economic system. Nevertheless, there are times when even the best-intentioned entrepreneur must be reined in.

---

*This is another example of where government tax policy is not based on an accounting theory so much as it is based on managing the economy by stimulating investment in property by allowing a fast write-off of the investment.

The pooling concept is a classic illustration of the application of the form and substance distinction discussed in Chapter 2. In its simplest form, a pooling occurs when two separate companies of about equal size, in *similar* businesses, agreed to combine their firms into a new company with the *same* stockholders by *exchanging* the *stock* of each company for stock in the new company. The intent would be a true merging of interests and management. In such a case, even the strict rules covering purchases versus poolings in effect today would recognize the merger as a "pooling of interests." The advantages of having this type of accounting, as opposed to a conventional purchase of one company by another, are significant. For example:

Under a pooling, the earnings of the two old companies are combined and become those of the new firm. This permits the earnings history of the old companies to be combined (pooled) and reported for the new company as though it had been in existence for as long as the two companies existed. On the other hand, under the purchase concept, the acquiring company could include the earnings of the acquired company only from the date of acquisition. Thus, under a pooling, the earnings history would be greater than under a purchase. Obviously the entrepreneur preferred the "pooling" of an acquisition rather than the purchase since the earnings trend line (and thus the probable appreciation in stock value) would be greater.

Furthermore, under a pooling, the assets of the new firm would be simply the sum of the two pooled companies, whereas under a purchase approach the market value of the acquisition would have to be determined and if it were in excess of the old book value of the acquired company, the excess (termed *goodwill*) would have to be either ascribed to the assets acquired, if possible, and depreciated over future years, or capitalized as an intangible asset and written off against future earnings. Neither approach was considered very desirable by the entrepreneur since the result was a charge to future earnings.

The concept of pooling was recognized as early as the 1920s[58] and interestingly enough, the first use of the concept occurred in hearings before the Federal Power Commission in 1943 in connection with rate case hearings, where it was applied to *void* increases in the asset base and, thus, *hold down* the rate increase.[59]

In the 1960s, however, the concept was widely used to boost earnings and provide "hype" to a company's stock. Bruce Willis, writing on business combinations, reports that "a significant increase in merger activity occurred during the 1960's, the so-called conglomerate era. During this period the size test criterion was so stretched that combinations of 100 to 1 were treated as poolings and the practice of part-purchase, part-pooling accounting developed. . . . Certain abuses also became evident. The successor of two pooled enterprises would occasionally sell off a significant operating asset of the smaller predecessor entity and obtain a dramatic boost in earnings. There is certainly nothing abusive about such a transaction normally, but when such sales occurred soon after a pooling was consummated and profits from the sale sustained a continued earnings growth by the combined company, there was a good deal of skepticism to say the least."[60]

Professor Abraham J. Briloff was not so kind when he wrote, "Further, I might fairly comprehend the application of pooling where, consistent with ARB 48 [the predecessor to Opinions 16 and 17 of the APB], the shareholders and managements of both component entities effectively combine their resources and talents to form the more perfect union. Instead, we find in practice that even where the combination or union is patently tenuous *the auditor will still follow management's* [emphasis added] propensity to pool. . . . As SEC Chairman Manuel Cohen has noted, this partiality toward pooling flows from its ability 'to create an appearance of earnings and growth when they are not really present,' and 'to increase a company's reported sales and earnings without improving performance! . . . In short, it is not that the pooling-of-interests method, per se, is not rationalizable with accounting theory generally; it is just that the way in which it has been applied has motivated my desire to see this accounting practice discredited and disowned."[61]

In making the comment "the auditor will follow management," Professor Briloff has struck a key point in the evolution of financial accounting and reporting—the lack of resolve on the part of the auditors in instances where the absence of any specific rule to cite as the reason for the auditor's disagreement with a client proposal. The abuses of the pooling concept could have been prevented under existing accounting conventions, such as form versus substance, if the practitioners, both managerial and public, had applied them with judgment and resolve.

Instead of waiting for restraint on the part of practitioners, more definitive rules in the form of Opinions Nos. 16 and 17 were issued by the APB. This action followed pressure from public accountants and the press. These two opinions effectively curtailed the use of the pooling concept and set a maximum standard of 40 years for the amortization of any goodwill arising from a purchase. However, the debate was bitter and severely damaged the status of the APB.

THE INVESTMENT TAX CREDIT REVISITED

No sooner was this issue resolved than another major controversy involving the APB broke out. In spite of the experience of the early 1960s with the first investment tax credit, the APB followed the same disastrous course when Congress revived the credit in 1971.

After asking the Treasury to not specify an accounting method, the APB issued an exposure draft of a proposed opinion that would have required that the cost reduction (deferral) approach be the sole method to be used, with the result that the credit would be deferred and amortized over the life of the related property. This approach, of course, greatly reduced the impact of the credit on earnings in the year of its origin.

When the government realized, however, that the impact of the investment credit on earnings would be greatly mitigated by this method, it objected. The Treasury wanted the immediate "shot in the arm" for the economy that they believed would be accomplished by the effect that the credit would have on profits. Thus, the Treasury forgot about remaining neutral and instead induced Congress to include the flow-through (immediate tax reduction) method, as well as the cost-reduction method, as acceptable accounting methods in the tax credit legislation.

APB Overridden Again

As a result, the Revenue Act of 1971 expressly provided "that no taxpayer shall be required to use any particular method of accounting for the credit for purposes of financial reports subject to the jurisdiction of any federal agency or reports made to the federal agency."[62] Of course, managerial accountants, applying the concept of realization and recognizing the close ties accrual-basis accounting should have to cash, overwhelmingly opted for the flow-through (tax reduction) method of accounting. Even today, those companies that chose the deferred method are dwindling as they realize that a deferred credit, outside of stockholders' equity for which they have long ago received the cash benefit, is distorting their debt-to-equity ratios, their cash flow analysis, and their reported net income.

THE END OF THE APB

The life of the APB was filled with such controversies and, finally, the AICPA decided it had to make still another try at establishing a forum for the setting of Generally Accepted Accounting Principles. In January 1971, the AICPA Board of Directors called a two-day conference to consider its standard-setting role. "Reflecting the mood of the conference, AICPA President Marshall Armstrong observed: 'If we are not confronted with a crisis of confidence in the profession, we are at least faced with a serious challenge to our ability to perform a mission of grave public responsibility'."[63]

This conference resulted in the formation of what were to prove to be two major studies in the accounting field. The first was *Establishing Financial Accounting Standards* (the "Wheat Report") while the second was the *Objectives of Financial Statements* (the "Trueblood Report"). The Wheat Report resulted in the formation of the FASB while the Trueblood Report became the basis for the FASB's conceptual framework project, which we will consider in Chapter 7.

The Wheat Committee

The Wheat committee, named after its chairman, Francis M. Wheat, was composed of the following leaders from the basic groups that were most concerned with the establishment of accounting principles:

Public Accounting (Auditing): John C. Biegler, CPA, senior partner, Price Waterhouse & Co.; Wallace E. Olson, CPA, executive partner, Alexander Grant & Co.; Arnold I. LeVine, CPA, national executive partner, J. K. Lasser & Co.

Investment Analysts: Thomas C. Pryor, senior vice-president of White Weld & Co.

Industry: Roger B. Smith, then vice president of finance (now chairman) of General Motors Corporation.

Academia: David Solomons, professor, Wharton School of Finance and Commerce, University of Pennsylvania.

Government: Francis M. Wheat, partner of Gibson, Dunn & Crutcher, attorneys-at-law; commissioner, Securities & Exchange Commission (1964–1969).

The committee conducted an extensive review of the standards-setting process for over one year. Its conclusions were quite critical of the APB and public accounting and called for a broader-based, full-time standards board with a full-time staff, adequately funded by the private sector.

Specifically, the committee found that the APB had fallen short, "in the following respects":

1 A part-time, volunteer APB will continue to be subject to doubts as to the disinterestedness of its members—their freedom from client and other pressures.
2 A part-time APB, however dedicated, cannot devote itself continuously and single-mindedly to the urgent problems confronting it.
3 Formulation of financial accounting standards would benefit from a broader base and perhaps a greater variety of skills than can be supplied by

a group chosen from among the members of a single professional organization, all of whom must hold the CPA certificate.

4 The research activities of the APB need more substantial and continuous direction than a part-time Board can provide.

We believe these imperfections call for more than minor modification of the present arrangement.[64]

It is interesting to note that many years later, Oscar S. Gellein, a board member of both the APB and the FASB, would explain the APB's failure in a somewhat different tone. "Claims were made that the APB had conflicts of interest and was indecisive, in that it bent by modifying or relaxing its proposals as pressure was exerted. There is no need to either defend or to castigate the actions of the APB, for there was a factor far more significant that thwarted the APB's commitment to advance the written expression of GAAP. *That factor was the need for a conceptual anchor* [emphasis added], a base about which few would argue. Time after time, as the APB considered financial accounting problems, the discussion would focus on the building blocks. They were argued from the beginning each time, of course, inconclusively. The result was inefficiency and difficulty in sustaining conclusions. Standard setting in the private sector must look to persuasion based on purpose, reason, and evenhandedness.

"Setting standards primarily by assertion requires muscle for compliance. whereas conceptually based standards have a built-in persuasiveness. The APB's problems stemmed more from a missing anchor than from conflicts of interests and part-time attention."[65]

Whatever caused the dissatisfaction with the APB, it is obvious that the Wheat committee thought that the solution lay in a foundation independent of the AICPA and a new board with broad-based support. The approach was akin to "getting all the critics into one boat in the hope they would be more interested in keeping it afloat." With these proposals, the era of the politicization of accounting standards began in earnest.

THE FASB FORMED

Following the recommendations of the Wheat committee, the Financial Accounting Foundation was formed in 1972 and the support of all the interested groups was obtained through pledges of support from the members of the original sponsoring organizations: the American Accounting Association (academia); American Institute of Certified Public Accountants; Financial Analysts Federation; Financial Executives Institute; and the National Association of Accountants. (The Securities Industry Association was added later.) The Foundation quickly formed the Financial Accounting

Standards Board and staff. The final step was the amendment, in 1973, of ethics Rule 203 by the AICPA. This rule was amended to require that members of the AICPA comply with the accounting standards established by the FASB. The SEC also endorsed the new FASB and issued Accounting Series Release No. 150 which designated the FASB as the sole recognized standards setter.

Although many noted academicians were quick to note the shift in the standards-setting process from the public-accounting base to a broad base composed of all interested parties, the FASB and its foundation have been reluctant to admit to such a change.

Thus, although Professor Charles Horngren would write (in 1973), "the setting of accounting standards is as much a product of political action as of flawless logic or empirical findings,"[66] the Structure Committee of the Financial Accounting Foundation would protest (in 1977) that, "the process [of standards-setting] can be described as political because there is an educational effort involved in getting a new standard accepted. But it is not political in the sense that an accommodation is required to get a statement issued."[67]

AICPA Not Pleased with Transfer of Standards-Setting

Moreover, the AICPA still is not very pleased with the delegation of standards-setting to the FASB. Shortly after the FASB was formed, the AICPA Executive Committee began issuing Statements of Position (SOPs) to which many public auditors attributed the status of GAAP.

In 1981 Dennis R. Beresford, then chairman of the AICPA accounting standards executive committee, defended the publication of SOPs and a new "issues paper," both of which are a way to document practice problems and to "offer guidance in areas too narrow for the FASB's attention or when a Board pronouncement will not be sufficiently timely to solve immediate problems."[68] However, after much discussion, the AICPA amended this practice on the proviso that the FASB would extract and publish standards based on SOPs, which occurred in 1981 and 1982.*

It seems clear that after ten years of the FASB the attitude of the public accountants who dominate the AICPA is much the same today as it was in 1969. At that time, Robert M. Trueblood (managing partner of Touche, Ross and later chairman of the AICPA Study Group on the Objectives of Financial Statements), speaking at the annual meeting of the AAA, said, regarding

---

*The tenuity of this agreement was illustrated in the hearing held by the FASB Task Force on Timely Financial Reporting Guidance in March 1983. Several representatives of public accounting recommended that the AICPA be permitted to "help" the FASB give guidance. Meanwhile, the AICPA has continued publishing SOPs, albeit at a reduced rate.

management's stake in accounting, "To the extent that the current practice of involving the business community in early discussions of projected APB opinions is helpful, well and good, but the circumstances and uses of accounting in business are so multivarious that to look to the business community for significant leadership in solution of the profession's larger technical problems is probably a mistake. To the extent other accounting organizations choose to conduct activities related to the formulation of accounting principles, again well and good. But this does not mean that the practicing profession (public auditors) can either share or delegate its own main responsibility."[69]

Thus the years of the FASB have been filled with political turmoil as its members struggled to maintain a balance of power among the SEC, the AICPA, and business. Oddly enough, the investment analysts have not been much of a factor in standards setting even though this group is supposedly the one everyone else is trying to serve.

FASB Far More Active and Detailed in Standards-Setting

The major points of disagreement are still the uniformity issue and the loss of relevancy in financial reporting. The FASB has pursued the uniformity goal with as much zest as the APB or the CAP, and possibly more. In the little over 10 years of its existence, the FASB has issued more statements (72) than the CAP did (51) in 20 years and more than twice as many as the APB issued (32) in its nearly 14 years. In addition, the FASB has issued over 3 dozen interpretations and added a procedure whereby staff technical bulletins are also issued from time to time.*

These statements, interpretations, and bulletins spell out such details as *Reporting Segment Information in Financial Statements That are Presented in Another Enterprise's Financial Report* (Statement No. 24), or *Reporting Tax Benefits Realized on Disposition of Investment in Certain Subsidiaries and Other Investees: An Interpretation of APB Opinion Nos. 23 and 24* (Interpretation No. 29).

Meanwhile the AICPA has continued in the de facto standards-setting business, issuing over 30 Statements of Position since 1974, and the SEC has also kept active with over 300 Accounting Series Releases to its credit.

Standards Overload

This flood of specific rules and regulations has created a third problem—standards overload. The small to medium-sized company, particularly one that does not come under the purview of the SEC, simply cannot afford the

---

*Some observers of the operation of bureaucracies have noted that such action was to be expected as an outgrowth of the need to support the funds-raising and staff requirements.

staff necessary to keep abreast of the rules and, thus, must rely on the public accountant to see that the company is in compliance with GAAP.

Moreover, the rules now are changing the internal accounting of a company (e.g., capitalization of interest), and, thus, increased costs are incurred to maintain the necessary records without any benefit to the management of the company.

The problem of standards overload has reached the point where the AICPA and the FASB are reviewing the possibility of big GAAP versus little GAAP.* In short, one set of standards would apply to the larger public companies while the smaller companies would be exempted. The better solution would be to simplify GAAP for everyone.

UNIFORMITY

Turning to the uniformity issue, there are two aspects to the question: The first involves outright abuses of the basic accounting concepts discussed in Chapter 3 and the second concerns the arbitrary imposition of a particular accounting method even though there is no specific need for it.

It is obvious to anyone who studies the pooling-of-interest era of the 1960s that the basic concepts of a true pooling (similar size, exchange of stock [no cash involved], similar businesses, and continuation of management) were being ignored, violated, and rationalized with little or no apparent resistance from the independent auditors involved. It is also obvious that, outright fraud aside, some managements will press for the most liberal interpretation of an accounting concept and, in the absence of a specific rule, the independent public accountants (and managerial accountants) will not hold a more conservative position. Bertrand N. Horwitz and Richard Kolodny noted that "some observers believe that the underlying reason for uniformity is that auditors prefer to operate in a tightly structured environment which minimizes judgment and, thus, the risk of legal liability. . . . An examination of the positions behind the 'uniformity vs. flexibility' debate reveals that a major concern has been whether possible legal liabilities would be less under uniformity than under practices which permit alternatives."[70]

Since experience shows that some managements will abuse the general concepts discussed in Chapter 3 and that many auditors will not take exception without some specific authority that can be cited, some rule-making is necessary.

The discipline involved in having standards-setters is quite beneficial so long as the standard-setters only step in when a clear distortion or abuse of an

---

*For example, see the *Report of the Special Committee on Accounting Standards Overload,* AICPA, New York, N.Y., February 1983.

accounting concept is involved. However, one of the basic problems in determining when the FASB should step in is the public accountants themselves. As noted earlier, it is always easier to cite a rule to a client than to base your opposition on judgment. This was illustrated at the March 1983 hearing of the FASB Task Force on Timely Financial Reporting Guidance in which the writer participated. The Task Force was formed by the FASB to consider both the need for more specific guidance for accountants and the ways by which such guidance could be furnished. Again and again those in public accounting cited the need for specific standards while many in business urged less of a "cookbook" approach. At one point in the hearings, one FASB staff member acknowledged that the great majority of the requests for guidance came from those in public accounting. It also became clear that the principal reason for such specificity by the public accountants was the desire to avoid conflicts with their clients and to prevent their clients from "shopping" for another public accounting firm more to their liking.

Trend Toward Absolute Rule Even When No Specific Abuse Noted

Thus, as we have seen, the standards-setters since the CAP, through the APB and the FASB, have steadily marched toward the elimination of judgment and the mandating of a single method even when no clear abuse of alternative methods could be established. We discussed examples of this trend earlier involving the CAP, and APB, and the FASB concerning leasing and pension accounting; two prime examples of the relentless thrust toward uniformity initiated by the FASB are Statement No. 2, *Accounting for Research and Development Costs* and Statement No. 34, *Capitalization of Interest Costs.*

Accounting for Research and Development Costs

From the viewpoint of simple logic, Statement No. 2 covering research and development costs is probably the worst standard ever established. Logically, no sensible business person spends money on research and development unless he believes that it is essential to do such work to maintain and expand the company's position and growth. In short, the money is spent with the intent of deriving future benefits. Such expenditures are so essential in a manufacturing business that one of the key ratios that an investment analyst will use is the percentage of R&D being spent per sales dollar. Of course, not all R&D proves to have future value. Many "blind alleys" must be pursued to find a Xerox patent.

The possibility of a certain percentage of "blind alleys" for every success in R&D brings us to the basic accounting question—how much of what is being spent on R&D should be capitalized as an asset with future value and how much should be expensed at once as valueless?

Reviewing the basic concepts discussed in Chapter 3, we see that several are involved in the resolution of this issue. First of all, there is the notion of materiality. The amount involved must be large enough so that the accounting decision will be of some significance. Second, there is the concept of matching related costs and revenues. If the R&D is successful, some revenue-producing product or service will result, and the costs associated with producing that revenue should be matched (offset) against the revenue in order to arrive at a reasonable calculation of the net profit (or loss) from the sale of the product or service.

However, it may be years until any revenue is received, and the need to report periodically the results of operations to date to the owners demands considerable judgment as to the future value of R&D expenditures made through a given period. In making this evaluation the concept of conservatism must be kept in mind; that is, it would be more conservative to understate current income by expensing any R&D costs to which a clear future value could not be assigned than to run the risk of capitalizing such costs and overstating current income.

This sort of evaluation generally makes public accountants uncomfortable. As Dane W. Charles puts it, "Until the mid-1970's [when Statement 2 was issued], R&D had been a chronically tacky area for accounting, some companies were expensing costs as incurred while others capitalized some or all of such costs."[71] Incidentally, this use of judgement probably resulted in a better matching of costs and eventual revenues than that accomplished under the present arbitrary standard.

The FASB solved "the tacky problem" quite simply. It required that, for all practical purposes, all R&D should be expensed, period! As a result, we have the paradox of amounts spent on R&D being expensed at once, as though the expenditures had no future value, when the decision to spend the money was based on the expectation of realizing future benefits. While the current standard has certainly made the independent public accountant's job easier, there is serious doubt that the result was necessarily good for business growth or investors, or whether it has even produced better accounting.

Professor Bertrand N. Horwitz and Richard Kolodny have conducted extensive research into "The Economic Effects of Involuntary Uniformity in the Financial Reporting of R&D Expenditures." They state that "based on the results of (1) statistical tests of the association of FASB Statement 2, Accounting for Research and Development Costs (ASR No. 178 of the SEC) with reductions in the level of R&D outlays of affected firms and (2) the responses to a questionnaire by key financial managers, we conclude that the evidence supports the premise that the expense-only rule *caused a relative decline in R&D outlays for small, high-technology firms* [emphasis added] which had previously used the deferral method of measurement."[72]

Capitalization of Interest Cost

However, an even better example of the mandating of a single method without any substantive need except uniformity for the sake of uniformity is Statement No. 34, *Capitalization of Interest Cost.*

The concept of cost of capital and the accounting for interest, both explicit and implicit, has been the subject of debate by theoreticians since the Industrial Revolution spawned the capital-goods industries. Until recent years, however, the actual inclusion of explicit interest expense in the costs of construction was limited to regulated utilities. Of course, in view of the rate-setting structure of public utilities, it makes sense to include *all* costs and expenses in their asset base.

However, other companies, notably real estate developers, began to capitalize and thus defer their interest expense as a part of the cost of the lots being developed. There is also considerable merit to this method's use by real estate companies since a far better matching of costs and revenues is obtained. However, the SEC became concerned by the growth of an accounting alternative that tended to increase income and adversely affect comparability. Thus, in 1974, the SEC issued Accounting Series Release No. 164, which placed a moratorium on the future capitalization of interest by anyone other than a regulated utility, a retail land sales company, or a savings and loan association which had adopted such a policy earlier. (Many savings and loan associations are involved in real estate activities, hence their special status.)

The FASB, unfortunately, got around to reviewing the subject in 1977 through a Discussion Memorandum and public hearings. In 1979, they issued SFAS No. 34, *Capitalization of Interest Cost,* which mandated the capitalization of interest incurred during the construction of an asset in specified circumstances, generally those assets built for an enterprise's use or discrete projects, such as ships, built for sale or lease. In issuing this statement, the FASB ignored the wide divergence of opinion in the responses they received. For example, the Committee on Corporate Reporting of the Financial Executives Institute was about evenly divided on this issue and filed a response that indicated its lack of consensus.

Clearly, there were no abuses to be corrected in this case. Even more clearly, the accounting literature (cited so well in the 1977 Discussion Memorandum itself) demonstrated that there was merit to both the capitalization and the immediate expense views. If ever there were an occasion for the existence of two different accounting methods, accompanied by the disclosure of the one selected, this issue was it. However, the FASB, by a narrow 4-to-3 vote, opted for the absolutism of one method. Uniformity won again.

Simple Majority of FASB Mandates Rule

The 4-to-3 voting margin is worthy of comment. Initially, the minimum required voting margin for the issuance of a standard by the FASB was 5-to-2, which closely paralleled the two-thirds margin required by the APB. However, in 1977 the Structure Committee of the Financial Accounting Foundation (which oversees the FASB) completed a review of the first four years of the FASB and made several recommendations that they believed would improve the efficiency of the FASB and its advisory council.

"The most significant recommendations were a change to a simple majority for the FASB to issue a standard and a change in the composition of the board so that no one constituent group is by plan committed to a majority of seats on the Board. . . ."[73] The change to a simple majority obviously makes it easier for the board to issue a standard. However, it also means that if only a bare majority voted for the issuance of the standard, then there is a strong possibility that the standard does not have broad support among the board's constituency and may well be a strong candidate for future revision—neither condition being very desirable.

The change in the composition of the board has not yet proved to be very significant, although it may be eventually. We have already considered the dissatisfaction of the AICPA with not having full control over the standards-setting process, and this change certainly did not ease that dissatisfaction. Initially, the public accountants dominated the board, holding four of the seven seats by plan. Since 1977, however, the foundation has modified this to the extent that today the public accountants' majority position has been lost, although three members are still from public accounting with the other four members from each of the other constituent groups.*

Returning to the other major point of disagreement between the standards-setters and many of the users of accounting—relevancy of the data—the FASB, like the APB, has continued to move away from accounting's basic cash/transaction orientation.

FOREIGN CURRENCY TRANSLATION

We have already discussed the struggles of the CAP, the APB, and the FASB over leasing as well as the fallacy of interperiod income tax allocation (APB Opinion No. 11). However, in 1976 the FASB issued a standard that represented such a departure from accounting's cash orientation that after five

---

*Donald Kirk, chairman, John March, and Ralph Walters are from public accounting, Frank Block is a former stock analyst, Victor Brown is a former businessman, Robert Sprouse is a former college professor, and David Mosso is from the government service.

hectic years the board issued a revision. Unfortunately, in revising the first standard the board (by a 4–3 margin) left the cash orientation even further behind and will probably soon be trying still another revision. The standards in question are Statement No. 8, *Accounting for the Translation of Foreign Currency Transactions and Foreign Currency Financial Statements,* and Statement No. 52, *Foreign Currency Translation,* issued in December 1981.

Assumes Stable Monetary Unit

In reviewing this subject there are a few basic points to keep in mind. First of all, one of the axioms of accounting is the assumption of a stable monetary unit. Obviously, the various monetary units around the world are anything but stable; therefore, any attempt to translate several different currencies into any given currency rests on an inaccurate assumption. Another point to keep in mind is that there has never been any dispute as to the correctness of charging or crediting foreign exchange gains or losses to operations that result from actual transactions at the local level. For instance, if a British company sells to a French company, some agreement must be reached as to whether payment will be in pounds (in which case the buyer assumes the exchange risk involved when he converts francs to pounds) or in francs (in which case the seller assumes the exchange risk).

Basis for Consolidation

The real point of conflict has to do with the noncash translation of the foreign company's financial statements into U.S. dollars (assuming the "parent" is a U.S. company) so its operations and balance sheet can be consolidated with that of its parent. Keep in mind, as discussed earlier, the accounting theory of consolidation of a parent company and its "controlled"* subsidiaries is a triumph of accounting substance over legal form conceived by Arthur Lowes Dickinson in 1901. Although today the United States income tax laws permit the filing (and levying of a tax) on the consolidated results of a company and certain of its subsidiaries, the law limits this to domestic companies in which the U.S. parent owns at least 80% of the voting stock. Thus, the consolidated result published in the annual report of a typical multinational company does not represent any legal entity basis; rather it is an attempt to present to

---

*Even the definition of control is quite subjective in theory if not in practice. Under existing accounting literature and standards it would be possible to consolidate a subsidiary in which a less than 50% interest was owned. (See *Handbook of Accounting and Auditing,* edited by Burton, Palmer & Kay, Chapter 31 by Robert Sack, pp. 31–33.) In actual practice, a more than 50% ownership interest in the voting stock is usually required in order to consolidate the financial statements of the subsidiary and its principal owner.

the stockholders of the controlling corporation the most reasonable representation of the assets and overall operations in which they have an ownership interest, albeit indirect, through ownership in the controlling company. In any application of substance over form, considerable judgment is involved and some compromise inevitable.

The consolidated financial statements then are generalizations designed to give a broad overview of the results of operations of the total related group of companies as though they were just one company operating in a world with only one currency. Unfortunately, many users and the FASB have seized on this broad generalization of results and attempted to make the consolidated financial statements serve purposes for which they were never intended. For example, the management of multinational companies do not use consolidated statements to judge the reasonableness of a given investment nor the performance of a given manager of an operating unit. Instead they look at the local currency results and the cash return.

It is important to remember that *all* investments are made with only one goal in mind—to maximize the return of cash. If then we were trying to devise a consolidation theory including foreign operations, we would immediately come to the conclusion that we should not even translate and consolidate the financial statements of the foreign subsidiaries. Instead we would only include the cash realized in U.S. dollars through the payment of dividend as income to the parent company. This would also mean that we would have to report the net investment in the foreign subsidiary as an asset in the parent company's balance sheet with some evaluation of the investment risk: for instance, if the investment was in Iran, we would certainly want to reduce the investment to a zero basis following the expulsion of the Shah in 1979.

Consolidation Tempered by Conservatism Prior to 1976

This approach, however, was considered too conservative by most accountants and, prior to 1976, the "current-noncurrent" method of translating the foreign currency statements for full inclusion in the consolidation was widely used* as representing a reasonable compromise of a simple cash received

---

*Other translation methods, or variations thereof, were also used prior to Statement No. 8 (1976). These were:

Monetary-Nonmonetary Method

First suggested by Professor Samuel R. Hepworth of the University of Michigan in a monograph, *Reporting Foreign Operations,* in 1956, this method specified that monetary items (defined as those fixed in terms of local currency such as cash, receivables, and payables, both long- and short-term) should be translated at current rates. Nonmonetary items (principally inventories and property) should be translated at historical rates, i.e., rates in effect at date of acquisition.

approach and a reasonable estimate of the earnings (future cash payments) for a given period. This method permitted the deferral of unrealized gains and losses arising in the translation process.

FASB Statement No. 8 Created Controversy

Statement No. 8, effective in 1976, stopped the deferral of these "paper gains and losses" and, instead, required that they be recognized in earnings cur-

---

Professor Hepworth maintained that monetary items were susceptible to *and immediately affected by* changes in the price of money, i.e., fluctuations in exchange rates; thus, these "gains or losses" should be reflected in net earnings for a given period. Nonmonetary items were not so affected based upon the premise that the changes in their value, caused by fluctuations in exchange rates, could be subject to recovery through changes in selling prices.

In 1965, the APB endorsed this method by concluding (APB Opinion No. 6) that long-term receivables and payables were to be translated at current rates "in many circumstances," which is their way of saying "always." Inventories, as a nonmonetary item, were to be translated at historic rates. Translation was not limited to this method, however, thus the current-noncurrent method was still used prior to 1976.

Temporal Method

In 1972, Leonard Lorensen built upon Professor Hepworth's thesis and developed the "temporal method" in Accounting Research Study No. 12, *Reporting Foreign Operations of U.S. Companies in U.S. Dollars* (AICPA, New York, N.Y.). Briefly the temporal method attempts to match the aspects of time with each transaction. Since U.S. accounting standards still require the use of historical cost, the temporal method is about the same as the monetary-nonmonetary method in application. It differs only in that it can be applied to any measurement base so long as the items carried at past, present and future prices can be determined. The temporal method became the basis for Statement No. 8 issued by the FASB in 1974, effective for calendar year companies in 1976.

Current Rate Method

Although this method was not permitted in the United States prior to 1981 (and Statement No. 52), it has long been the preferred method by European and Canadian accountants. Basically, this method treats foreign operations as though they existed separate and apart from the parent and, thus, the historical cost could only be expressed in the local currency and, in effect, all items were to be considered as monetary, i.e., immediately affected by changes in the price of money (exchange rates), whenever they were translated into another currency.

This method has strong ties to the debate over the effect of inflation on accounting data. Basically, the long-term fluctuations of exchange rates among currencies reflect the relative stability of the currencies being exchanged. A key factor in this relative stability is the inflation rate in the respective countries, which, in turn, is a broad gauge of the economic soundness of the country. Generally, the country with an inflation rate higher than another country will have a currency that is weaker. Thus, advocates of some form of current-value accounting argue that the foreign currency statements be adjusted to current value by use of an appropriate local country index and then the current rate could be applied and the current value in U.S. dollars determined. Initially the FASB proposed this approach for hyperinflation countries (i.e., an inflation rate in excess of 100% over three years) in its revision of Statement No. 8. The final statement abandoned this approach, however.

rently. This requirement caused the greatest discontent with Statement No. 8, although the "yo-yo" effect of the change in inventory translation described in the following paragraph has resulted in a goodly share of controversy too.

Unrealized "gains and losses" have been described as "paper" since no cash ever changes hands nor probably ever would. Briefly, such gains (or losses, depending on the relative positions of the currencies being measured) result from the change in the relative positions of the currencies from the point of the initial transaction. Thus, if a British subsidiary borrows 1000 pounds when the exchange rate is one pound equals $2.00 and the money is invested in property, the translated U.S. dollar values will be $2000. However, if at the next month-end, the exchange rate has changed to one pound equals $1.90, Statement No. 8 would require that a gain of $100 be included in the consolidated earnings. The "gain" supposedly results from the translation of the debt into $1900 U.S. dollars since theoretically that is all the dollars it would now take to buy 1000 pounds and pay off the debt. Of course, neither the British company nor its parent has any intention of paying off the debt immediately. If the exchange rate bounces back to $2.00 by next month-end, the "gain" disappears and, if it goes to $2.10, a "loss" suddenly appears even though there is still no intent to use U.S. dollars to buy pounds and pay off the debt.

It is this unrealistic and capricious charging or crediting "paper gains and losses" to earnings that occurs under Statement No. 8 that caused such a storm of criticism. It is analogous to a person who earns a comfortable salary as a professional accountant having to include in his earnings the market price fluctuations of 1000 shares of a stock he has owned for ten years and has no intention of selling.

Some defenders of Statement No. 8 have maintained that management's great objection is that they wish to manage earnings and that Statement No. 8 disrupts this goal. Such critics fail to realize that management is not as concerned with the management of earnings as they are with being able to forecast and anticipate what earnings will be—whether up or down—and also what the cash flow will be from those earnings. Statement No. 8 disrupts both of those analyses.

The statement also changed the translation of inventories from current to nonmonetary with the result that the effect of an exchange rate change on inventories was deferred until the inventories were sold. This created the controversial "yo-yo" effect in which a gain on a net liability position would be recognized at once as the U.S. dollar strengthened against other currencies while the loss on the higher inventory cost would be delayed for a few months until the inventory was sold. Such a "yo-yo" effect simply aggravated the problem of forecasting earnings and cash flow referred to earlier.

Statement No. 52 a Poor Compromise

The new Statement 52, issued in December 1981 by another 4-to-3 margin, will do little to resolve the issue of the translation of foreign currency financial statements. If anything, it will add to the controversy since it introduces a new concept, that of "functional currency" and also introduces the special reserve out of stockholders' equity as a kind of "holding tank" for debits and credits that cannot be classified as assets, liabilities, or earnings.

The concept of functional currency is defined in the statement according to a variety of guidelines, but basically if a foreign operation is in effect a branch of the U.S. operations, then the concepts of old Statement No. 8 are still applied with all of their marvelous vagaries. If, however, the foreign operation is reasonably independent, then the current rate (see preceding footnote) is applied, except that all unrealized translation gains or losses are stored in the special reserve out of equity rather than charged or credited to earnings. This does resolve the problem of unpredictable fluctuations in earnings, but it also raises questions as to just what those debits and credits in the special reserve are. Finally, for those subsidaries operating in hyper-inflation countries (an inflation rate of at least 100% over three years), the concepts of old Statement No. 8 will still be in effect.

Conservatism and Realization Would Have Been Better Guides

What should the FASB have done with the problem of foreign currency translation? They would have had a far better chance of gaining broad support from analysts and businessmen alike if they had adhered to the cash orientation, realization concepts.

The current-noncurrent method widely used until 1976 with the deferral of unrealized gains and losses *prior* to recognition in the income statement was a far better compromise of the conceptually correct nonconsolidation of foreign currency financial statements than any method required since 1976.

SUMMING UP—GAAP

To sum up: (1) While there is no comprehensive set of Generally Accepted Accounting Principles, there are broad concepts (discussed in Chapter 3) that have formed the basis for the practice of accounting (not auditing) for centuries; (2) managerial accountants, using these general concepts, could meet the basic goal of accounting—to record, classify, and summarize transactions and events and interpret the results thereof—without any assistance from regulatory agencies, either private or public; (3) the goal of standards-setters and public accountants is the elimination of alternatives (judgment) in the *reporting* of results. To the degree this requires uniformity in accounting practice, so much the better; (4) standards-setters, both the SEC and FASB, are overconcerned with the supposed "needs" of the short-term investor, that is, the speculator rather than the long-term investor; (5) whenever standards-setters (or practitioners) depart from the basic cash-transaction basis of accrual-based accounting, problems arise; (6) the plethora of rules, standards, and interpretations is causing an overload that even public accountants, as well as business, are objecting to; (7) however, it is necessary to have standards-setters and public auditors to curb abuses and frauds and to attest to the representations of management; (8) the FASB at least should be more representative of the actual practitioners of accounting—the managerial accountants—instead of the public auditors; and (9) the emphasis in financial reporting must change from a concentration on specific rules to that of disclosure and analysis of results if the accounting profession is to survive and grow.

With this background on accounting concepts and GAAP, let us move to the field of accounting that has become synonymous with the profession in the minds of most people—public accounting or, more correctly, auditing.

REFERENCES

1. Hendriksen, *Accounting Theory*, p. 54.
2. John Maynard Keynes, "The State of Long-Term Expectations," *The General Theory of Employment, Interest and Money*, Harcourt Brace & Co., New York, 1960, chap. 12.
3. Ibid., p. 152.
4. Ibid., p. 153. This was written in 1935 but is certainly still true today.
5. Ibid., pp. 153–154.
6. Ibid., pp. 154–155.
7. John Kenneth Galbraith, *The Great Crash*, The Riverside Press, Cambridge, Mass., 1954.
8. Ibid., p. 174.
9. Ibid., pp. 182–187.
10. *Memoirs and Accounting Thought of George O. May*, Paul Grady, ed., Ronald Press, New York, 1962, p. 46.
11. Carey, *The Rise of the Accounting Profession*, vol. 1, p. 161.
12. *Memoirs*, p. 147.
13. *Memoirs*, p. 58.
14. Carey, *The Rise of the Accounting Profession*, vol. 1, p. 163.
15. *Eric Louis Kohler*, W. W. Cooper and Yuri Ijiri, eds., Reston Publishing Co., Reston, Va., 1979, p. 49.
16. Ibid., p. 35.
17. *Memoirs*, pp. 73–74.

18. Samuel Eliot Morison, *The Oxford History of the American People,* Oxford University Press, New York, 1965, pp. 937–939.

19. Franklin D. Roosevelt Inaugural Address, *The World of Business,* vol. 3, March 4, 1933, Simon & Schuster, New York, 1962, p. 1576.

20. Adolph A. Berle, Jr., and Gardiner C. Means, *The Modern Corporation and Private Property,* Harcourt, Brace & Co., New York, 1932.

21. Ibid., p. 182.

22. Ibid., pp. 182–183.

23. Ibid., pp. 271–272.

24. Carey, *The Rise of the Accounting Profession,* vol. 1, p. 169.

25. Morison, *The Oxford History,* p. 958.

26. Ibid., p. 958.

27. Galbraith, *The Great Crash,* p. 83.

28. Ibid., p. 83.

29. *Eric Louis Kohler,* p. 35.

30. Carey, *The Rise of the Accounting Profession,* vol. 1, pp. 171–172.

31. Ibid., p. 173.

32. Ibid., pp. 185–186.

33. Ibid., p. 182.

34. Weldon Powell, "Putting Uniformity in Financial Accounting into Perspective," in AFM Exploratory Series No. 6, *The Development of Accounting Principles—A Study in Diversity,* G. D. Pound, editor, University of New England, N.S.W., Australia, 1979, p. 124.

36. Ibid., p. 201.

37. Paton, *Paton on Accounting,* pp. XI and XII.

38. *Eric Louis Kohler,* p. 37.

39. Ibid.

40. Ibid.

41. Kripke, *The SEC and Corporate Disclosure,* p. 34.

42. Previts and Merino, *A History of Accounting in America,* pp. 85–86.

43. Carey, *The Rise of the Accounting Profession,* vol. 2, chap. 4.

44. Ibid., p. 59.

45. Ibid., p. 74. From a speech before the Philadelphia Chapter of the Financial Analysts Federation.

46. Ibid., p. 81.

47. Statement by the APB, April 13, 1962.

48. Carey, *The Rise of the Accounting Profession,* vol. 2, p. 98.

49. Ibid., p. 103.

50. Ibid., p. 105.

51. Ibid., p. 109.

52. Ibid., p. 113.

53. Ibid.

54. Ibid., p. 114.

55. Ibid., pp. 122–124.

56. *Establishing Accounting Principles—A Crisis in Decision Making,* Arthur Andersen & Co., Chicago, Ill., 1965.

57. Accounting Research Bulletin No. 43, Committee on Accounting Procedure, AICPA, New York, 1961, chap. 14, par. 7.

58. Arthur R. Wyatt cites John R. Wildman and Weldon Powell, *Capital Stock Without Par Value, 1928,* in Accounting Research Study No. 5, *A Critical Study of Accounting for Business Combinations,* AICPA, 1965, p. 19.

59. Ibid., p. 22.

60. John C. Burton, Russell B. Palmer, and Robert S. Kay, eds., *Handbook of Accounting and Auditing,* Warren, Gorham & Lamont, Boston, Mass., Copyright © 1981. Chapter 30-4 reprinted by permission of Warren, Gorham & Lamont. All rights reserved.

61. Abraham J. Briloff, Specified excerpt from *Unaccountable Accounting,* by permission of Harper & Row, New York, Copyright © 1972, p. 65.

62. D. Larry Crumbley, *Income Taxation and Its Impact on Financial Reporting—An Historical Overview,* Haskins History Seminar, New York University, 1978.

63. *Establishing Financial Accounting Standards: The Report of the Study on Establishment of Accounting Principles,* AICPA, March 1972. (The so-called Wheat report, after the study's chairman, Francis M. Wheat.)

64. *Establishing Financial Accounting Standards,* p. 8.

65. Burton, Palmer, and Kay, *Handbook of Accounting and Auditing,* Chap. 2-8.

66. Charles Horngren, "The Marketing of Accounting Standards," in Essays in Honor of William A. Paton, *Journal of Accountancy,* October 1973, p. 61.

67. *The Structure of Establishing Financial Accounting Standards,* Financial Accounting Foundation, April 1977, p. 19.

68. Dennis R. Beresford, "Emerging Problems: How the Profession is Coping," *Journal of Accountancy,* February 1981, pp. 57–60.

69. Robert M. Trueblood, "Ten Years of the APB," AAA annual meeting, August 27, 1969. Reprinted from *Tempo,* September 1969.

70. Bernard N. Horwitz and Richard Kolodny, "The Economic Effects of Involuntary Uniformity in the Financial Reporting of R & D Expenditures," *Journal of Accounting Research,* vol. 18, Supplement 1980, Institute of Professional Accounting, 1981, p. 42.

71. Burton, Palmer, and Kay, *Handbook of Accounting and Auditing,* chap. 21, p. 2.

72. Horwitz and Kolodny, "The Economic Effects," in *Journal of Accounting Research,* vol. 18, Institute of Professional Accounting, 1980, p. 62.

73. *The Structure of Establishing Financial Accounting Standards,* Report of the Structure Committee, The Financial Accounting Foundation, April 1977, p. 34.

five

PUBLIC ACCOUNTING AND CORPORATE RESPONSIBILITY

PUBLIC ACCOUNTING–A GROWTH INDUSTRY

One of the little known growth industries of the past 50 years or so has been the public accounting profession. This sector of accounting, which initially was concerned with auditing alone, has expanded into such areas as management consulting, tax planning and return preparation, systems review and installation, and personnel recruitment.

The statistics alone dramatically illustrate this growth. In 1930 there were about 14,000 CPAs in the United States but only about 2500 were in the AI(CP)A.[1] By 1981 the number of CPAs had grown to over 200,000 with the great majority (196,000) members of the AICPA about half of whom practice public accounting. Even if we assume all 2500 CPAs in 1930 were in public accounting, the number in *public* accounting has grown 4000% in about 50 years!

The "Big Eight"

Although there are thousands of people (many who are not CPAs or CPAs who are not members of the AICPA) practicing some form of public accounting, including bookkeeping services and tax return preparation,* a

---

*The role of the public accountant in the taxation field was the subject of a long dispute between the lawyers and public accountants. John L. Carey devotes an entire chapter to this dispute which was not resolved until 1965, after over 30 years of disagreement, with the passage of Public Law 89–332 which provided that, "any person who is duly qualified to practice as a certified public accountant . . . may represent others before the Internal Revenue Service." (John L. Carey, *The Rise of the Accounting Profession,* volume 2, AICPA, New York, NY, 1970, p. 257.)

great deal of this growth has been concentrated in the so-called Big Eight—the eight international public accounting firms of Coopers & Lybrand; Price Waterhouse & Co.; Peat, Marwick, Mitchell & Co.; Arthur Andersen & Co.; Deloitte Haskins & Sells; Ernst & Whinney; Touche Ross & Co.; and Arthur Young & Co.* A study, done in 1976 by the Congressional Research Service for the Subcommittee on Reports, Accounting, and Management (the Metcalf Committee) found "85% of the 2,641 corporations listed on the New York Stock Exchange and the American Stock Exchange are clients of the 'Big Eight' firms. Those clients accounted for one-half of the . . . sales for the Nation's manufacturing, trade, and retail sectors and about 84% of the . . . corporate profits after taxes, using average annual data for the years 1974 and 1975."[2]

An even more specific analysis of the significance and growth of public accounting is provided by the annual reports of some of the "Big Eight." Coopers, Peat, PW, and Touche have each published an annual report at least once since the skirmish with Senator Metcalf's committee in 1977, which we will review later in this chapter. Andersen began publishing a report in 1974, whereas the other three firms have chosen to maintain the privacy of their data.

Coopers & Lybrand's report for the year ended September 30, 1980 states, "Overall, our Firm's average annual growth rates for the past five years have been 19.2% in worldwide billings and 6.8% in aggregate partners and staff. Highlights of 1980 contributions to this growth are:

Worldwide billings for 1980 rose 19.0% to $846 million from $711 million for 1979.

Aggregate earnings for 1980 was 20.8% to $208 million from $172 million for 1979.

At September 30, 1980, personnel, including those of associated firms, totaled

---

*The description "Big Eight" is widely used by American accountants, but it should be noted that precise rankings are impossible because most firms do not publish their financial statements. Based on a survey done in 1980 by Vinod B. Bavishi and Harold Wyman, both of the University of Connecticut, the Klynveld, Main, Goerdeler Group (Netherlands) may be the eighth largest firm based on the number of multinational corporations audited. They audit 44 versus only 31 by Touche Ross & Co. Viewed another way, based on total dollars of assets of client firms, Showa Audit Corporation (Japan) and Treuarbeit AG (West Germany) may be the sixth and seventh largest audit firms in the world. Incidentally, by these standards, Price Waterhouse & Company are number one by a wide margin with 109 multinational clients and assets of $687 billion versus Peat, Marwick, Mitchell & Company's 78 multinational clients and assets of $435 billion (for second place). Since Peat, Marwick and Price Waterhouse also publish total revenues, the difficulty in using the number of clients or assets as a test of size can be illustrated since Price Waterhouse with $850 million in revenues trails Coopers & Lybrand ($998 million), Peat, Marwick ($979 million) and Arthur Andersen & Co. ($973 million). (*New York Times*, January 3, 1982.)

approximately 25,100, including 1,960 partners, as compared to 23,500, including 1,830 partners, at the preceding year end.

In 1980, 23 offices and three countries were added to the Coopers & Lybrand network . . . Global coverage now includes 395 offices in 93 countries."

Another less accurate although representative illustration of the growth is a comparison of the Big Eight's estimated gross revenues and partners for 1959, as done by *Fortune,* with published (in most cases) 1981 results. (As noted, Table 5.1 is only representative since it should be understood that some of the growth is due to worldwide mergers during the two decades of the sixties and seventies.)

And, although as mentioned earlier, public accounting has expanded into

Table 5.1   Estimated Gross Revenues of the Big Eight

	1959[a]		1981[b]	
	Partners	Gross Revenues (in millions)	Partners	Gross Revenues (in millions)
Peat, Marwick, Mitchell & Co.	190	$ 45	1,931	$ 979
Arthur Andersen & Co.	171	40	1,400	973
Ernst & Ernst (now Ernst & Whinney)	132	36	1,600	706
Price Waterhouse & Co.	101	35	1,613	850
Haskins & Sells (now Deloitte Haskins & Sells)	176	33	2,000	800
Lybrand, Ross Bros. & Montgomery (now Coopers & Lybrand)	126	28	2,010	998
Arthur Young & Co.	104	26	1,944	750
Touche, Ross, Bailey & Smart (now Touche Ross & Co.)	71	17	1,979	700
	1,071	$260	14,477	$6,756

[a]"The figures on partners shown are not strictly comparable, since some firms have several classes of partnerships and others do not; however, these and other figures do at least make it clear that the relative sizes of the firms have changed a lot since 1939. The figures are FORTUNE's estimates and are based on information from a wide variety of sources. None of the firms' names have confirmed these figures, but several have acknowledged that they are in the right range." *Fortune, The Auditors Have Arrived* by T. A. Wise, Copyright © 1960 by Time, Inc. All rights reserved.

[b]*The Year of the Accountant,* by Leslie Wayne, The New York Times, January 3, 1982. (As noted, Ernst & Whinney, Deloitte Haskins & Sells, and Arthur Young & Co. do not publish annual reports; hence their figures are estimated.)

such areas as taxation and management consulting, the bulk of the work performed, at least by the Big Eight, is still auditing. Although Coopers's annual report does not give a breakdown of their revenues, the report of Price Waterhouse for 1980 does and is probably representative of the Big Eight.*

Price Waterhouse reports that in 1976, 81% of their revenues in the U.S. came from auditing services while 14% were from tax services and about 5% from management advisory services (MAS). Significantly for 1980 these percentages had shifted to 75%, 18%, and 7%, respectively, reflecting the growth of tax services and MAS. No data are available for similar percentages for the hundreds of smaller public accounting firms but, since the Big Eight have such an overwhelming share of the major companies (85% of those listed on the NYSE and ASE), it is quite probable that the revenues from tax services, in particular, as well as MAS, would be far more significant in the smaller public accounting firms.

In fact the expansion of public accounting has been so broad and far-ranging that the SEC found it necessary to issue two Accounting Series Releases (No. 250 in 1978 and No. 264 in 1979) dealing with the question of a possible conflict of interest and the disclosure of the extent of nonaudit services in the proxy statement. Although both releases were subsequently rescinded (in 1981 and 1982), their issuance illustrates the extent of the nonaudit services by public accounting firms and the SEC's concern.

Ironically, this multibillion dollar business almost did not survive its early years in the United States. As mentioned earlier, public accounting in the U.S. began in the late nineteenth century as an outgrowth of contemporary industrialization, which brought the English and Scottish public accountants to the U.S. to audit British-owned companies.† In fact, the 1902 annual report

---

*According to questionnaires completed for 1975 by the Big Eight for the Subcommittee on Reports, Accounting, and Management (the Metcalf Committee) of the Senate Committee on Government Operations, the percentages ranged from a low of 62.2% (by Touche, Ross) to Price Waterhouse's 76% (81% per PW's annual report) from accounting and auditing revenues, while tax services revenue ranged from 15% (Haskins & Sells) to 23.5% (Touche, Ross), and management advisory services revenue ranged from a low of 5% (Haskins & Sells) to 16% (Arthur Andersen). (See *The Accounting Establishment,* A Staff Study, Committee on Government Operations, U.S. Government Printing Office, Washington, D.C., December 1976, Appendix A.)

†Although auditing, i.e., the review of another person's work in some form, dates back as far as accounting, the modern public accountant is a corollary of the development of the modern corporation. As Robert L. Kane, Jr. writes in *The CPA Handbook,* "In those days (sixteenth century) therefore, public accounting was little more than public bookkeeping. No doubt there were occasions, perhaps many of them, when partners in the spice trades or in silk importing disagreed among themselves over their shares of profits, or creditors disagreed with debtors over amounts due, and an independent person with skill and experience in accounts was called in to learn the *facts* [emphasis added] and render a decision. Their names, too are lost to history, and literature gives them little recognition." (*CPA Handbook,* vol. 1, edited by Robert L. Kane, Jr., American Institute of Certified Public Accountants, New York, N.Y., 1952 and 1956, p. 2.)

of the new United States Steel Corporation was the first by an American Company to be accompanied by an auditor's report.[3]

Over the next 30 years, the passage of federal corporate income tax laws (1909 and 1913) by Congress, the growth of equity financing through public sale of stock, and the growing involvement of the U.S. government in regulating business (e.g., the formation of the Interstate Commerce Commission, the Federal Trade Commission, and the Federal Reserve Board) provided impetus for the growth of public accounting to fill the need for an independent, third-party attestation to absentee stockholders of the stewardship of management and to assist in income tax return filings.

1933 Congressional Hearings Ignored Public Accountants

Then in 1933, following the 1929 debacle and the Pecora investigation described in Chapter 4, Congress began hearings that would result in the Securities Act of 1933. The public accountants were virtually ignored. The only reference to them in the first draft of the bill was a provision to the effect that the Federal Trade Commission could, at its discretion, request an audit by independent accountants if the FTC had any doubt about the financial statements being submitted with a company's application to register its securities. (Administrative authority was initially given to the FTC, prior to the formation of the SEC in the 1934 act.)

John Carey reports that "on the day following the publication of [the] draft [legislation], the Institute dispatched a letter to the appropriate Congressional committee, suggesting that it might be desirable to extend the provision for independent audit to all financial statements filed for purposes of registration."[4]

Carter Testimony Pivotal

Although the suggestion of the American Institute of (Certified Public) Accountants was adopted and the draft bill so amended, the Senate Committee on Banking and Currency, which had the oversight responsibility, was not so quick to agree. We have already noted that the institute chose to not appear at the Senate hearings, but that Colonel Arthur H. Carter, then managing partner of Haskins & Sells and also president of the New York Society of Certified Public Accountants, was not so reticent. Judging from the exchange reported by Carey, it was a good thing for the public accountants that he was not reticent. Senator Alben Barkley, in particular, took some convincing. Colonel Carter's testimony is quite interesting since it touches on the issues still sensitive today—auditor independence, government auditors versus public accountants, cost/benefit relationships, uniformity and comparability of financial statements, valuation of a company, and government establishment of accounting standards. The testimony, as reported by Carey, is as follows[5] (portions have been italicized for emphasis):

Mr. Carter:	At the end of subsection 4-A of section 5 on page 8, I would suggest that the following be added after the words "actual business"· "The accounts pertaining to such balance sheet, statement of income and surplus shall have been examined by an independent accountant and his report shall present his certificate wherein he shall express his opinion as to the correctness of the assets, liabilities, reserves, capital and surplus as of the balance sheet date and also the income statement for the period indicated."
Senator Barkley:	How much more and additional employment would that give to certified accountants?
Mr. Carter:	*Eighty-five per cent of the companies that are listed on the exchanges in New York today are examined.*
Senator Reynolds:	Do you think it proper to insert in there that these independent public accountants should be privileged to state their opinion as to the *value* of securities or the condition of the company?
Mr. Carter:	We are unable to express an opinion as to the value of securities. *I think the impression generally prevails that one who reads a balance sheet and an income statement regards the figures* in such a statement *as a defensible definitely ascertainable* fact, whereas, as a matter of fact *in reality it can only be an opinion based upon certain accounting assumptions* which must be applied to the opinion of some individual as to values. . . .
Senator Barkley:	In other words, after the statement has been filed by the officers of the company you want an independent organization to go over it and then report to the Federal Trade Commission whether that is correct or not?
Mr. Carter:	I mean that that statement itself should have been the subject of an examination and audit by an independent accountant.
Senator Gore:	Before filing?
Mr. Carter:	Before filing.
Senator Gore:	Is that patterned after the English system?
Mr. Carter:	Yes, sir.

Senator Reynolds:	Together with an opinion.
Mr. Carter:	That is all they can give; that is all they can give. That is all anyone can give as to a balance sheet.
Senator Wagner:	Well, basically, are not these facts that have got to be alleged rather than an opinion?
Mr. Carter:	Under the terms of the bill it has to be given under oath. *I do not see that anyone can certify under oath that a balance sheet giving many millions of dollars of assets is as a matter of fact correct. He can state his opinion based upon a thorough investigation.*
Senator Barkley:	In other words, before the officers of the company that is issuing stock shall file that statement that is contained in this bill with the Federal Trade Commission the company must call in outside independent accountants and give them the job of going over it and passing on whether they have told the truth or not. *Well, I am not for your amendment, I will say that now. . . .*
Mr. Carter:	. . . But there is in the bill a provision which gives the Commission a right to demand such an investigation and demand such a report as a result of such investigation. My point is to put that in the application in the beginning.
Senator Barkley:	*Do you not think it is more in the interest of the public that is to buy these securities, if there is to be any checkup or any guarantee as to the correctness, that it be done by some government agency rather than by some private association of accountants?*
Mr. Carter:	I think it is an impractical thing for the government agency to do it effectively.
Senator Reynolds:	Why?
Mr. Carter:	Because it involves such a large force. It involves the question of time.
Senator Reynolds:	Well, it would not require any more time on the part of the government officials to make a checkup and audit than it would by private individuals, would it?
Mr. Carter:	I think the public accountant is better equipped to do that than the average government agency would be able to do that. . . .
Senator Barkley:	*Is there any relationship between your organization with 2,000 members and the organization of controllers, represented here yesterday with 2,000 members?*

Mr. Carter: None at all. We audit the controllers.

Senator Barkley: You audit the controllers?

Mr. Carter: Yes; the public accountant audits the controller's account.

Senator Barkley: *Who audits you?*

Mr. Carter: *Our conscience.*

Senator Barkley: I am wondering whether after all a controller is not for all practical purposes the same as an auditor, and must he not know something about auditing?

Mr. Carter: He is in the employ of the company. He is subject to the orders of his superiors.

Senator Barkley: I understand. But he has got to know something about auditing?

Mr. Carter: Yes.

Senator Barkley: He has got to know something about bookkeeping?

Mr. Carter: But he is not independent. . . .

Senator Reynolds: Why should your members ask that they be permitted and empowered to check these accounts?

Mr. Carter: Because it is generally regarded that an independent audit of any business is a good thing.

Senator Reynolds: All right. Then, after it goes to the Commission they have to check up to see who is right; they have to go through and audit again. There has to be a government audit, as suggested by Senator Barkley. Would it not be creating more difficulty and more expense and more time for the government if auditing organizations in-erest themselves in these various and sundry corpora-tions? . . . *Could they do it more economically than the government?*

Mr. Carter: I think so.

Senator Gore: There would not be any doubt about that.

Senator Reynolds: Why?

Mr. Carter: We know the conditions of the accounts; we know the ramifications of the business; we know the pitfalls of the accounting structure that the company maintains. You have got every kind of business to deal with.

Senator Reynolds: *Suppose that we decide in the final passage of this bill here to employ five or six hundred auditors from your organization,* that would be all right, then, would it not?

Mr. Carter:	I do not think the government could employ five or six hundred independent accountants.
Senator Reynolds:	Why could they not?
Mr. Carter:	I do not think the type of men that are in the public practice of accountancy would leave their present practice to go in the government employ. . . .
Senator Adams:	How much of a burden is this going to put on the comparatively small company? You were speaking a while back of the companies whose stocks are listed being independently audited. Now coming under the control of this bill are going to be thousands of small companies putting out an issue for their original financing. How much of a burden and cost is that going to put on them?
Mr. Carter:	Very little measured in value to the investor and to them.
Senator Gore:	What would be the range?
Mr. Carter:	My experience would be that the average company pays around $500 or $600 or $700 for its auditing [this was 1933], that is taking the large and small together. . . . And the largest organizations of our country do it and have been doing it for the last 15 years.
Senator Gore:	*Have had these independent audits made?*
Mr. Carter:	Have had these independent audits made, yes.
Senator Gore:	But they have not been available for any public authority to examine and afford no safeguards?
Mr. Carter:	They have been published in their annual reports and distributed to all of their stockholders, to the newspapers and anyone who calls for them.
Senator Gore:	*And have not done any good?*
Mr. Carter:	Yes, sir; I think they have.
Senator Gore:	*We have had all this debacle here in spite of that. . . .*
Mr. Carter:	Eighty-five percent of all the companies listed on the New York Stock Exchange have independent audits. . . .
The Chairman:	This bill covers all of them, those listed and those not listed.
Mr. Carter:	Those are the ones that should be independently audited.

Senator Reynolds: Which ones?

Mr. Carter: Those that are not listed.

Senator Reynolds: All right; the ones that are not listed are the little fellows, are they not?

Mr. Carter: Yes, sir.

Senator Reynolds: Could they pay you $75 a day to go into their books? . . .

Mr. Carter: It does not cost them $75 a day.

Senator Reynolds: How much do you charge a day, then?

Mr. Carter: It would cost them an average of, I should say $25 a day.

Senator Kean: What big companies charge $25?

Mr. Carter: That is about an average.

Senator Kean: Marwick, Mitchell & Co. cost more than that.

Mr. Carter: I am giving you an average.

Senator Kean: Waterhouse & Co. cost more than that. What companies do you know of that charge only $25 a day?

Mr. Carter: I said that was an average for all. The rates range from $100 a day for a partner down to $15 and $20 a day for a junior. The average scale of rates that are charged are $35, $30, $25, $20, and $15, depending upon the class of men. . . .

Senator Gore: *Don't you think we have got to establish some sort of standard of bookkeeping for different lines of industry before we can make any comparison?*

Mr. Carter: *I think it is very hard to establish a standard of bookkeeping. You can rely upon principles of accounting. . . .*

Senator Gore: I mean the bookkeeping would be standard there so that you could compare one with another, and if they are not standardized *give this Commission the power to require them to conform to it?*

Mr. Carter: Take the automobile industry. You could have the reports of the various companies and you could find a great similarity in their bookkeeping.

Senator Gore: I know, *but unless there is a substantial similarity I do not see how any comparison could be made.* You take the textile companies: I presume they may have standards now that they all conform to, but if they do not, don't you think it would be necessary?

Mr. Carter: I think you would have to take each industry itself and . . . provide a system in which they would set up their accounts peculiar to that particular industry.

Senator Gore: That is what I mean, some sort of standard or set of principles so that each industry and individual instances in each industry could be compared with each other. . . . Is this mandatory in England, the requirement that an independent accountant shall check up?

Mr. Carter: All companies in England are required to be audited by an independent accountant, who is present at the stockholders' meeting and is available to answer any questions the stockholders wish to put to him. . . .

The subsequent legislation incorporated the suggestions of the institute and Colonel Carter with regard to the inclusion of the opinion of an independent public accountant in every registration.

SECURITIES ACT OF 1933 VITAL TO PUBLIC ACCOUNTING

As significant as this action was, it was not without cost to the public accountants. The legislation greatly extended the liability provisions regarding public accountants. Many law suits and court decisions were necessary before the harshness of the initial law was mitigated to some extent, although recent cases have kept open the question of the auditor's liability.

Furthermore, as we have seen, Congress provided that a governmental agency (initially the FTC, then the SEC) should establish uniform accounting standards, and it was not until 1938 that this was delegated to the AICPA, although the SEC still closely oversees the process.

However, in spite of these drawbacks, the benefits to public accounting of the Congress's action are almost incalculable. We would certainly still have some type of practice of public accounting even if Congress had created a governmental agency to audit securities registrations, but it is doubtful in such a case that public accounting would have achieved the prestige, power, and financial status that it has today.*

Thus, by the slimmest of margins, the budding, independent public ac-

---

*As a point of interest, Congress already had an audit agency, the General Accounting Office (GAO). Although the GAO can trace its ancestry back to the legislative system of appropriations established by the British Parliament in 1688, it came into existence as a separate entity with the passage of the Budget and Accounting Act in 1921. The act established the GAO as an agency, "independent of the executive departments" to review, control, and audit government accounts, and report on operations throughout the federal government. (*GAO 1966–1981; An Administrative History,* by Roger L. Sherry, Timothy D. Desmont, Kathi F. McGraw, and Barbara Schmitt, U.S. GAO, 1981.)

However, it was during the 15-year term (from 1966 to 1981) of Elmer B. Staats, as comptroller general of the U.S. (and head of the GAO), that the agency matured and reached the

counting field was not just spared virtual extinction in 1933 but actually given a potential for growth of almost limitless scope by the action of Congress in *requiring* audits for all publicly traded companies.* Of course, this "grant" was not irrevocable and, as we shall see, the public accountants and the Big Eight, in particular, are very sensitive to the mood of Congress and the SEC.

PUBLIC ACCOUNTANTS ARE NOT ADVOCATES OF CLIENTS

This sensitivity is due also to the paradoxical relationship of independent auditors and their audit clients. The public accountants must maintain absolute independence while, at the same time, collecting the fees for their services from the very companies and management that they are charged with auditing. No other profession must deal with such a paradox. Lawyers are acknowledged *advocates* of a particular client's position. They are not responsible for ascertaining the reasonableness of the other side's position—judges, other attorneys, and juries are responsible for that determination.

Managerial accountants too occupy an advocate's position and develop the reasonableness of the accounting policies and practices for their company. Independent public accountants then must perform the role of judge

---

stature it has today as an outstanding professional auditing and management review staff. Nevertheless, the GAO has always been Congress's fact-finder, never competing in the private sector with public accountants.

*Homer Kripke, Chester Rohrlich Professor of Corporate Law at New York University and an outspoken critic of the SEC and public accountants, describes this as an "exclusive franchise." "It is hard to think of another situation where the government in granting a license (i.e., access to the public securities markets), requires the licensee to use the services of a specified profession as intermediary. There is no comparable requirement that the documents be prepared by lawyers, or by printers instead of duplicators. It is worthwhile to emphasize the extraordinary aspect of this exclusive franchise. The public accounting profession has the license to take toll at the gates for everyone who wants to use the markets in the issuance or trading in securities. . . . The ascendancy of the independent public accountant introduces a fourth party with his own risks and motivations into the trilateral disclosure system of issuer, investor and SEC. The costs of introducing the independent public accountant as a fourth party are substantial." (*The SEC and Corporate Disclosure: Regulations In Search of a Purpose,* Law & Business, Inc., New York, 1979, pp. 276–277.)

Another interesting analysis of the auditor and the 1933–1934 securities acts was done by J. Wiesen for the Cohen Commission. "The author assembles evidence and develops arguments to show that Congress did not carefully consider the auditor's role during the legislative hearings on the 1933 and 1934 securities acts. . . . Congressmen displayed a lack of knowledge about auditing and 'less than vigorous' interest when the topic was raised in the hearings. The reaction of the SEC in 1934 appears to have been a substitution for profound thinking about the duties of auditors." (*The Commission on Auditors' Responsibilities,* AICPA, New York, 1978, p. 163.)

and jury as they judge the reasonableness of a particular position taken by the managerial accountants. Of course, the independent public accountant must also concern himself with the possibility that his client might switch to another "judge/jury" more compatible with the company's views. In any event, the independent public accountant must concern himself with the mundane but necessary problems of collecting a fee from a client dissatisfied with his judgment and decisions.

This relationship is further complicated by the fact that most companies either rely on their public accountants to give them advice on the appropriate accounting for any out-of-the-ordinary transaction or at least request their concurrence with the method decided upon by management.

AUDITING TOO LACKS BROAD, THEORETICAL BASE

What then does an auditor do that so distinguishes his work from the managerial accountant and that permits him to command fees comparable with those of other professions?

As we have seen, accounting developed from a practical need for some system of reckoning without any clearly defined body of standards, postulates, or generally accepted principles for that system. The growth of auditing paralleled this development. In his book *Theory of Auditing,* Professor Charles W. Schandl comments, "In no other discipline can we find less literature in the last 150 years than in the field of auditing."[6]

Various attempts have been made to develop a broader theoretical base for auditing. In 1973, the Committee on Basic Auditing Concepts of the American Accounting Association published *A Statement of Basic Auditing Concepts* in which four conditions were listed that create a demand for auditing. These were discussed by Professor Wanda Wallace in her study of the economic role of the audit and are as follows:

1 Conflict of interest: Conflict between an information preparer and a user can result in biased information.
2 Consequences: Information can have substantial economic consequences to a decision maker.
3 Complexity: Expertise is often required for information preparation and verification.
4 Remoteness: Users are frequently prevented from directly assessing the quality of information.[7]

These concepts have also been defined as (1) the agency theory of the stewardship hypothesis; (2) the information hypothesis (i.e., the public good); and (3) the insurance hypothesis. The last stems from the legal liability exposure that has grown markedly in the past decade or so.[8]

Lack of Base Led to Misunderstanding of Auditing

In spite of these efforts, however, the lack of broad, definitive literature early in the developmental stages of public accounting has contributed to a wide gap in the general understanding of what an auditor does and what his report represents. The Commission on Auditors' Responsibilities (the Cohen Commission, named after its chairman, Manuel F. Cohen), formed by the AICPA in 1974 to study this problem following the Watergate disclosures of foreign bribes, states, "The Commission . . . was charged to develop conclusions and recommendations regarding the appropriate responsibilities of independent auditors. It should consider whether a gap may exist between what the public expects or needs and what auditors can and should reasonably expect to accomplish. If such a gap does exist, it needs to be explored to determine how the disparity can be resolved. . . . After considerable study of available evidence and its own research, the Commission concludes that such a gap *does* exist. However, *principal responsibility* does *not* appear to lie *with* the *users* of financial statements"[9] [emphasis added]. Instead the commission placed the blame on the failure of the public accounting profession to evolve rapidly enough to keep pace with the American business environment, that is, to develop definitive audit standards—more rules!

The commission may have been too polite to the users of financial statements. Later in its report, it notes that "a survey conducted for Arthur Andersen & Co. [in 1974] indicated that 66% of the investing public believes that 'the most important function of the public accounting firm's audit of a corporation is to detect fraud.' "[10]

Initially Detection of Fraud Was Considered Goal

Of course, as the Cohen Commission concludes, this is really the fault of the public accountant in not explaining and better defining his work. In fact, initially the public accountant was taught that the detection of fraud and errors was a chief object of his audit in such textbooks as L. R. Dicksee's *Auditing: a Practical Manual for Auditors,* published in 1898.[11] As the implications of such shortsighted goals dawned on the public accountant, the auditing textbooks began to ease away from them. *Montgomery's Auditing,* probably the most widely used text, which has been through nine editions (1916 through 1975), charts this change.[12]

The reason for the change is quite practical; the cost of any audit designed to detect all fraud and errors in a company of any size would be prohibitive and even then might fail, leaving open the danger of legal liability should any person be damaged as the result of the undetected fraud. This denial of any primary responsibility to detect fraud by the public accountant is a continuing source of confusion to the users of financial statements and of embarrassment to the public accountant. For if the purpose is not specifically to detect frauds or errors but to attest to the reasonableness of the data, how can a person state that the data are reasonable (i.e., "presents fairly") if material errors or frauds have gone undetected?

The SEC and the courts have not been very sympathetic toward the public accountants' position either. In Accounting Series Release No. 19, "In the matter of McKesson & Robbins, Inc." (1940) the SEC stated, "Moreover, we believe that, even in balance sheet examinations . . . accountants can be expected to detect gross overstatements of assets and profits whether resulting from *collusive* [emphasis added] fraud or otherwise. . . . Without underestimating the important service rendered by independent public accountants in their review of the accounting principles employed in the preparation of financial statements . . ., we feel that the discovery of gross overstatements in the accounts is a major purpose of such an audit even though it be conceded that it might not disclose every minor defalcation."[13] In 1974, this position was reiterated by the SEC in ASR No. 153.

Reliance on Internal Control and Integrity of Management

How do the public accountants solve this conundrum? Surprisingly enough, to a great extent the public accountant places a great deal of reliance on the basic integrity of his clients. Many readers will scoff at this, including some accountants, both public and private. Yet as we analyze the techniques employed by the auditor, the complexity and sheer volume of the transactions involved, the effect of collusion on any system of control, and the cost of a "foolproof" control system, we come to the realization that the auditor places more trust in the integrity of his clients than is generally assumed.

Montgomery's Auditing, Ninth Edition (1975) contained the following observation: "Most managers are conscientiously interested in strong internal controls, sound accounting principles, and the best possible presentation of financial information to the public. Responsible managers recognize the social and legal necessity of an audit to lend credibility to their representations. They know that sound reporting enhances both the company's and its management's standing in financial circles. They expect, and often insist on receiving, advance counsel from auditors about prospective changes in accounting systems and controls, accounting principles to be used for prospective transactions, and all of the other decisions that ultimately affect financial statements. The integrity of the accounts and financial statements depends on and reflects the integrity of management."[14]

In short, if the public accountant does not believe he can trust his client, then the accountant had better sever the relationship because if the client really wants to cheat, the chances are that he will succeed, at least for a time. Of course, we are writing of top management, not the defalcations of an employee within the company. However, the latter are rarely significant enough to affect the general financial position of a company and, accordingly, do not affect the auditor's representation as to the fairness of the presentation of the financial statements as a whole. Most of the frauds that have a significant impact on the public accounting field are those of a scale that only top management could perpetrate (e.g., Ivar Krueger, McKesson-Robbins, and Equity Funding).

Over-Optimistic Management

A more subtle problem, however, is that of overoptimistic management who influence the judgment involved in choosing the accounting method so as to get the most liberal method possible, thereby misleading investors with their excessively liberal accounting. The real estate companies of the fifties and sixties who reported sales of fully developed lots on which they had done little of the development work and for which they had only received nominal down payments on long-term sales contracts, are one example. The franchise companies of the sixties who reported the entire franchise fee as income at the time of receipt even though they had considerable work to do to assure that the fee would be earned, are another example.

A classic illustration of overaggressive management in recent times was reported in the *Wall Street Journal* in May 1982 as the Datapoint Corp. disclosed that it reversed "a significant amount of sales recorded in the current and prior quarters—a sign that its hard-driving sales force probably recorded as firm sales equipment valued at perhaps millions of dollars that its customers later either would not or could not pay for." (*Wall Street Journal,* May 3, 1982)

The *Journal* articles (May 3, May 13, and May 27, 1982) do not give an indication of any fraud but instead refer to an obsession with growth. " 'By that time quarter-to-quarter growth had become a religion at Datapoint, and it was either sell or get fired,' says one current regional marketing manager. So Datapoint marketing people pushed through shakier and shakier orders." (*Wall Street Journal,* May 27, 1982) It is far more difficult for the public accountant to deal with honest but overoptimistic management than it is to deal with outright fraud.

McKESSON-ROBBINS

The basic need for integrity has been dramatized again and again by major frauds, but probably the most dramatic was the McKesson-Robbins case, which broke in 1938.[15] It might be said that what the 1929 crash did for Generally Accepted Accounting Principles and uniformity of accounting, McKesson-Robbins did for Generally Accepted Auditing Standards (GAAS).

In December 1938, a complaint charging certain officers and directors of McKesson-Robbins, a well known drug and chemical company, with fraud was filed in the U.S. District Court in Hartford, Connecticut. The fraud was quite complex, involving fictitious purchases of drugs from five imaginary vendors and subsequent "sales" through imaginary commission agents. All of this was perpetrated by the Musica brothers, under various aliases: as F. Donald Coster (Philip Musica), president of McKesson-Robbins; George Vernard (Arthur Musica), representative of W. W. Smith & Co.; and Manning & Co., the "commission agents"; George Dietrich (George Musica), assistant treasurer of McKesson-Robbins; and Robert Dietrich (Robert Musica), in charge of the shipping department of McKesson-Robbins. Two brothers-in-law of Philip Musica and another man (not related) were also involved. All pled guilty and served sentences except Philip Musica, who committed suicide as the U.S. marshal came to arrest him.

The fraud, which had been going on since 1923, resulted in a loss of $2.9 million in cash while the company's assets (principally receivables and inventories) were overstated by about $21 million, or about 25% of the total assets. The fraud was uncovered by the treasurer, Julian Thompson, who, of course, was not involved. During 1936 and 1937, Mr. Thompson, recently promoted to treasurer, attempted to realize some of the purported sales of the drug division in the form of badly needed cash rather than having it apparently put back into financing increased receivables and inventories of the drug division. After several rebuffs by the assistant treasurer (George Musica), Thompson became suspicious and began some investigations on his own which were quite successful as well as quite startling.

SEC Investigates

As the details of the fraud became public, the SEC stepped in to conduct a full investigation. One of the most respected public accounting firms in the world, Price Waterhouse & Company, had been the auditors for McKesson-Robbins for many years and had not been aware of the fraud. As the AICPA's official publication, *The Journal of Accountancy,* put it, "Like a torrent of cold water the wave of publicity raised by the McKesson-Robbins case has shocked the accountancy profession into breathlessness."[16]

How could such a fraud have escaped detection for so long? In January 1939, the SEC began public hearings aimed at answering that question. As the 1932 Pecora investigations had explored the question of uniformity of accounting standards, the 1939 SEC hearings dealt with the question of "the adequacy of the safeguards inherent in generally accepted practices and principles of audit procedure to assure reliability and accuracy of financial statements."[17] Twelve of the most well-known certified public accountants were called as expert witnesses and their testimony ran to more than 1500 pages. The topics covered were to be echoed nearly 40 years later in the hearings that led to the passage of the Foreign Corrupt Practices Act: the nature of auditing, internal check and control, and disclosure of fraud.

More Specific and Uniform Audit Standards Resulted

However, several topics covered were to lead to major changes in auditing practices as well as more specific audit standards. As the investigation proceeded, it became evident that although the collusion of key officials made the detection of the fraud difficult, it might have been discovered through an audit if the auditor had either requested direct confirmation of the bogus receivables or, more importantly, had attempted to physically inspect the inventories supposedly stored in various warehouses. Both these procedures were *suggested* in the AICPA's bulletin *Examination of Financial Statements* (published in 1936 as a part of the institute's responses to the events taking place in the accounting field from 1932 through 1935). Obviously not all public accounting firms deemed them to be necessary, nor were they mandatory at that time (1936).

Of course, with the benefit of hindsight the AICPA should have required the direct confirmation of receivables and the physical observation of inventories in all cases where they were significant. In May 1939, then, the Special Committee on Auditing Procedure of the AICPA filed a report with the Executive Council on Extensions of Auditing Procedure that required those two verification procedures as well as two other new procedures.

The last two covered the selection of the auditors and the form of the auditor's opinion covering his examination. Up to then, the selection of the auditors had not been a cause for concern, but following the McKesson-Robbins hearings, the committee recommended that the selection be made annually by the stockholders rather than management. This more clearly established to whom the auditor was responsible, although as a matter of practice, the stockholders virtually always ratify the auditor recommended by management.

The change in the form of the auditor's opinion was made in an attempt to avoid any negative connotation in the opinion. The phrase, "but we did not make a detailed audit of the transactions" was omitted from the form that had been approved in 1934 as a part of the AICPA/New York Stock Exchange discussion covered in Chapter 4.

Committee on Auditing Procedure

These were major, radical changes. The AICPA, however, was not finished. The SEC was quite disturbed and left no doubt in the minds of the institute's leaders that the rather casual approach to auditing standards, practices, and procedures was not satisfactory.[18] Ever sensitive to the desires of the SEC, the institute established a standing committee on auditing procedures. Over the next eight years the committee reviewed existing practices and procedures, issued 22 Statements on Auditing Procedures covering specific problem areas, and, then in 1947, published what have become general auditing standards in the *Tentative Statement of Auditing Standards, Their Generally Accepted Significance and Scope*. As we shall see, the general standards, standards of field work, and standards of reporting spelled out in this report are still the basic concepts of auditing followed today.

Auditing Standards Board

The Committee on Auditing Procedure (CAP) continued in existence until 1972 when it was replaced by the Auditing Standards Executive Committee (AudSEC) when the FASB was formed. The AudSEC, in turn, was replaced by the more formal Auditing Standards Board (ASB) in 1978 following the tumult caused by the Metcalf and Moss investigations in the post-Watergate period, which we will review later in this chapter.

Little Controversy Over Auditing Standards

An interesting aspect of the work of the AICPA through the CAP, AudSEC, and, currently, the ASB is that although a total of almost 100 statements on auditing procedure have been published over the last forty-plus years, there has been little controversy over them. Basically managerial accountants have not been concerned with the increasing codification of auditing quite simply because it does not affect their accounting practices.* On the other hand,

---

*At the FASB's 1980 Symposium on the Conceptual Framework for Financial Accounting and Reporting project, Professor Maurice Moonitz spoke of this contrast between the success enjoyed by the public accountants in establishing a broad set of fundamental auditing standards with the various groups' lack of success in establishing a conceptual framework of accounting

Congress and the SEC have been extremely sensitive to auditing procedures and every time a major fraud is discovered, an outcry occurs for stricter auditing procedures.

Corporate Audit Committees

The McKesson-Robbins case also resulted in the SEC recommending that an audit committee composed solely of outside (nonemployee) members of a company's board of directors be formed.[19] This committee could then provide the means by which the public accountants, through direct contact with this committee, could be insulated from possible pressures exerted by company management. Although a few companies did form such committees at that time, the idea did not really take hold until after Watergate.

EQUITY FUNDING

However, in spite of all of this activity, the fact remains that, to this day, a well-planned fraud conducted by a group of persons in key positions cannot be detected by auditors until the size of the fraud grows out of control. This is illustrated again and again by the periodic, sensational major frauds that occur. Nearly 40 years after McKesson-Robbins, the Equity Funding fraud gave the most dramatic evidence of this fact.

Equity Funding Corporation of America (EFCA) and its subsidiaries, notably Equity Funding Life Insurance Company (EFLIC), had started business in 1959 with the merger of two small securities and insurance marketing organizations. Basically, it was an independent sales company that marketed mutual funds shares, life insurance programs, and funded programs combining the two. Substantially all of its income was from commissions.[20] For the next few years it showed the growth in earnings that the stock market is so fond of and became a "high-flyer" growth stock.

Then, in early 1973, a disgruntled former employee reported to the New York State Department of Insurance and an insurance stock analyst that the earnings and assets were fraudulent.[21] Fictitious funded-loans receivables and insurance policies had been recorded on the books to create commission income. A giant "pyramid club" had been created, since, in the absence of

---

that met general acceptance. Professor Moonitz noted (quite correctly) that "to go to the heart of the matter, management will not willingly bear the responsibility for the soundness of financial statements without having a key role in framing the accounting and disclosure rules which underlie it." (Transcript, Symposium—Conceptual Framework for Financial Accounting and Reporting, FASB, June 24, 1980, p. 223.)

genuine cash flows, each year's fraud required an even larger fraud the following year and the fraud had been started as early as 1964! The magnitude of the case was even more stunning to the public accounting profession than McKesson-Robbins. Although the dollar amounts involved were large—estimates range from $150 million to $300 million—the number of persons involved was even more surprising. Indictments were returned against 22 people, including some of the officers and directors, for conspiracy to commit various federal crimes including stock fraud. All either pled guilty or were convicted of one or more counts against them. Furthermore, it seems apparent that many other employees were probably aware of the fraud but "did not get involved."[22]

In May 1973, the board of directors of the AICPA appointed a special committee "to study whether the auditing standards which are currently considered appropriate and sufficient in the examination of financial statements should be changed. . . ."[23]

The findings of this special committee bring out another facet of all professions—inadequate execution of customary procedures. Although the special committee refrained from directly criticizing the public accountants, the committee's conclusions were that with a minor exception, present auditing standards were adequate and that "the committee believes that customary audit procedures properly applied would have provided a reasonable degree of assurance that the existence of fraud at Equity Funding *would be detected*"[24] [emphasis added].

Both McKesson and Equity were massive management frauds involving significant portions of both companies' assets and earnings. Both frauds, of course, were so large that the financial statements of the companies were misrepresentations of material facts and thus, if known, would have affected the auditor's opinion dramatically (probably to the extent that disclaimers would have resulted).

The sensitive payments issue so disturbing to the nation and Congress generally was not of a magnitude to affect the representations of the company's financial position and, thus, the auditor's opinion as to the fairness of presentation of the financial statements, and consequently were not even the subject of his audit. This disturbs many people, but the point is that the auditor was hired to attest to the reasonableness of the financial position and the results of operations, not judge the relative merits of one nation's business practices versus another.

Management Versus Employee Fraud

What it comes down to is that, to a degree not recognized by the general public, the public accountant relies on the basic integrity of management.

The AICPA formally acknowledged this in Statement on Auditing Standards No. 16 when they concluded, "Unless the auditor's examination reveals evidential matter to the contrary, his reliance on the truthfulness of certain representations and on the genuineness of records and documents obtained during his examination is reasonable" (AU 327.12). All of the frauds of which critics such as Professor Briloff write with such hyperbole only prove the point. As sensational as McKesson-Robbins and Equity Funding were, they are the *exception*, not the rule. Thousands of companies are audited each year and the broad management-directed frauds, such as McKesson-Robbins or Equity Funding, are extremely rare.

The number of frauds, thefts and embezzlements committed by lower-level individuals each year, of course, is far greater. However, as deplorable as these crimes are, and as much as companies attempt to set up internal control systems to prevent them, the fact is that these lower-level frauds are rarely significant enough to affect the reasonableness of the financial position being attested to by the public accountant. Thus, while the general public has a difficult time understanding why such defalcations are not discovered by the public accountant, the truth is that he was not specifically looking for them—nor should he. The cost of such a fraud detection audit would be substantially greater than present audit costs with no assurance of discovering a well-concealed fraud.

MATERIALITY IN AUDITING

This last point—cost/benefit—is a difficult concept for many to understand, including the U.S. Congress (during the 1970s at least). In 1973, as an outgrowth of the investigation done by the Office of the Watergate Special Prosecutor, the SEC became aware of the widespread use of corporate funds for illegal political contributions. Subsequent investigations revealed that questionable,* if not actually illegal, payments beyond political contributions were being made by U.S. companies both in the U.S. and overseas. In the latter case, the possible bribery of foreign officials to induce favored treatment or to secure business was discovered. In 1975, the SEC announced a program whereby companies could voluntarily disclose questionable activities. Under this program more than 450 corporations admitted† making questionable or illegal payments exceeding $300 million.[25]

---

*The word "questionable" came into use because, in many cases, companies would pay independent agents and not actually know what ultimately was done with the funds, although the vagueness of the transaction was enough to raise a "question."
†Although there is no question of the illegality of payments made by many major corporations, not all of the corporations that filed statements (usually in the form of a commentary in their

These disclosures shocked many people, notably Senator William Proxmire (D-Wisconsin) and Congressman John E. Moss (D-Calif.) and ultimately led to the passage by Congress of the Foreign Corrupt Practices Act (FCPA) in December 1977. We will discuss this act later in this chapter; the point here is that most nonaccountants were amazed to learn that not only did the public accountants fail to discover, or disclose if they did discover, the questionable payments; they weren't even looking for them! Nor did the auditors' failure to discover the payments have any effect on the auditors' attestations even after the payments were disclosed!

The concept of materiality discussed in Chapter 3 is the basic concept involved. The simple fact is that $300 million spread across 450 large companies as well as several years is not material to the public accountant. The auditor who *is* concerned is the one often overlooked—the internal auditor. In fact, the internal auditor is attempting to do what most people believe the public accountant should do. In short, the general public has the responsibilities of the two auditors confused.

Internal Auditor Versus Public Accountant

Although there are many similarities in the work done and in the basic academic background required by the public accountant and the internal auditor, the difference in the product of their work dictates different procedures and methods. The internal auditor's* goal is defined in the *Standards for the Professional Practice of Internal Auditing:* "The scope of the internal audit should encompass the examination and evaluation of the adequacy and effectiveness of the organization's system of internal control and the quality of performance in carrying out assigned responsibilities. . . . The primary objectives of internal control are to ensure: 1) The reliability and integrity of information; 2) Compliance with policies, plans, procedures,

---

Form 10-K, the annual report filed with the SEC) were actually admitting they had made illegal payments.

Instead, a sophisticated legal point was involved in the "voluntary" disclosure program. As noted earlier, the term "questionable" was used to describe the payments because in many cases such payments had been made to independent brokers (which *could* have involved "laundering") and thus the corporation involved could not be certain of the ultimate use of the funds. However, under the amnesty-like provisions of the voluntary disclosure program, it was to a corporation's advantage from a legal point of view to disclose any and all possible "questionable" payments in order to forestall possible future legal action.

*The internal auditor is represented through The Institute of Internal Auditors, Inc., an international association dedicated to the continuing professional development of the individual internal auditor and the internal auditing profession. Founded in 1941, it now serves more than 21,000 members through 145 chapters in 85 countries.[26] The institute also has a certification program, the Certified Internal Auditor Program. Through 1980, more than 2000 members had successfully completed the four-part examination.[27]

laws and regulations; 3) The safeguarding of assets; 4) The economical and efficient use of resources; 5) The accomplishment of established objectives and goals for operations or programs."[28] Most nonauditors, including accountants, would tell you this is what they expect from the public accountant.

But if the public accountant does not set out to accomplish the same goals as the internal auditor, what are his goals? These too are clearly spelled out in the formal auditing standards of the AICPA, the pertinent parts of which are as follows:

Standards of Field Work

3　Sufficient competent evidential matter is to be obtained through inspection, observation, inquiries, and confirmations to afford a reasonable basis for an opinion regarding the financial statements under examination.

Standards of Reporting

1　The report shall state whether the financial statements are presented in accordance with generally accepted accounting principles.
2　The report shall state whether such principles have been consistently observed in the current period in relation to the preceding period.
3　Informative disclosures in the financial statements are to be regarded as reasonably adequate unless otherwise stated in the report.
4　The report shall either contain an expression of opinion regarding the financial statements, taken as a whole, or an assertion to the effect that an opinion cannot be expressed. When an overall opinion cannot be expressed, the reasons therefor should be stated. In all cases where an auditor's name is associated with financial statements, the report should contain a clear-cut indication of the character of the auditor's examination, if any, and the degree of responsibility he is taking.[29]

Presents Fairly Not Exactly

The result of the execution of these standards is that the public accountant can conclude that the representations of management expressed in the financial statements "present fairly" the financial position and results of the company—not present *exactly* but *fairly*. What does that mean? It means that there are no *material* errors or misstatements. And, of course, no satisfactory definition of *material* exists, the "prudent man" concept discussed in Chapter 3 being the best attempt.*

---

*The SEC's Regulation S-X (which covers specific accounting rules of the commission) defines materiality: "The term 'material' when used to qualify a requirement for the furnishing of information as to any subject, limits the information required to those matters as to which an *average prudent investor ought reasonably to be informed* [emphasis added] before purchasing the security registered." "Newly Emerging Standards of Auditor Responsibility." (*The Accounting Review*, January 1976, p. 26.)

Very few nonauditors understand this, and even fewer accept it even if they profess to understand. The history of public accounting is full of landmark court decisions involving aggrieved parties' frustration with the lack of certainty in an auditor's report. What is even worse, however, is that in the early stages of auditing, the auditors encouraged the myth of certainty. The early auditor's opinions spoke of financial statements as being "true and correct." And part of the mystique of auditing was the deterrent implicit in the understanding that an auditor would be reviewing the books of account. Of course, the *successful* embezzler knew that the auditors were not as perfect as they seemed to indicate they were, but the embezzlers were not about to tell anyone of their success in deceiving auditors (and management).

Ultramares Case

The most significant legal case concerning a public accountant's responsibility for fraud is *Ultramares Corporation vs Touche et al.,* decided in the New York Court of Appeals in 1931 with a decision handed down by Judge Cardozo. Briefly, the background is as follows:[30] Touche, Niven and Company, certified public accountants, audited Fred Stern and Company, Inc.'s balance sheet and with the exception of an income tax question gave a clear opinion on same.* The president of Stern Company later used the audited balance sheet as support for a loan from the Ultramares Company, which was subsequently granted. Stern went bankrupt in January 1925 and in November 1926, Ultramares sued Touche, Niven alleging negligence inasmuch as a careful audit should have disclosed the insolvency of Stern and stating that they, Ultramares, had relied upon the auditor's work. Later, fraud was also alleged by the plaintiff.

Cardozo Limited Liability to Third Parties

Judge Cardozo's opinion confirmed the common law concept that a public accountant should not be held liable to third parties for negligence: "The defendants owed to their employer a duty imposed by law to make their certificate without fraud, and a duty growing out of contract to make it with the care and caution proper to their calling. Fraud includes the pretense of knowledge when knowledge there is none. To creditors and investors to

---

*The auditor's certificate actually stated that the balance sheet gave a "true and correct view." The full opinion read: "We have examined the accounts of Fred Stern and Company, Inc., for the year ending December 31, 1923, and hereby *certify* that the annexed balance sheet is in accordance therewith and with the information and explanations given us. We further *certify* that, subject to provision for federal taxes on income, the said statement, in our opinion, presents a *true and correct* view of the financial condition of Fred Stern and Company, Inc. as of December 31, 1923" [emphasis added].[31]

whom the employer exhibited the certificate, the defendants owed a like duty to make it without fraud, since there was notice in the circumstances of its making that the employer did not intend to keep it to himself. . . . A different question develops when we ask whether they owed a duty to those to make it without negligence. If liability for negligence exists, a thoughtless slip or blunder, the failure to detect a theft or forgery beneath the cover of deceptive entries, *may expose accountants to a liability in an indeterminate time to an indeterminate class.* The hazards of a business conducted on those terms are so extreme as to enkindle doubt whether a flaw may not exist in the implication of a duty that exposes to these consequences" [emphasis added].

Gross Negligence Could Be Fraudulent

Judge Cardozo, however, then went on to develop a new concept, at least as it applied to public accountants: "Our holding does not emancipate accountants from the consequences of fraud. It does not relieve them *if their audit has been so negligent* as to justify a finding that they had no genuine belief in its adequacy, for this again is fraud" [emphasis added].[32] Thus, gross negligence could be construed as fraud.

As it turned out, the Court of Appeals did not find the defendants guilty of fraud due to gross negligence, and it affirmed the trial judge's dismissal of the cause of action based on negligence alone. However, it did reverse the trial judge's dismissal of a cause for action based on fraud and granted a new trial. None was ever held, an out-of-court settlement having been made instead.[33]

SEC Rule 10b-5

Shortly after this case, the 1933–1934 securities and exchange acts were passed, and a new rule was included that formed the basis for numerous suits over the years. Section 10(b) of the 1934 act and Rule 10b-5 thereunder provide that: "It shall be unlawful for any person . . . by the use of . . . interstate commerce . . . to make any untrue statement of a material fact or to omit to state a material fact necessary in order to make the statements made, in the light of the circumstances under which they were made, not misleading. . . ."[34] This rule is so broad and vague that it has become the basis for many of the lawsuits our litigious society fosters. However, the trend toward a more liberal interpretation of the public accountant's liability than established in *Ultramares* was arrested with the U.S. Supreme Court decision in *Ernst & Ernst vs Hochfelder* in March 1976.

Hochfelder Case

As J. Jay Hampson puts it in *The Journal of Accountancy,* "Before *Hochfelder,* the case law on accountants' liability under 10b-5 was in a state of flux.

Some courts interpreted the rule to encompass both negligent and intentional conduct, whereas others held that the rule was aimed at only intentional participation in a fraud. . . . before *Hochfelder,* courts had imputed a negligence standard into SEC Section 10(b), but the Supreme Court rejected such an interpretation."[35]

The case is a classic in the concept of negligence. Ernst & Ernst (now Ernst & Whinney) had audited First Securities Company of Chicago, a brokerage firm, from 1946 to 1967 and given clean opinions that were used in the appropriate filings with the SEC. In 1968, Leston B. Nay, president of First Securities and owner of 92% of its stock killed himself, leaving a note that his company was bankrupt. Subsequent investigation revealed that Nay, after receiving funds from customers to invest, had diverted them to his own use. The defrauded customers, headed by Olga Hochfelder in the class action suit, accused Ernst & Ernst of "inexcusable negligence"[36] in the performance of their audit. The U.S. Supreme Court rejected this claim and, in effect, reverted to the basic concepts implicit in *Ultramares:* that is, to find that auditors were liable for all management fraud regardless of the circumstances would expose the auditors to such a broad liability as to render them practically useless.[37]

Now there is no question that if the public accountant knowingly acquiesces to client fraud then the public accountant can be held liable. The basic issue involved in *Ultramares, Hochfelder,* and other similar cases is whether the auditor should be held liable if he had no knowledge of the fraud and performed his audit in conformance with the required professional standards. The answer in most decisions to date is "no."

Public Still Persists in Holding Public Accountants Liable for Fraud

However, even if the courts seem to accept the limitations of an audit, the general public has not. In November 1981 a federal court jury in New York found that Arthur Andersen & Company was guilty of fraud in 1968–1970 against a mutual fund called Fund of Funds and ordered the public accountants to pay $80 million to the shareholders of the mutual fund now in liquidation. The alleged fraud involved the purchase of natural resource assets by Fund of Funds during 1968–1970 from two concerns controlled by John King, a Denver oil and gas drilling fund promoter. The mutual fund alleged that the assets were sold at "unrealistically high and fraudulent prices"and that Andersen "had knowledge of or recklessly disregarded the fraudulent activities," basing its claim on the fact that Andersen had for a time been the auditors for both the King concerns and the Fund.[38] Such action makes public accountants very cautious.

Professor Kripke notes that "the statutory provisions and the SEC's infatuation with liability necessarily make the public accountant run scared and he has evolved a formidable apparatus to protect himself. He has organizations to determine Generally Accepted Accounting Principles and . . . Generally Accepted Auditing Standards. . . ."[39]

PUBLIC ACCOUNTANTS FUNCTION AT PLEASURE OF CONGRESS AND SEC

Professor Kripke's book, *The SEC and Corporate Disclosure*,[40] succinctly sums up the basic problem in accounting today. The public accounting profession functions at the whim and pleasure of Congress and the SEC. Every time a major fraud is discovered, that relationship is tested. Consider the problem that public accounting faces: Here we have a virtually unlimited growth business for which the demand can only grow because of the increasingly complex financial reporting and income tax rules. Two major threats, however, must be dealt with constantly—that of total government regulation and that of crippling, if not fatal, lawsuits. This combination drives the major public accounting firms (as the ones with greatest exposure) to seek safety in more and more specific rules. (As we shall see later, this thrust has created two paradoxes: the experiment with summary annual reports and the impetus by smaller public accounting firms to exclude their clients from the more sophisticated standards, such as capitalization of interest.)

The ebb and flow of fraud and abuse, rules and regulation, has been going on since the modern corporation and absentee ownership were conceived. The 1933–1934 securities and exchange acts were the most dramatic manifestation of government regulation. However, the 1970s virtually equaled the 1930s. Several related, although separate reviews, all stemming from Watergate, made changes in the structure of public and private accounting, the ultimate effects of which will not be known for many years.

WATERGATE AND QUESTIONABLE PAYMENTS

During the Watergate investigations in 1973, 17 companies confessed that they had knowingly broken the law that prohibits corporations from making political contributions in federal elections from corporate funds. The SEC, among others, began to investigate whether or not the disclosure provisions of the securities laws were broken also. During the investigations, in February 1975, Eli Black, chairman of United Brands, leaped to his death from his office on the 44th floor of the Pan Am Building rather than face the disgrace of the imminent revelation of a $1.25 million bribe paid in 1974 by United Brands to a Honduran official to induce him to reduce the export tax on bananas.[41] Mr. Black's death dramatized a growing scandal in illegal domestic political contributions and bribes of high foreign officials. As the SEC continued its investigation (which led to the voluntary disclosure program discussed earlier), Congress and the AICPA also began their own reviews.

In October 1974 the AICPA formed The Commission on Auditors' Responsibilities (the Cohen Commission). The commission issued a *Report of Tentative Conclusions* early in 1977 with a final report, *Conclusions, and Recommendations,* the next year. Much of its work is still being studied by the public accounting sector. However, its recommendations concerning a voluntary oversight program, including peer reviews, were promptly implemented, as we shall see.

Moss Subcommittee

Then, early in 1976, Congressman John E. Moss (D-Calif.), chairman of the House Commerce Committee's Subcommittee on Oversight and Investigation (with oversight responsibilities over the SEC) began investigating not only public accounting and corporate ethics, but the effectiveness of the SEC itself. In October 1976 the subcommittee issued a report on federal regulation and regulatory reform that included a scathing criticism of accounting, corporate management, and the SEC.[42] The regulator itself (SEC) was placed in jeopardy along with the public accounting profession.

The Moss subcommittee did not hold public hearings and, in fact, based much of its report on the testimony of the lone witness, Dr. Abraham J. Briloff, Emanuel Saxe Distinguished Professor of Accountancy at the Baruch College of the City University of New York. Professor Briloff is a very articulate, outspoken critic of accounting and financial reporting in general and the author of several books highly critical of management and public accounting. In his testimony before the Moss subcommittee,[43] Professor Briloff made several revolutionary proposals. First, he proposed the creation of an "independent disciplinary" board: "The oligopolistic stranglehold by the Big Eight firms over the AICPA must be broken.... While [the FASB] is independent on paper, its principal reliance on the (public accounting) profession's oligopoly for funding and other support subject it to pressures corresponding to those on the AICPA, and the erstwhile APB."

He then went on to "urge that the SEC use its disciplinary procedures more aggressively, more even-handedly and more openly." Of course, he also urged "that the SEC use its legislated authority to establish and implement standards of accounting. . . ." He recommended a far stronger definition of "present fairly" by the SEC and that to be consistent, Congress should "act promptly to make clear that its 1933 and 1934 Acts intended all professions bearing upon the issuance or trading of securities be held to a high standard of responsibility. . . ." In short, overturn the *Hochfelder* decision.

Finally, he proposed that Congress establish a super bureau—the Corporate Accountability Commission—that would oversee the Securities and Exchange Commission, the Federal Trade Commission, the General Accounting Office, the Interstate Commerce Commission, the Federal Communications Commission, the Federal Power Commission, the Civil Aeronautics Board, the Cost Accounting Standards Board, The Comptroller of the Currency, the Federal Deposit Insurance Corporation, and perhaps, the Internal Revenue Service!

With this testimony as background, it was not surprising that the Moss report was quite critical of the SEC's delegation of its accounting principles responsibility (to the AICPA) in 1938 and of the failure of the private sector since that time to develop uniform standards. "The FASB has accomplished virtually nothing toward resolving fundamental problems plaguing the profession. These include the plethora of optional 'generally accepted' accounting principles, the ambiguities inherent in many of those principles, and the manifestations of private accountants' lack of independence with respect to their corporate clients. Considering the FASB's record, the SEC's continued reliance on the private accounting profession is questionable. Recent disclosures of illegal and questionable corporate payments show that the protection of investors requires more than uniform accounting principles. Public investors and the public generally need the protection afforded by effective, well-enforced internal corporate controls; responsible corporation directors; and independent auditors."

The Moss subcommittee concluded from the disclosures made in the Watergate investigation and under the SEC's voluntary compliance program "that the inadequacy of internal controls contributed significantly to the incidence of corporate illegality and unaccountability." It cited the fact that in 46 of the first 95 companies that disclosed to the SEC illegal or questionable payments or practices, top management had knowledge of the payments or practices. Furthermore, "In a number of cases, for example, Gulf Oil, Lockheed, Northrop and United Brands, the illicit payments were in fact engineered by executives in the top hierarchy. . . ."

The subcommittee cited ineffective financial controls, noting that "one of the primary purposes of such controls is to prevent practices such as over-billing or over-invoicing, kicking back the excess to purchase agents or suppliers, or laundering through off-the-book bank accounts—practices which crop up repeatedly in payoff disclosures."

The report did note that the SEC report included a recommendation to require "management to establish and maintain its own system of internal accounting controls designed to provide reasonable assurance that corporate transactions are executed *in accordance with management's general or specific authorization. . . ."* [emphasis added]. The fundamental point that everyone ignored in making such recommendations (which were to lead eventually to the Foreign Corrupt Practices Act of 1977) is that the best internal accounting control system possible would be ineffective if managed by persons intent on making illegal payments. In short, the system would reflect the transactions *in accordance with management's general or specific authorization* which, in many of the questionable payment cases, was to bribe foreign officials. Thus, the effectiveness of any system rests on the basic integrity of those who manage it.

The Moss report then concludes with five recommendations concerning corporate accountability which the SEC was instructed to implement.

1 Accounting standards, principles and practices: "to the maximum extent practicable, the SEC should prescribe by rule a framework of *uniform* accounting principles. . . ."

2 Internal controls: Seven rules were proposed covering codes of conduct, the elimination of off-book entries, penalties for falsification of records, and the attestation of independent auditors as to the quality and enforcement of internal controls in the annual report.

3 Boards of directors: Six rules were proposed covering the assurance of independence from management of the board.

4 Auditing standards: Three rules were proposed requiring the SEC to set auditing standards and codes and finally to draft legislation that would overturn the Hochfelder decision.

5 SEC enforcement of federal disclosure laws.

The subcommittee then specifically requested the SEC to vigorously pursue the disclosure of all relevant facts and, where appropriate, to refer cases to the Department of Justice and to inform the public of the extent of illegal and questionable activities of corporations.[44]

In the words of Michael N. Chetkovich, then incoming chairman of the AICPA, "It [the Moss report] was brutal."[45]

Senate Action

At the same time, various senators were pursuing a separate course of corrective action. At first, there was some confusion as to how to attempt to address the problem. In March 1976, Senator Proxmire introduced legislation to amend the 1934 Securities Act to require the SEC to promulgate rules requiring issuers under the act "to maintain accurate books, records, or accounts of all transactions," but no mention was made of the illegal foreign payments per se. In May 1976, Senators Church, Clark, and Pearson introduced legislation that was directed at prohibiting such payments. Entitled the International Contributions, Payments, and Gift Disclosure Act, it would have required companies to file highly detailed sworn disclosure statements.[46]

Also in May 1976, the SEC forwarded its *Report on Questionable and Illegal Payments and Practices* to the Senate Committee on Banking, Housing, and Urban Affairs. In its report the SEC identified three critical components for any legislative action: a prohibition against the falsification of corporate accounting records, a prohibition against the making of false and misleading statements to those persons conducting audits, and the requirement that management establish and maintain an effective system of internal accounting controls. (Ultimately the SEC report was to form the basis for the Foreign Corrupt Practices Act.)

An interesting aspect of these three strictures is that all in the private practice of accounting in industry had always considered the first two prohibited activities to be illegal while the third has always been the keystone to the successful management of any company of any size whatsoever. As we shall see, the basis for any internal management information system, which is needed to operate and manage business operations, is an effective system of internal control that includes the accounting controls.

Metcalf Subcommittee

As the corrupt practices gained national attention, Senator Lee Metcalf* (D-Montana), chairman of the Subcommittee on Reports, Accounting, and Management of the Committee on Government Operations, began an investigation of accounting and the SEC in the fall of 1975. In December 1976, the subcommittee's staff issued *The Accounting Establishment*[47] which was even more critical of public accounting, the FASB, and the SEC than the Moss report. Although the study (termed the Metcalf report) was never formally adopted by the subcommittee, the effect on the public accountants was dramatic as we shall see.

The tone and theme of the Metcalf staff report are set early in the 1760-page book. The accounting establishment is defined as being "primarily comprised of the Nation's eight largest accounting firms, certain influential CPA professional organizations and business lobbying groups, and a few Federal agencies—most notably the Securities & Exchange Commission." It goes on to state that "the Financial Accounting Foundation (FAF) is the non-profit

---

*Senator Metcalf died in 1978 and was succeeded by Senator Thomas Eagleton (D-Missouri).

corporation *organized by the AICPA* [emphasis added] and co-sponsored by four [now five] other private interest groups to operate the Financial Accounting Standards Board (FASB), which sets accounting standards. Those groups are the Financial Executives Institute, the National Association of Accountants, the American Accounting Association, and the Financial Analysts Federation [the Securities Industry Association was added in October 1976]. *None of these private interest groups is suited to control the setting of accounting standards* [emphasis added] which affect the Federal Government and the public."[48] That certainly is clearly enough stated! Since every private group—academia, business, and analysts—is represented, their exclusion from being "suited to control the setting of accounting standards" leaves only the government as being suited. The staff study went on to recommend 16 actions "in order to achieve efficient and effective accounting practices that will promote corporate accountability." Briefly these were:

1 Congress should exercise *direct* authority to achieve proper accounting practices. "Broad delegation of legislative authority to Federal agencies, which in turn delegated broad authority to private interest groups, has been a major factor in the establishment of accounting practices which have benefited special interests at the expense of the Federal Government and the public."

2 "Congress should establish comprehensive accounting objectives. . . . The lack of such objectives has . . . contributed to the failure to establish uniform and meaningful accounting standards for publicly-owned corporations during the past 40 years. The Cost Accounting Standards Board [a government Board established in 1970 to set arbitrary government contract cost accounting standards and then disbanded in 1980] has benefited from its specific statutory mandate to achieve 'uniformity and consistency' in cost accounting standards. . . . A comprehensive set of Federal accounting objectives should encompass such goals as uniformity, consistency, clarity, accuracy, simplicity, meaningful presentation, and fairness in application. . . . Congress should establish specific policies abolishing such 'creative accounting' techniques as percentage of completion income recognition, inflation accounting [I am not sure what the problem was with this], 'normalized' accounting [presumably, this means the matching of costs and revenues], and other potentially misleading accounting methods." [Apparently, accrual basis accounting was suspect. In many respects, the staff's approach to accounting was closer to that used by the Internal Revenue Service.]

3 "Congress should amend the Federal securities laws to restore the right of damaged individuals to sue independent auditors for negligence. . . .

[This] is necessary to overturn the holding of the U.S. Supreme Court in *Ernst & Ernst v. Olga Hochfelder,* et al., . . . that 'scienter'—the intent to deceive, manipulate, or defraud—is a necessary requirement of private actions for damages. . . ."[49]

4 "Congress should consider methods of increasing competition among accounting firms for selection as independent auditors. . . ." [The Federal Trade Commission's antitrust unit also pursued this aspect of public accounting, and "in early 1979, in the light of legal advice questioning the legality of the long-standing prohibition against direct uninvited solicitation and the prospect that the ban would be challenged by the United States Department of Justice, the . . . AICPA voted . . . to eliminate the ban.][50]

5 "The Federal Government should directly establish financial accounting standards for publicly-owned corporations. . . . The SEC's long association with the private accounting establishment and insistent determination to rely upon its accounting pronouncements cast substantial doubt on the SEC's ability to establish accounting standards which would restore public confidence in corporate financial reporting. . . . Public participation and strong oversight by Congress are essential to safeguarding the public interest in any standard-setting procedure adopted.

6 "The Federal Government should establish auditing standards. . . .

7 "The Federal Government should itself periodically inspect the work of independent auditors. . . . Periodic quality reviews could be conducted by the General Accounting Office, the SEC, or a special audit inspection agency." [As we shall see, this recommendation was complied with by the AICPA as a part of the formation of an SEC Practice Division for CPA firms.]

8 "The Federal Government should restore public confidence in the actual independence of auditors . . . by promulgating and enforcing strict standards of conduct. . . ." Of particular concern to the Metcalf staff was the "representation of clients' interests" in income tax and management advisory services. [SEC Accounting Series Release Nos. 250 (1978) and 264 (1979), since rescinded, were directed specifically to this point.]

9 "The Federal Government should require the Nation's 15 largest accounting firms to report basic operational and financial data annually." [As noted earlier, Arthur Andersen began publishing an annual report in 1974, while this recommendation encouraged Coopers; Peat, Marwick; Price Waterhouse; and Touche Ross to publish some type of report at least for a while.]

10 "The Federal Government should define the responsibilities of independent auditors so that they clearly meet the expectations of Congress, the public, and courts of law." [This is almost a truism. Certainly
the independent auditors would appreciate such a definition. Presumably the 1933 to 1934 securities and exchange acts attempted to do
exactly what the Metcalf staff recommended.]

11 "The Federal Government should establish financial accounting standards, cost accounting standards, auditing standards and other accounting practices in meetings open to the public." [Although the
government has not taken over the standards-setting task yet, in 1977 the
FASB did change its procedures to provide that all meetings where a
majority of the board was present would be held in the "sunshine," i.e.,
as open meetings.]

12 "The Federal Government should act to relieve excessive concentration
in the supply of auditing and accounting services to major publicly
owned corporations.

13 "The Federal Government should not contract with accounting firms for
the performance of management advisory services. [Evidently the Metcalf staff believed that public accountants were becoming too friendly
with their regulators.]

14 "The SEC should treat all independent auditors equally in disciplinary
and enforcement proceedings. . . ." [Here, the Metcalf staff objected to
what they perceived to be favoritism toward the Big Eight.]

15 "The membership of the Cost Accounting Standards Board [now dis-
solved] should not be dominated by representatives of industry and
accounting firms which may have vested interests in the standards [being
established].

16 "Federal employees should not serve on committees of the AICPA or
similar organizations. . . ."[51] [Again, the regulators should not get
friendly with those they regulate.]

After reading these recommendations, there can be little doubt about the
feelings of the Metcalf staff—only the government can be trusted and even
then the SEC was suspect as being too cozy with the public accountants.
Professor Briloff or that redoubtable iconoclast, Admiral Hyman G. Rickover, could not have said it better. Professor Briloff, of course, did reach the
same conclusion in his testimony before the Moss subcommittee while Admiral Rickover was to testify in May 1977 before the Metcalf subcommittee
to the same effect.[52]

The AICPA, understandably, took strong exception to the Staff's conclusions, particularly those which implied an excess concentration of power in

the Big Eight and their dominance of both public accounting and the FASB. "An examination of the staff study discloses a significant gap between the purported evidence and the recommendations."[53]

During April, May, and June 1977 the subcommittee held eight days of public hearings on the issues raised in the staff study. Interestingly enough, although the majority of the witnesses disagreed with the staff study, several of the recommendations were ultimately adopted (as noted above in the author's parenthetical comments following the recommendations).

Moreover, John Biegler, then senior partner of Price Waterhouse & Co., astonished the public accounting profession by recommending that the SEC assume "greater control over (public) accounting firms by (1) requiring registration of most CPA firms that audit publicly-held companies, (2) publishing annual financial statements by firms, (3) initiating peer reviews under the aegis of the SEC and (4) establishing SEC guidelines for management consulting."[54] There is no doubt that many people in public accounting took the threat of total government control quite seriously, as well they should have.

One other point of continuing interest: In November 1977, Senator Metcalf's subcommittee filed a report with Senator Abraham Ribicoff (D-Conn.), chairman of the Committee on Governmental Affairs. In that report, Senator Metcalf comments that "the inquiry was initiated because of general concern over unexpected failures and wrongdoing by publicly-owned corporations which were either undetected or not disclosed by the accounting firms. . . . The subcommittee *also received complaints from academics and representatives of small accounting firms* that the . . . 'Big Eight' firms *were dominating the profession's private standard-setting* organizations, and that . . . *was detrimental to the interests of both the general public and* the [public] accounting profession as a whole" [emphasis added].[55] This schism between the major public accounting firms and the smaller firms is very real and is more of a problem in the 1980s than it was in the 1970s.

Responding to the intense pressure of the Metcalf and Moss subcommittees and the SEC (which was also under severe criticism from Congress), the statements of such leaders in the profession as John Biegler of Price Waterhouse, and the likelihood of new legislation regulating public accounting, the Executive Council of the AICPA acted swiftly (some would say hastily) to avert, once again, the threat of total government regulation.

AICPA Reaction—Public Oversight Board

In September 1977, the council, without seeking a vote of the full AICPA membership, established as divisions of the AICPA by firms the SEC Practice Section and the Private Companies Practice Section, and also a Public

Oversight Board (POB) to exercise continuing oversight of the SEC Practice Section with specific regard to a new requirement for peer review, that is, a review of a firm's practices and procedures by another public accounting firm. The radical nature of these changes can be gauged by the fact that, prior to the Council's action, the AICPA was organized only as individual (not firm) members and all such actions were accomplished by a vote of *members*.

A distinguished panel was selected to form the Public Oversight Board. John J. McCloy, a renowned lawyer, diplomat, and public servant, was named chairman. The other members are Ray Garrett, Jr., and William L. Cary, both former SEC chairmen, and John D. Harper and Arthur M. Wood, retired board chairmen of the Aluminum Company of America and Sears, Roebuck and Co., respectively. (Robert K. Mautz, director of the Paton Accounting Center at the University of Michigan and a noted accounting professor and author, was appointed to fill the vacancy created by the death of Ray Garrett, Jr., in 1980.)

In spite of this blue-ribbon panel, however, the success of the POB is still open to question. As the Public Oversight Board stated in their annual report for 1980–1981 (p. 16), "In the aggregate, the number of firms, especially those with SEC clients, that joined the [SEC] Section during the past two years is disappointing and is evidence that the changes made in Section requirements to attract or retain smaller firms were not effective. The Board notes with interest that 1,600 firms belong only to the Private Companies Practice Section and that over the past year the number of such firms that audit SEC clients has increased from 58 to 107." (The SEC section had 515 firms on March 31, 1981 who audited 91% of the estimated 9000 companies required to file financial statements with the SEC.)

Many of the smaller public accounting firms have never been in favor of the division of firms. Initially, a lawsuit was filed against the AICPA in September 1977 by 18 members, alleging that the council had exceeded its powers. The plaintiff subsequently lost the suit. Then in 1980, the scheduled publication of a directory of members of the division for CPA firms was delayed until summer 1982. The following appeared in the POB's annual report for 1980–1981: "Some AICPA members express serious concerns about the establishment of the division with two sections. Some believe it has led to an inappropriate distinction among firms. Some members that do not audit SEC clients fear that a directory will be used by competitors to solicit their privately-held clients."[56]

Although the debate concerning the Divison for Firms is still going on within the AICPA, the fact is, for the time being, expanded federal regulation of public accounting has been thwarted. In June 1978, Congressman Moss did indeed introduce a bill entitled The Public Regulatory Act. "The Act would establish a National Organizaton of Securities and Exchange Commission Accountancy with which independent public accounting firms would be required to register in order to furnish audit reports with respect to financial statements filed with the SEC. This new organization would, under SEC oversight, review the audit work performed . . ., investigate audit inadequacies . . . and take disciplinary actions where necessary. The Act would clarify and strengthen the authority of the SEC to develop and issue accounting principles and auditing standards."[57]

This legislation never got very far as the interest of Congress diminished following the AICPA's action in September 1977 creating the POB, the passage of the Foreign Corrupt Practices Act in December 1977, and the SEC's strong defense of the AICPA's actions in their July 1978 report to the Eagleton subcommittee on the accounting profession. The SEC concluded "that the progress during the past year has been sufficient to merit continued opportunity for the profession to pursue its efforts at self-regulation." However, the SEC warned that, "the process of demonstrating that accountants themselves rather than government should (i) retain primary authority to regulate their profession, (ii) ensure and instill confidence in their professionalism and objectivity, (iii) maintain control over the quality of the work of the profession's members and discipline those who fail to adhere to its standards, and (iv) formulate appropriate accounting and auditing standards, is one which will demand the profession's and Commission's commitment for many years to come. If the profession or the Commission lose sight of these objectives, the public generally and *accountants specifically will, in the long run, be the losers*"[58] [emphasis added]. But if the public accountants "dodged the bullet" of outright government regulation once again, the accounting profession—in the broader definition—was not so lucky.

Foreign Corrupt Practices Act Passed

As mentioned earlier, Senators Proxmire, Church, and others had initiated legislation intended to curb the practices disclosed by the Watergate and SEC investigations. As noted, the SEC had concluded that the system of corporate accountability had been frustrated inasmuch as "millions of dollars of funds have been inaccurately recorded in corporate books and records to facilitate the making of questionable payments."[59]

This conclusion was an unfortunate one indeed because it omitted consideration of the basic problem with questionable payments and resulted in the misdirection of the efforts of Congress. The resulting legislation (the FCPA) would ultimately add millions of dollars to the cost of regulation, cause the loss of many more millions in legitimate foreign sales (and thus adversely affect the nation's economic trade balance), and all this without actually addressing the problem.

For the basic problem involved in the questionable payments issue was one of integrity of management. As noted, the best system of internal accounting controls is only as effective as the integrity of management. As the history of major top management frauds has shown (McKesson-Robbins, Equity Funding, etc.) if management wants to do something illegal, no system of internal control can stop it. All control systems are basically designed to stop, or at least minimize, lower-level fraud, but since they rest on management's integrity, they will be ineffective to prevent broad-scale frauds by top management. Thus, if any legislation were even necessary,* such legislation certainly need not have been directed at accounting. Professor Kripke comments on the lawyers' domination of the SEC that left a narrowed moralistic perspective rather than a pragmatic one: "Of all the new disclosure topics that have commanded the Commission's attention in recent years, questionable payments' looms largest. Sometimes the amounts involved *were* large enough to be material in some companies by ordinary standards. Cloak-and-dagger transmittals of cash and falsification of books justified the SEC's attention. But the Commission's persistence, even after the Griffin study† for the Advisory Committee Report showed the events were not really material in the minds of investors, revealed a moralistic purpose and seizure of an opportunity to stake out for the Commission a claim in the area of corporate governance. Undoubtedly, the facts disclosed presented serious issues of governance, given the complicity of leading officials in some companies and the supine role of independent directors. But the integrity of the books and character of management had not been among the Commission's prime concerns in disclosure until the revelations gave the Commission a moral posture from which to press for changes in corporate governance. Once this moralism was invoked, the situation was on 'the slippery slope of materiality,' as Commissioner Sommer pointed out."[60]

However, in spite of the Griffin study, the SEC and Congress pressed on. The result was that the scope of the legislation was far more encompassing than just foreign bribes. Section 102 of the FCPA, signed into law by Pres-

---

*Subsequent experience and consideration in a less-heated atmosphere than prevailed in the immediate post-Watergate period makes this need doubtful. At the September 1981 hearings held by the House Subcommittee on Telecommunications, Consumer Protection, and Finance on a proposed amendment to the FCPA (H.R. 2530), former SEC Chairman Roderick M. Hills said that he supported the bill's proposal to limit the scope of disclosure under the FCPA. He said the "criminalization" of the issue was one step too far and, as a result, the whole program is now suspect. Without the FCPA, Hills said, there are laws sufficient to deal with corrupt practices. (*Executive Disclosure Guide, SEC Compliance,* Commerce Clearing House, Chicago, September 23, 1981.)

†Paul A. Griffin, "Sensitive Foreign Payment Disclosures; The Securities Market Impact," *Report of the Advisory Committee on Corporate Disclosure to the SEC,* 1977.

ident Carter in December 1977, was codified by the SEC early in 1978 as Section 13(b)(2) of the Securities Exchange Act of 1934. The new law set *accounting requirements* for *all* business activities and *all* U.S. companies that have to register with the SEC (nearly 9000 companies) *regardless* of foreign activities. Thus, while the thrust was ostensibly foreign bribery, the result was rigid rules governing all financial records and internal accounting controls for the everyday activities of all SEC-registered companies in the U.S.

As the American Bar Association's Committee on Corporate Law and Accounting put it: "Congress moved hastily on the accounting provisions of the 1977 Act; technical problems of day-to-day accounting were pale stuff compared to the red-hot moral-political issues of bribery that commanded the attention of Congress. . . . As a result—the language of the accounting mandate of section 13(b)(2) is simplistic and vague. If it is not interpreted by the courts and responsible official agencies with thoughtful deliberation and care, it could lead to results that are terribly costly, unproductive, unfair and unintended by Congress."[61]

What are the words for which such dire consequences were predicted? They really are quite brief; the act is several pages long, covering primarily foreign bribery prohibitions, but the accounting standards section covers only a few lines as follows (emphasis added):

Accounting Standards

Sec. 102 Section 13(b) of the Securities Exchange Act of 1934 (15 U.S.C. 78q(b)) is amended by inserting "(1)" after "(b)" and by adding at the end thereof the following: 15 U.S.C. 78l Post, p. 1500. Records, maintenance.

(2) Every issuer which has a class of securities registered pursuant to section 12 of this title and every issuer which is required to file reports pursuant to section 15(d) of this title shall

   (A) *make and keep books, records, and accounts, which, in reasonable detail, accurately* and *fairly reflect* the *transactions* and *dispositions of the assets* of the issuer; and

   (B) *devise and maintain a system of internal accounting controls sufficient to provide reasonable assurances that—*

      (i) *transactions are executed in accordance with management's general or specific authorization;*

      (ii) *transactions are recorded* as necessary (I) to permit preparation of financial statements *in conformity with generally accepted accounting principles* or any other criteria applicable to such statements, and (II) to *maintin accountability for assets;*

      (iii) access to assets is permitted only in accordance with management's general or specific authorization; and

      (iv) the *recorded accountability for assets is compared with the existing assets at reasonable intervals and appropriate action is taken with respect to any differences.*[62]

The final wording is virtually the same as that recommended by the SEC in its May 1976 Report to the Committee on Banking, Housing, and Urban Affairs (pp. 63–64); only the words "in reasonable detail" were added to modify "accurately and fairly."

Even more interesting is the fact that the wording of part (B) is virtually a copy of the AICPA's definition of internal accounting control.[63] This really is not surprising since the AICPA testified extensively at the various hearings held by both the SEC and Congress.* However, with the FCPA, the more or less informal auditing literature was now made a part of law with criminal prosecution as a potential consequence.

Moreover, in spite of extensive expert testimony to the contrary, the perception of the public accountant as being responsible for discovering fraud remained unchanged and, if anything, the public accountants only lost respect for their failure to do just that in the cases disclosed by the SEC questionable-payments investigation. Over a year after the passage of the act, Senator Charles H. Percy (R-Ill.) would state in an interview for Deloitte Haskins & Sells's *The Week in Review:* "The profession has a great responsibility to find illegal payments. I discovered that the SEC had flushed out enough rare instances to make it almost a pattern. I cannot help but feel that detecting those activities was the responsibility of the accounting firms."[64]

THE PARADOX OF AUDITING

This comment illustrates just how formidable the task of explaining what an auditor does really is. As mentioned earlier, one of the paradoxes of the double-entry system of bookkeeping upon which accounting rests is the combination of the precision of the entries coupled with the subjectivity of the decisions that precede them.

The practice of auditing compounds this paradox. Its very roots are deep in the discipline of precise choices,† for instance: are the transactions, representations, and events being recorded by management as they are purported to be and is that way conceptually reasonable (some would say correct)? Thus, the auditor initially seems to state that he *is* going to verify the accuracy of the company's records and financial statements and then appears to back

---

*In fact, one participant (who had testified at the Congressional hearings) at a seminar later made the comment that it was fortunate they (the AICPA) were able to limit the FCPA to "internal *accounting* control" rather than all administration controls!

†"Ever since double-entry has been in use, textbook instructions have been given for checking the recorded data for error; and some of the earliest advice in this respect is still sound as far as it goes." (A. C. Littleton, *Accounting Evolution to 1900*, Accounting History Classic Series, University of Alabama Press, 1981. (Reprint of the 1933 original edition, published by American Institute Publishing Co., New York.)

off and say his goal is not to discover fraud. Small wonder that the nonaccountant gets confused and becomes skeptical of the accountant's integrity.

This apparent emphasis on precision is often perpetuated by the approach taken by the junior auditors (and, unfortunately, some senior auditors) in an engagement. The discipline of double-entry bookkeeping often attracts those of a more structured, precise temperament and early in their auditing career they tend to overemphasize that trait.* (This is the "failure to see the forest for the trees" syndrome which is not peculiar to just the auditing field.) Then too juniors are not granted the latitude (because of inexperience) to make the subjective evaluations involving materiality, for example, that the senior accountant or partner must make.

Auditing, properly performed, is very subtle and very complex. The auditor must not only be skilled in the use of audit techniques and procedures but must, of necessity, be a sound accounting theoretician since he will be judging (or calling the attention to) the subjective decisions the managerial accountant has made. In addition, the proficient auditor should be particularly adept at displaying tact since in most of his work he will be questioning and even challenging the decisions of others.

As mentioned earlier, the audit rests on the integrity of management. Basically, in performing an audit, the auditor begins by making certain assumptions and then proceeds to perform various tests and reviews that are designed to prove or disprove the validity of the original assumptions.

The first assumption is that the company is composed of people (both management and staff) who are honest, ethical, and competent. The second assumption follows naturally then; that is, the financial data that the auditor has been engaged to review are a fair representation of the company's activities for the period being audited. Having so placed his trust in the company, the auditor then begins to perform tests, reviews, and analyses to ascertain if his trust is well-placed. Determining the extent of the testing deemed necessary to reach that conclusion is part of what differentiates the art from the science of auditing.

Basically, the decision is based on an evaluation of the client's control system, that is, the internal flow of data, the documentation, the authorizations, the "checks and balances" that help insure that the internal system will reflect the actions and results as well as the policies of the company.

Another factor in this control system which has become increasingly important in the past decade has been the widespread growth of corporate audit committees. Although a few companies had audit committees for over

---

*I still recall my dismay, 25 years ago, upon learning that an assistant, auditing a subsidiary company of a large, multicompany audit I was supervising, had insisted that the controller of the subsidiary record a ten cent ($.10) adjustment to correct an error in the bank account the auditor had discovered.

75 years it was not until the McKesson and Robbins case that the concept gained attention by those outside the companies. In its 1939 report on the case the New York Stock Exchange strongly endorsed (although they stopped short of requiring) audit committees as a means of assuring auditor independence. Shortly therafter (in 1940) the SEC also endorsed such action in Accounting Series Release 19. Through such a committee, composed of outside (non-employee) directors, direct access to the Board of Directors is available to the public accountants. Such a procedure alleviates the pressure from management sometimes experienced by the public accountants and thus enhances their independence.

However, it was not until the problems of the 1960s described in Chaper 4, that the audit committee gained wide acceptance. By 1973, 72% of the large industrial corporations who responded to a Korn/Ferry International survey, reported that they had audit committees. Then in 1977 the New York Stock Exchange amended its policy regarding audit committees to that of *requiring* such committees effective June 30, 1978. This action, plus the continuing strong interest of the SEC, has resulted in virtually all public companies having such committees.

It is possible, although rare, that in some instances the internal system of controls is so poor that the auditor concludes that no reliance can be placed in the system and that *all* material transactions and data have to be examined in order for the auditor to conclude that his initial assumptions were correct and that the financial statements "present fairly" the company's results and position. In the mid-1960s, the author performed such an audit on a small real estate joint venture company. In order to be satisfied, it was necessary to trace down the disposition of every lot in the real estate tract being developed. Obviously, internal controls were nonexistent; no procedures were in place, the controller was incompetent, and management was too concerned with the development/marketing effort to notice. Management was composed of honest (if exuberant) salesmen, and, after discovering and correcting several duplicate payments, we were able to verify all of the data and render a clear opinion. The more typical situation is the existence of some form of internal control system. Naturally, the larger and more complex the company, the more sophisticated the system of internal control.

NEED FOR INTERNAL CONTROL SYSTEM

The reason for the system of internal control is not to make an auditor's job easier (although the better the system, the easier his work will be and the lower the cost) but to provide management with the reliable data and control it needs to plan and succeed—the discipline of accounting mentioned earlier.

A review of the basic concepts of control illustrates the obvious need for the system, regardless of auditing requirements. A good overview of these concepts was provided in 1979 in the Report of the Special Advisory Committee on Internal Control done for the AICPA:

> The effectiveness of a company's organizational structure depends on how well it serves as a framework for direction and control of company activities. An effective structure would give appropriate consideration to the following matters:
>
> Competence of personnel and provision of appropriate resources to discharge the responsibilities assigned, together with a system of measurement of, and accountability for, performance.
>
> Assignment of responsibility and delegation of authority to deal with matters such as goals and objectives, operating functions, organization form, management style, regulatory requirements, and financial reporting standards.
>
> Budget and financial reports to facilitate the discharge of assigned responsibilities and monitor the activities at each level in the organizational structure.
>
> Checks and balances that separate incompatible activities to preclude absolute control by any single individual or unit, provide for supervision by higher levels of management, and provide for monitoring of overall company activities.

Obviously, every manager wants to achieve these basic goals. Of course, the cost of achieving them must always be balanced against the benefit gained. This is not really a matter of concern insofar as competent personnel are concerned—competence is always cost-effective. The two goals of assigning responsibility and adequate budgeting are also not in question. It is the last, "checks and balances," where the most serious cost/benefit evaluations come into play.

If, for example, there is little risk of loss of an asset for whatever reason, theft, damage, and so on, then the control over the asset could be minimal. Thus, whereas a diamond distributor might find it worthwhile to station numerous guards to control strictly the movement of diamonds in and out of his store, the distributor of cement blocks may find that a simple fenced area and a single clerk is all the control that is necessary. As Kenneth P. Johnson and Henry R. Jaenicke put it, "While internal accounting control aims at preventing and detecting errors, absolute prevention or 100 percent detection is costly and probably impossible. Since controls have a cost in both time and money, management must always make economic judgments as to whether a further degree of risk reduction is worth the cost of providing it."[65]

The long-standing importance of control to management (long before the

FCPA) was borne out in the major findings of the landmark research study done by R. K. Mautz, director of the Paton Accounting Center, and six other members of the faculty at the University of Michigan, from 1977 to 1980:

"(i) Control is seen by most executives as an integral part of the management process, and a key management responsibility which they accept. Many executives expressed resentment at the implication which they feel underlies the accounting provisions of the Foreign Corrupt Practices Act, that U.S. corporate executives as a group are not adequately attentive to control practices within their companies. They also feel that they are being burdened unduly for the transgressions of a relatively few companies."[66]

Statistical Sampling

The auditor tests the adequacy of the company's control system in order to determine the reasonableness of his own reliance upon its ability to produce reliable financial data. In a large corporation the extent of this testing is actually quite small—in many cases less than 1% of the total transactions. As small as this percentage is, however, today it is based on sound statistical sampling concepts developed initially by Kenneth W. Stringer* of Deloitte Haskins & Sells (DH&S) in the early 1960s. Until that time, the extent of testing deemed necessary varied widely, even within a single accounting firm, based on the temperament and conservatism of the individual auditor in charge of the engagement.

However, two major factors made such a casual approach untenable. These factors were increased litigation involving public accountants and increased pressure from clients to keep audit costs under control. We discussed the litigation problem, which is still very much a problem; the time/cost question is another factor affecting the quality of audits. The Cohen Commission reports that "a disturbingly high proportion (approximately 50 percent) of the respondents to the Commission's survey replied that pressures induced by time budgets had a negative effect on the quality of audits and that such pressures were increasing."[67] These pressures (lawsuits and time) made a more scientific approach to auditing imperative.

Maurice S. Newman, retired partner of Deloitte Haskins & Sells, and a

---

*Mr. Stringer could be called the "father of modern auditing." In 1981, the Auditing Section of the American Accounting Association presented its first Distinguished Service in Auditing award to Mr. Stringer, citing the numerous auditing innovations introduced to the profession during his tenure with DH&S. These innovations include: (1) A statistical sampling plan that is particularly efficient and effective in low-error situations characteristic of auditing populations, (2) use of a regression-analysis package for analytical review that is integrated with the sampling plan for tests of details, and, (3) the first widely-applicable computer auditing software package.

pioneer with Kenneth W. Stringer in the application of statistics to accounting and auditing, writes of its development, "Within the broad area of finite sampling, two fields of major interest to accountants can be distinguished. One field, estimation sampling, is the subject of [my] book. The other field, audit sampling, is a more specialized form of finite sampling, dealing with rare occurrences and therefore of considerable importance to auditors and others engaged in the auditing function. Inasmuch as audit sampling has been developed to a high degree by Haskins & Sells, in particular by my partner, Kenneth W. Stringer, many people who know of this pioneering research might assume that [my] book deals with the subject of audit sampling. While the fields overlap to a slight degree . . . [my] book covers only the more general and classical field of estimation sampling."[68]

Without attempting to instruct the reader as to the specific application of statistics to auditing, suffice it to say that basically the auditor makes a basic decision as to how large an error he can tolerate (i.e., the materiality factor) and then applies mathematical formulas so as to select a representative sample from the data being examined (the "population"), for instance, a listing of the accounts receivable that must be confirmed through direct correspondence at least on a test basis. Based on the errors discovered in the sample, the auditor can extrapolate (again, based on mathematical formulas) the probability and amount of errors in the entire population along with a degree of certainty (reliability). As the amount of the tolerable error the auditor is willing to accept decreases or the degree of reliability increases, the sample size increases.

After the furor over the Watergate disclosures and the FCPA, many public accountants began reviewing their audit procedures and new terms such as *transaction flow auditing* or *cycle audits* sprang into use, and some firms and writers have publicized these as "new" concepts. It may well be that to some firms they are new, but Mr. Stringer and his associates were teaching "test of transactions" auditing in staff training sessions in the 1950s.

What did happen was that some public accounting firms had emphasized the analysis of the balance sheet and devoted little time to the income statement, assuming that if the beginning and ending balance sheets were reasonable, the income statement that "bridged" the two must be also. This was a reasonable assumption to some degree and its use for decades illustrates another interesting facet of auditing.

Because the great majority of frauds, thefts, embezzlements, and so on, are committed by employees *against* a responsible, reputable management, the auditor runs a relatively low risk of liability regardless of the competency or completeness of his audit. In short, most managerial accountants can maintain a satisafctory set of accounts and prepare fair and reasonable financial statements *without* outside help. Instead, the major problems encountered by auditors result from frauds *by* management (e.g., McKesson-Robbins, Equity Funding, etc.).

FCPA Created Need to Reconsider Control System

Nevertheless, with the passage of the FCPA, companies were forced to reconsider their internal control systems. As an attorney associate put it, the vagueness of the law (FCPA) and the state of the art in accounting and auditing meant that the application of the FCPA would be determined by case law (i.e., through litigation). This, in turn, meant that one of the cornerstones of the defense would be the documentation by management of the existence and adequacy of a system of internal control, including internal accounting control.

The report to the Congress on the impact of the FCPA by the comptroller general of the General Accounting Office (GAO) (March 1980) found that "over 60 percent of the respondents [to the GAO questionnaire] reported that they have increased the amount of control documentation to a moderate or a greater extent. . . . Further, almost 40 percent reported that as a result of the Act, they had increased routine testing of accounting or control systems to a moderate or a great extent. . . [O]ver 20 percent of the respondents said that to a moderate or a great extent, they have increased their internal audit staff's (1) responsibility, (2) size, (3) training, and (4) independence from management.* . . . More than 30 percent reported that they have increased the number of special reviews or investigations to a moderate or a great extent. . . . The role of the audit committee has also undergone change. . . . [S]ome committees have become involved in monitoring compliance with . . . codes of conduct . . [and] their interest in monitoring the effectiveness of internal accounting controls has increased." However, about 55% of the respondents "reported that their compliance efforts resulted in costs that exceeded the benefits."[69] The GAO report then concluded that Congress should repeal the criminal penalties associated with the act's accounting provisions and, instead, establish such penalties for "knowing and willful falsification of corporate books and records."†

As companies reacted to the legal implications of the FCPA, the public accountants stepped in with marketable programs for evaluating internal accounting control or guides to the establishment of a system of internal accounting controls. The result was that the cost of regulation increased

---

*Although it isn't stated, the respondents probably meant independence from *financial* management, i.e., those that the internal auditors audit.

†In 1981, Senator John H. Chaffee (R-R.I.) led a determined effort to moderate the FCPA, which died in committee. Then in 1983 similar legislation was reintroduced.

without a commensurate benefit. A survey done by the Financial Executives Institute in 1979 found that "five hundred thirty-four respondents with an aggregate sales volume of $880 billion and annual audit fees of $264 million estimated the FCPA costs to date [1978] at $31 million for an average cost of $58,000 per company . . . equivalent to 12% of the annual audit fees."[70]

A year later, Professor Michael W. Maher of the University of Michigan, and a member of the previously mentioned Mautz research team, performed a research study called *The Impact of Regulation on Controls: Firms' Response to the Foreign Corrupt Practices Act.* Professor Maher's conclusion was: "These hypotheses, that the regulation would not directly affect the level of internal accounting controls, but would affect the expenditure of resources for efforts to 'prove' compliance with the law, were generally supported by the empirical results."[71] Professor Maher also notes that "the law has reportedly led to an 'increased awareness' by top management and operating managers of the importance of internal control in many companies. This, in itself, could lead to improved control, according to the interviewees."[72]

This last point, if sustained over time, is probably the only benefit of the FCPA. And it is doubtful that the cost is worth that benefit. The reason is that the purpose of internal control systems is to limit frauds and thefts by employees against management and provide a discipline by which exuberant, overoptimistic managers can be controlled. Internal control systems were necessary before the FCPA and will be necessary should it be modified or repealed. It was not necessary, and was in fact wasteful, to add the threat of criminal action to the requirement for internal control. This legal "club" only stimulated a defensive reaction by reputable companies while the relative few who are not ignored (or evaded) the law. In short, it increased the cost of those who are not a problem while missing those who are.

GOVERNMENT PRESSURE EASED

In the early 1980s, the intense pressure on the public accountants eased as the Reagan administration deemphasized government regulation. In 1981, the new commissioner of the SEC John F. Shad addressed the annual meeting of the American Accounting Association and told the attendees, "With specific reference to the accounting profession, I believe the private sector can regulate itself much more effectively than the government can. . . . The Commissioner's role should remain one of oversight rather than regulation."[73]

However, this pause is only that, and will last until the next McKesson-Robbins or Equity-Funding-type scandal. The ever-present threat of government regulation combined with the hazard of legal liability and the desire for growth in a highly competitve, expanding "industry" (public accounting, consulting, and tax planning) have caused the major public accounting firms to seek safety in such courses of action as uniform, specific accounting rules that can be cited, the creation of more formal quasigoverning bodies such as the Auditing Standards Board and the Public Oversight Board with its peer review program, and the division of practice into two sections. As these actions are taken, the gap between big and little public accounting firms grows, paradoxically driving the latter to abandon costly audits based on rules-setting and peer review.

PUBLIC ACCOUNTANTS SHOULD BROADEN VIEW

What is needed instead is for public accounting to broaden its viewpoint from a narrow numbers-oriented, rules-constrained one to a more qualitative, analytical one. Narrative disclosure and analyses of the reasons for the different applications of an accounting method should be used instead of the arbitrary elimination of subjectivity and judgment involved in selecting among several methods (e.g., the requirement that imputed interest during construction *must* be capitalized).

The great advantage of (and need for) auditing, whether public or internal, is discipline; it tends to curb honest but exuberant managers, and it also forces the documentation of reasons for actions. As we will see in the next chapter, the heart of a good management program is the reliability of its system of internal communication and control. The discovery of fraud is incidental to this system of control, and auditors must constantly emphasize this point; that is, both internal and public auditors are giving assurance as to the overall reliability of the data, incidental errors or occasional frauds notwithstanding.

REFERENCES

1. Carey, *The Rise of the Accounting Profession*, vol. 1, p. 1 (facing chart).
2. *The Accounting Establishment*.
3. Burton, Palmer, and Kay, *Handbook of Accounting and Auditing*, chap. 39, p. 3.
4. Carey, *The Rise of the Accounting Profession*, vol. 1, p. 184.
5. Ibid., pp. 185–190.
6. Charles W. Schandl, *Theory of Auditing*, Scholars Book Co., Houston, Tex., 1978, p. 13.
7. Wanda A. Wallace, *The Economic Role of the Audit in Free and Regulated Markets*, Touche, Ross & Co. Aid to Education Program, 1980, p. 8.

8. Ibid., pp. 12–21.

9. Manuel F. Cohen, chairman, *The Commission on Auditors' Responsibilities: Report, Conclusions, and Recommendations,* AICPA, New York, 1978, pp. 11–12.

10. Ibid., p. 31, reference 2.

11. Ibid., p. 33, reference 7.

12. Ibid., pp. 33, 34.

13. Ibid., pp. 32, 33.

14. Philip L. Defliese, Kenneth P. Johnson, and Roderick K. Macleod, eds., *Montgomery's Auditing,* 9th ed., Ronald Press, New York, 1975, p. 13.

15. The analysis of this case was based principally on a review of two books: J. J. Staunton, *The Case of the Crude Drug Wizard: Mr. Musica of McKesson & Robbins,* AFM Exploratory Series no. 4, Dept. of Accounting and Financial Management, University of New England, Armidale NSW, Australia, 1977; and Carey, *The Rise of the Accounting Profession,* vol. 2.

16. John L. Carey, Editorial, *The Journal of Accountancy,* February 1939.

17. Testimony of Expert Witnesses at SEC Hearings, *The Journal of Accountancy,* April 1939.

18. Carey, *The Rise of the Accounting Profession,* vol. 2, p. 36.

19. Ibid., p. 36.

20. *Report of the Special Committee on Equity Funding,* AICPA, New York, 1975.

21. Kerry Cooper and Steven Flory, "Lessons from McKesson and Equity Funding," *The CPA Journal,* New York Society of CPA, New York, April 1976.

22. John L. Gillis, "Equity Funding—A Continuing Saga," *Financial Analysts Journal,* May/June 1981.

23. *Report of the Special Committee,* p. 7.

24. Ibid., p. 27.

25. *Impact of Foreign Corrupt Practices Act on U.S. Business,* Report to Congress by the Comptroller General of the United States, AFMD-81-34, March 4, 1981, p. 1.

26. *Standards for the Professional Practice of Internal Auditing,* The Institute of Internal Auditors, Altamonte Springs, Florida, 1980.

27. *Certified Internal Auditor,* The Institute of Internal Auditors, Inc., Altamonte Springs, Florida, 1980, p. 3.

28. *Standards for the Professional Practice of Internal Auditing,* pp. 300–301.

29. *Statement on Auditing Standards,* Codification of Auditing Standards and Procedures, Committee on Auditing Procedure, AICPA, New York, 1973, p. 150.02.

30. James Don Edwards, *History of Public Accounting in the United States,* Accounting History Classic Series, University of Alabama, 1978, pp. 141–145.

31. Ibid., p. 141.

32. Carey, *The Rise of the Accounting Profession,* vol. 1, p. 257.

33. Ibid., p. 257.

34. Defliese, Johnson, and Macleod, *Montgomery's Auditing,* p. 51.

35. J. Jay Hampson, "Accountants' Liability—The Significance of Hochfelder," *The Journal of Accountancy,* December 1976, p. 69.

36. Ibid., p. 69.

37. Supreme Court of the United States, Syllabus, *Ernst & Ernst v. Hochfelder et al.,* in *The Accounting Establishment,* pp. 1538–9.

38. "World Accounting Report," *The Financial Times*, London, January 1982; *New York Times*, November 5, 1981.

39. Kripke, *The SEC and Corporate Disclosure*, p. 271.

40. Ibid.

41. *The Accounting Establishment*, p. 1754.

42. U.S. Congress, House Commerce Committee's Subcommittee on Oversight and Investigation, *Federal Regulation and Regulatory Reform*, October 1976, chap. 2.

43. "The Establishment and Implementation of Accounting Standards," Statement by Abraham J. Briloff in testimony before the House Commerce Committee's Subcommittee on Oversight and Investigation, May 20, 1976.

44. *Federal Regulation and Regulatory Reform*, chap. 2, pp. 32–33.

45. *New York Times*, October 21, 1976.

46. *A Guide to the New Section 13 (b)(2), Accounting Requirements of the Securities Exchange Act of 1934*, The Committee on Corporate Law and Accounting, American Bar Association, Chicago, 1978.

47. *The Accounting Establishment*.

48. *The Accounting Establishment*, pp. 1–24.

49. Ibid.

50. *Report of the Special Committee on Solicitation*, AICPA, New York, 1981, p. 5.

51. *The Accounting Establishment*, pp. 20–24.

52. *The Week In Review*, May 27, 1977.

53. *The Week In Review*, April 1, 1977.

54. *The Journal of Accountancy*, July 1977, p. 4.

55. *Improving the Accountability of Publicly Owned Corporations and Their Auditors*, Report of the Senate Committee on Governmental Affairs, Subcommittee on Reports, Accounting and Management, GPO, November 1977.

56. *Annual Report 1980–81*, Public Oversight Board, AICPA, p. 19.

57. U.S. Congress, House, Congressional Record, June 16, 1978, 5744.

58. *SEC Report to Congress on the Accounting Profession and the Commission's Oversight Role*, GPO, July 1978, pp. 46–49.

59. *SEC Report on Questionable and Illegal Corporate Payments and Practices*, May 12, 1976, in *A Guide to the New Section 13(b)(2) Accounting Requirements*, p. 24.

60. Kripke, *The SEC and Corporate Disclosure*, pp. 19–20.

61. *A Guide to the New Section 13(b)(2) Accounting Requirements*.

62. Ibid., p. 38.

63. *The Auditor's Study and Evaluation of Internal Control*, Statement on Auditing Procedure No. 54 (Auditing Research Monograph 3), AICPA, New York, 1972, pp. 27–28.

64. Senator Charles H. Percy, "A Senator Speaks," *The Week In Review*, March 10, 1978.

65. Johnson and Jaenicke, *Evaluating Internal Control*, New York, 1980, p. 14.

66. R. K. Mautz, W. G. Kell, M. W. Maher, A. G. Merten, R. R. Reilly, D. G. Severance, and B. J. White, *Internal Control in U.S. Corporations: The State of the Art*, Financial Executives Research Foundation, New York, 1980, p. 7.

67. *The Commission on Auditors' Responsibilities: Report, Conclusions and Recommendations*, AICPA, New York, 1978, p. 117.

68. Maurice S. Newman, *Financial Accounting Estimates Through Statistical Sampling By Computer*, Wiley, New York, 1976, Preface, p. x.

69. *Impact of Foreign Corrupt Practices Act on U.S. Business,* Report to the Congress, U.S. GAO, March 1981, pp. 10–12.

70. *Bulletin,* Financial Executives Institute, New York, No. 285, September 20, 1979.

71. Michael W. Maher, "The Impact of Regulation on Controls: Firms' Response to the Foreign Corrupt Practices Act," 1980 Competitive Manuscript Award, *The Accounting Review,* American Accounting Association, October 1981, p. 751.

72. Ibid., p. 768.

73. John F. Shad, Speech at AAA meeting, August 1981, in *Journal of Accountancy,* October 1981, p. 50.

six

MANAGERIAL ACCOUNTING, INFLATION, AND CAPITAL FORMATION

CONTROL OF OPERATIONS IS STILL BASIC FUNCTION OF ACCOUNTING

As pointed out in earlier chapters, accounting developed from the owner/manager's basic need for a systematic, disciplined means of maintaining control of his current business and to assist in the formation of future plans. Accrual-basis accounting, as opposed to the pure cash-basis recording of events and transactions, evolved as business became more sophisticated and the need arose to match and control dollars being spent today with dollars to be received later. These needs still exist today.

Typical Planning Process

Let us review how accounting is used internally in a typical capital-intensive business and then analyze the effect inflation has on this process. (We will concentrate on a capital-intensive business because low-capital businesses are little affected by inflation insofar as their financial data are concerned since most of the transactions are in the same reporting period.)

We will also assume that the business has been in operation for some time because the decision whether or not to begin operations is far different from decisions concerning the continuation of operations. For example, in beginning a new operation, the promoters will (or should) have analyzed the potential market for the proposed product or service, evaluated the management/employee group, studied the capital needs, and finally, the expected rate of return. If the expected return is comparable with other possible investments, after giving consideration to the degree of risk, the promoters will be able to attract investors.

As mentioned in Chapter 4, however, once the investment is made, the investors are "locked in" to the extent that the business must now succeed so that dividends or appreciation in the investment (increase in stock price) can be realized. Otherwise, they will lose a portion or even all of their investment. Of course, it is possible that the enterprise may just stumble along, breaking even, in which case the investors will not be receiving a satisfactory return. This would prevent them from "cashing out," except at a loss large enough to make it possible for new investors to earn a reasonable return on their investment. As reviewed later in this chapter, this "locked-in" aspect of an investment is also a major factor in how a company copes with the impact of inflation.

But for now, let us assume that we are managing a company that has been successful up to now in manufacturing and selling a major consumer product. Furthermore, this product is affected by the energy supply, as well as the availability of financing. The planning involved in this type of company involves the evaluation of many factors and several disciplines.

Market Research

The first, and most important, is the continued marketability of the product. For in truth, in spite of all the myths about financial people's ability to "manage earnings," there is no substitute for sales for making a company profitable. Thus, we must start with a review of the market for the next one to five years. This review would involve such disciplines as marketing, psychology, politics, economics, engineering, demography, and finance.

Outside research firms may be employed. For example, the University of Michigan's index of consumer confidence is widely used as one measure of the attitude of the potential customer toward making the commitment involved in a "big ticket" purchase. This analysis of attitude illustrates the "self-fulfilling prophecy" syndrome. To a degree, if enough people perceive economic conditions as being unfavorable, and thus react accordingly (i.e., reduce spending, pay off debts, etc.), the effect in itself could produce a decline in the economy.

Demography

The demography of the society is another vital area of study. We must know the historical use of our product by age and income group and then must analyze and project the future composition of the population of our market. For example, since World War II, one of the most dramatic shifts in the working force of the United States has been the growth of two-income families, as the women joined the men in lifelong careers. This, coupled with medical discoveries in the area of birth control, changed the level of affluence as it reduced the average number of births per family. These factors, along with the knowledge that mankind now has the terrible power to end life as we know it on earth, has, in turn, changed the very life style, expectations and spending habits of the post–World War II generations.

Other Factors

Engineering, politics, and economics, as well as marketing, must all be considered in analyzing the type of product the customer will buy. The psychic as well as the more practical needs of the customer, coupled with the compromise involved in balancing "wants" with "needs" and the ability to pay, must all be studied. Outside forces involving such broad issues as the stability of the political conditions in the Middle East, for example, and its influence on world energy prices must be considered. The interplay of world trade, relative inflation among nations, and the stability of various foreign currencies and the effect all these factors have on interest rates are another essential area of study. Of course, the same evaluation must be made of the domestic fiscal and monetary policies of the government in relation to both domestic issues, such as inflation, social unrest, unemployment, defense spending, and foreign relations must also be included in any long-range planning.

Out of this complex analysis various sets of assumptions will emerge, and at least three plans will be developed—an optimistic view (the "up-side" potential), a pessimistic view (the "down-side" hazard), and, naturally, the "most probable" view.

Forecasting Hazards

The hazards of long-range forecasting should be obvious from a considera-tion of the volatile nature of many of the factors involved (e.g., the political instability of the critical Middle East). This volatility points up the most critical factor—the need for flexibility coupled with a continual evaluation and updating of the plan of action developed.

For example, consider the problems faced by the Chrysler Corporation in the late 1970s and early 1980s. In the late 1970s, faced with bankruptcy, the company obtained government support, restructured the entire company, and geared to produce a small, fuel-efficient vehicle on the broad, long-range assumption that gasoline costs would continue to rise toward $2.00 a gallon by the early 1980s. This view was widely recognized and supported by independent analysts. However, in the early 1980s a worldwide recession developed (for many other complex reasons) that, coupled with the startling success of energy conservation and the discovery of more oil following decontrol, resulted in what was termed "a glut of oil."

As supply rose and demand dropped, we learned, once again, the fundamental economic law of supply and demand, and the price of gasoline actually decreased in 1982. While most "experts" believe the excess of supply is only temporary, the existence of the excess forced Chrysler to once again change plans; keep a larger vehicle in their product line and to restructure their capital once again.

In spite of the repeated failure of the most thorough and capable analysts to predict the "most probable" future course of the world's economics, the myth persists that the managers of companies are able to plan and control their companies' destinies, when, in fact, the most successful are the most flexible and adaptable to changing conditions rather than the best forecasters.*

Options Reviewed

Nevertheless, after studying all the various factors, we, as managers of our hypothetical company, have developed the three plans mentioned earlier. Thus, we have an estimate of the products we will need to produce and a range of the volumes we expect to sell. We have attempted to keep our options open to the fullest extent possible as to how customer preferences might develop, so several variations of the product mix are in our overall plan.

We refine the broad market analysis for the elasticity of demand, that is, what volumes can be sold at various prices. We then must consider our estimated production costs in relation to the various volumes and the productivity of the facilities available. Out of this analysis will come some conclusions as to the need to build more modern, highly mechanized facilities or perhaps to renegotiate labor contracts, or the availability and feasibility of obtaining additional long-term capital either in the form of equity (stock), debt, or a combination of both.

In this phase of our review, we might even decide that the future market potential of our product is such that so much new capital will be required that it may be that a better course of action is to investigate other areas of investment. †

---

*For an excellent analysis of the hazards of long-range planning in a capital-intensive industry, see *The Wreck of the Auto Industry* by William Tucker, *Harpers*, November 1980.

†One of the boons of the computer age, which must be used judiciously, is the capability, through computers, to develop various planning models and alternatives not previously possible because of the sheer volume and complexity of the variables involved.

For example, the General Electric Company employs a well-publicized program for "Coping with Inflation." We will not go into this in depth here, but briefly, it involves evaluating all possible investment opportunities and putting the new capital into growth sectors of the economy while managing the mature, low-growth sectors of the business to slowly liquidate themselves over a long period of time—the latter process being termed the "harvest theory" of managing those sectors. Again, this may not be possible, even if desirable, because of the extent of the investment and the inability even to liquidate that investment without extensive losses greater than the cost of trying to keep going (e.g., the Chrysler condition).

Another interesting "twist" to the growth versus "harvest" theory of coping with inflation is the social implications associated with the choices of management by the public, the unions, the government, and the media. For example, Winston Williams reported in *The New York Times* ("Steel: To Diversify or Rebuild?," November 23, 1981) that the "domestic [steel] producers are modernizing many of their facilities, but apparently they have finally accepted with resignation their diminishing importance in the world steel industry . . . [and] have shown dissatisfaction with their long-term prospects . . . [and] have turned to other industries." The most notable change cited was U.S. Steel's $6.4 billion bid (eventually successful) for Marathon Oil Company. Mr. Williams noted, "These actions have upset supporters of 're-industrialization,' who thought that the breaks in the new tax bill would permit the steel sector to modernize and expand. . . . [N]ow many Congressmen, government officials and labor leaders who vigorously backed steelmakers' demands for help feel betrayed." Thus, the steel industry finds itself in the untenable position of having to choose between an investment choice to move out of a capital-intensive sector, in which inflation (caused by governmental policies) makes the possibility of earning a reasonable return for its stockholders almost impossible, and face national criticism (and perhaps punitive tax legislation or regulation), or stay in the steel sector and fail to meet the expectations of its stockholders.

Management Ability Critical Factor

Still another vital factor in the planning process, which I believe is the single most important one, is the sheer talent and ability of top management. The history of business is full of once successful companies which failed because of the unwise decisions management made even in the face of good advice. It is difficult to find the entrepreneur who has the vision to see the potential of a new product or service and at the same time not to overreach. The May 3, 1982 issue of *Fortune* includes an article on *How DeLorean Dashed His Dream,* which illustrates this very point.

And how many customers were out there waiting for the DeLorean experience? The company needed 10,000 (unit) sales per year to break even, and its marketing department said it could sell 12,000 at most, even if it drew customers away from Porsche, Mercedes, Cadillac, and every high-class make in between. Beguiled by a backlog of 7,000 orders at the dealerships, DeLorean aimed higher. Just as the Dunmurry plant was settling into a routine of meeting production schedules and quality standards, DeLorean cranked the plant up to 80 cars a day, doubling its production rate to roughly 20,000 cars a year.

The marketing department said, once again, that it didn't need that many cars; the financial department reported that the company couldn't sustain the increased overhead for long;* and the manufacturing people were worried about so many workers coming on line without sufficient training. But De-Lorean kept the plant going at high speed. "I guess we got carried away," he says now.[1]

Estimate of Future Costs

At this point let us explore in more depth the essential area in our evaluation most closely related to managerial accounting—the estimate of our future production cost. While, as we shall review later, costs are far from the principal factor in the setting of prices, the ability of a company to produce a product at a cost less than the price it finds to be marketable, will obviously determine whether or not a profit is earned.

Chapter 3 described how cost accounting evolved separately from the financial reporting concepts over which the AICPA, the FASB, and the SEC labor so assiduously. Professor H. Thomas Johnson has done extensive research in the history of management accounting and has concluded that "between 1903 and 1912 executives at E. I. du Pont de Nemours Powder Company developed what was probably the first management accounting system used for planning and control in a vertically integrated industrial firm."[2]

Professor Johnson goes on, "The basic criterion used by the Powder Company to evaluate these steps toward vertical integration was return on investment. Basically, an investment in outside supply sources was approved only if it was judged likely to earn at least 15 percent per annum. . . . The estimated return, or 'profit,' on such a manufacturing process was calculated by deducting the estimated unit cost of production from current market price."[3] This method, developed nearly 80 years ago, is still widely used today.

In evaluating our hypothetical company's product then, we must calculate the estimated future production costs. In doing this we should use estimates

---

*Presumably they assumed that only inventory, not sales, would result.

of the material prices and usage at the time of production, as well as the direct labor costs, wages and related benefits, such as health care and pensions, in effect at that time also.

These labor costs will be affected by the type of production methods used: For instance, will an older facility be used or a new, more highly mechanized facility? The material costs will be influenced by the engineering design: For instance, will the ratio of steel versus aluminum change? However, the most difficult cost to estimate are the indirect costs. Although certain of these costs are relatively fixed, such as depreciation, most will be variable depending upon production (e.g., the cost of heating and lighting). As noted in Chapter 3, the basic concept of the matching of costs and revenues originated with managerial accountants and industrial engineers in response to an obvious need to develop a system of evaluating the alternative investment opportunities available to management.

After we have developed our estimated production cost, we can compare them to the estimated sales price we believe the market will accept. If the return on our investment is satisfactory, or if *any* return is more desirable than an attempted liquidation, we can continue with the new product planning.

Specific Plans and Budgets Prepared

We can now begin to make specific, detailed plans. The market research group should develop the most probable volume of sales by year, and based on that, the manufacturing group can plan where the product will be made, order any new equipment needed, hire and train any new workers, and schedule delivery of the raw materials needed. The treasurer will arrange any necessary financing for the new equipment and the build-up of inventories.

The controller will develop a specific budget for the first full year of production, working from the marketing group's estimates of sales and the manufacturing group's estimate of facilities and people required. This budget will bear some resemblance to a conventional income statement inasmuch as sales, costs, expenses and a net profit (or loss) from operations can be derived. However, at the departmental level, it may well exclude the allocation of such corporate expenses as interest expense and management salaries. Moreover, the format will typically be more functional to enhance the control aspect of the budget. Thus, the categories would most likely include:

Sales	Overtime premiums
Volume	Payroll taxes and insurance
Mix	Heat, light, water, and power
Direct labor	Supplies
Indirect labor	Repairs and maintenance

Material used	Taxes and insurance
Scrap material	Over/Under-absorbed burden
Depreciation	Miscellaneous

The essential feature of such a budget is that any area of cost or expense that management considers sensitive could be set out so that a variance analysis against actual operations can be done.

The development of the specific annual operating budget is a time-consuming task. Done properly, it will take several months and involve all of the various functions concerned down to the basic operating unit, namely, the individual departments and foremen. This is essential since the success of the operation depends to a great extent on the attitude of everyone toward the budget, and their involvement in its preparation helps in obtaining their cooperation in its execution.

In addition to developing the detailed operating budget, we will need to develop a forecast of our working capital with particular regard to our liquidity position throughout the operating year. This forecast will not be done in nearly as much detail as the operating budget, being limited to the major divisions of our hypothetical business, specifically, those with full working capital elements: receivables, payables, and inventories. (Cash, in most cases, will be managed by the corporate treasurer.) This forecast will assist our treasurer in estimating his short-term loan needs.

A separate corporate forecast of capital expenditures and long-term debt and/or equity requirements will also be prepared by our financial staff. The capital budget will be prepared by the controller's staff working with the requests for facilities which, in turn, are based on the products in the approved forward plan. The treasurer's staff will then incorporate this capital budget into the working capital forecast and analyze the funding requirements.

Performance Monitored

Once developed and approved, the annual operating budget will be monitored virtually on a daily basis, at least at the plant department level. Key variances, such as labor efficiencies, scrap material, burden savings, and overtime premiums, will be reported daily at the plant level. Obviously any unfavorable variances will be investigated, explained, and corrected, if possible. Every plant will have assigned accountants who will work directly with the foremen and superintendents, analyzing and assisting in the resolution of production problems.

The consolidated plant reports, based on the actual data and performance, will be reported monthly to those in the headquarters of our hypothetical company. The various reports will be consolidated into a corporate report, and comparisons will be made with the monthly and year-to-date budget as originally prepared. Explanations based on actual sales volumes and product mix and actual manufacturing performance will be prepared, along with possible alternative courses of action (e.g., increasing capacity to handle increased volume by adding a second shift). All of this will be presented to top management for consideration and decisions.

Forecast Updated Regularly

At the time this budget-to-actual review is going on, our marketing people will be monitoring the actual success of our products in the market. I mentioned the need to maintain flexibility. This is reflected in another phase of the management process—the monthly update of the budget. To avoid confusion at the plant level, we will hold the original budget and term our monthly update a forecast.

This forecast will not be done in nearly as much detail as the budget; instead, it will be based on our revised sales estimates, which translate into new production schedules. We will update this forecast monthly for from six to eight months out, depending on the lead times needed to ensure an uninterrupted material and parts supply based on the revised volumes. Thus, each month our controller's staff will also be preparing a similar analysis of actual results to the revised forecast as well as the original budget.

PROLIFERATION OF STANDARDS IMPINGING ON MANAGERIAL ACCOUNTING

The preceding is *managerial accounting** and represents applied accounting as practiced by thousands of managers of companies throughout the world. Professor Montgomery expressed this quite well in his textbook *Managerial Accounting Information.* "Managerial accounting is primarily

---

*The National Association of Accountants, after remaining in the background for many years (see Chapter 3) initiated a program in 1981 directed toward a more definitive role in accounting for managerial accountants. The Management Accounting Practices Committee of the NAA issued the first of a new series of *Statements on Management Accounting* designed to develop guidelines on management accounting concepts, policies, and practices. In addition, the committee will, "express the official position of NAA on relevant accounting matters to other professional groups, government bodies, the financial community, and the general public." (Statement No. 1A, *Definition of Management Accounting,* NAA, New York, March 19, 1981.)

concerned with the various techniques and systems for planning and controlling a firm's activities, with providing the informational tools with which managers at various levels can manage the firm. Since a significant portion of management activity is devoted to anticipating, minimizing, and controlling costs, the logical starting point in the study of managerial accounting is the study of costs. Cost accounting refers to that portion of accounting concerned with the gathering, classifying, recording, summarizing, and reporting of cost information. . . . With the development of the more structured activities of managerial accounting, and with the increasing use of cost information in decision-making in all functional areas of business, the role of the cost accountant has expanded."[4] Professor Montgomery goes on to draw a sharp distinction between financial and managerial accounting: "Except for the cost accounting data supplied to financial accounting, GAAP (Generally Accepted Accounting Principles) does *not* apply to managerial accounting."[5]

This is an overstatement. It is possible for a company to maintain an internal management reporting system separate from the external reporting system (as it must for differences between income tax return requirements and GAAP), but it is not a practical approach.*

The impractical nature of such an approach is the cause of the growing dispute within the AICPA concerning the applicability of GAAP to smaller businesses. Smaller firms in the AICPA, calling the issue "big GAAP" versus "little GAAP," have been concerned with the burden of complying with the plethora of standards coming out of the FASB for several years. Serious consideration started in 1974 with a study by the Werner committee on whether any variances in the application of GAAP were appropriate. The committee's report (1976) found that the same measurement principles should be applied in the general-purpose financial statements of all entities, but required disclosures should be distinguished from those that merely provide additional or analytic data. The report was an advisory one only, and no action was taken by the FASB, the SEC, or the ASB (Auditing Standards Board).

Still dissatisfied, in 1978 the Special Committee on Small and Medium-sized Firms (the Derieux committee) was formed at the AICPA's annual meeting to study the question of "big versus little GAAP" again. This com-

---

*Interestingly enough, Professor William Beaver represents the opposite extreme as he redefines accounting as being virtually a branch of economics: "Accounting, broadly conceived as the measurement and communication of economic information relevant to decision makers, has undergone dramatic changes during the past decade." *Financial Reporting: An Accounting Revolution*, Prentice-Hall, Inc., Englewood Cliffs, N.J., 1981, p. xiii.

mittee urged the FASB to reconsider burdensome standards for small companies and also suggested that small, nonpublic companies be permitted to
use a strict income tax basis of accounting and still receive a clear,
unqualified opinion from their auditor. This time, discussion papers were
issued by both the AICPA and the FASB.

The National Association of Accountants has also received complaints
from small businesses: Excerpts of representative letters were published
in the May 1981 issue of *Management Accounting:* "One issue which concerns me is financial reporting rules that are oppressive. . . . We are
rapidly approaching the era of three sets of books for a company—one
for the IRS, one for finanical reporting, and one for really knowing what is
going on."[6]

The most significant action to date has been the report of the Technical
Issues Committee of the AICPA Private Companies Practice Section Division for CPA firms. This committee was appointed by the AICPA in 1981 to
"consider alternative means of dealing with accounting standards overload."[7] Their report, published in 1982, found that "the FASB and its
predecessors did not give adequate consideration to the needs of private
companies before issuing certain standards. . . . The remainder of this report
discusses the specific GAAP requirements that we believe either should not
apply to private companies or do not sufficiently benefit the users of private
companies' financial statements to justify their costs. . . . We do not believe,
however, that exempting private companies from accounting standards that
are not relevant or cost-effective for them is the same as establishing two sets
of GAAP."[8] (This position was reinforced in February 1983 by the *Report of
the Special Committee on Accounting Standards Overload* of the AICPA.)

Private Companies Seek Exemption

The report goes on to recommend that private companies be exempt from the
following standards, which they believe are either not relevant or
cost-effective:[9]

Deferred income taxes (APB Opinion No. 11)

(Capitalization of) leases (FASB Statement No. 13 and seven amendments
and six interpretations)

Capitalization of interest (FASB Statement No. 34)

Imputed interest (APB Opinion No. 21)

(Accrual of) compensated absences (FASB Statement No. 43)

Business combinations (APB Opinion No. 16)

Troubled debt restructurings (FASB Statement No. 15)

(Disclosure of) research & development costs (FASB Statement No. 2)

Discontinued operations (APB Opinion No. 20)

(Reporting) Tax benefit of tax loss carryforward (APB Opinion No. 11)

(Disclosure of method for) investment tax credit (APB Opinion Nos. 2 and 4)

As the reader will note, public companies too have the same complaints about the relevancy and cost-effectiveness of those same standards. It is significant that the first five represent notable departures from the cash/transaction orientation of accounting. The remainder deal with disclosure questions that the committee believed were not cost-effective.

Efficient Market Theory May Obviate Need for Detailed Reporting of Major Companies

A paradox in the movement underway to have private companies exempt from onerous standards is the growing recognition by the SEC and the FASB that the concept of stock market efficiency may be valid for the major companies listed with the SEC, which could lead to less reporting by such companies as well.

Professor Beaver, who has written of this concept a great deal, credits its origin "with respect to financial statements . . . in the practice of security analysts, [searching for] mispriced securities. . . . The [stock] market is efficient with respect to some specified information system, if and only if security prices act as if everyone observes the information system."[10]

The information system referred to is the regular flow of data about a company in the form of press releases, news stories, news conferences, analysts reports, stockholder forums, and financial reports and statements. If a company's stock is in the "efficient" class, then the stock market adjusts its price to its "intrinsic value" virtually daily. On this basis, the possibility of the financial statements containing anything not already conveyed to the market and discounted by it is remote.

Deloitte Haskins & Sells prepared a research study for the Financial Executives Research Foundation in 1982–83 on the feasibility of only requiring "efficient market" companies (defined as those eligible to utilize the SECs minimum registration rules) to publish summary annual reports in which such detail as footnotes to financial statements would be omitted. If this concept is accepted by the SEC and the FASB, we may have the paradox of the large and small companies being exempted from onerous reporting, leaving only some middle group of companies which must struggle with the reporting burden!

ACCOUNTING AND INFLATION

Returning to our hypothetical company: in our long-range planning, we did not use conventional financial statements or historical costs. We did use cost-estimating techniques that require the combination of industrial engineering skills and accounting in order to develop standard labor and material costs and burden absorption at various assumed levels of production. All of these costs were based on the expected costs at time of production, that is, adjusted for any inflationary trends.

In his book *Managing in Turbulent Times*, Peter F. Drucker sharply criticizes American businessmen [and indirectly the accounting field] for failing to give recognition to inflation's effects in the data they use for decision making: "But executives today . . . do not know the facts. What they think are facts are largely illusions and half-truths. The reality of their enterprise is hidden, distorted and deformed by inflation. . . . In the Western countries and in Japan, business after business these last ten years has announced 'record profits' year after year. In fact, very few businesses (if any) in these countries can have a profit at all. Making a profit is by definition impossible in an inflationary period, because inflation is the systematic destruction of wealth by government. . . . But the illusion of 'record profits' also leads to the wrong actions, the wrong decisions, the wrong analysis of the business. It leads to gross mismanagement. . . . All this is known to most executives. Yet few so far have even tried to correct the misinformation inflation creates."[11]

Management Aware of Problem of Inflation

While the "illusion of record profits" is still a political and psychological problem for some companies in the troubled 1980s, I suspect that Professor Drucker is exaggerating for emphasis. Most companies are well aware of the hazards of inflation and are taking what actions are open to them to combat its effect. The problem, however, is not so simple that all we have to do to make it disappear is index our historical cost data, or write our balance sheets up (or down) to some estimate of current value.

Professor Andrew M. McCosh of the Manchester Business School spoke on this topic at the plenary session on inflation at the 1981 annual meeting of the American Accounting Association. Commenting on the various solutions proposed by his American counterparts, he observed that we could experiment with such solutions while we had only a 10 to 12% annual inflation rate but that when it reached 25 to 30%, as it had in England, all of our analysis would only prove that no one should be in a capital-intensive industry with its long-term fixed capital investments under such conditions.

William M. Agee, former chairman of the Bendix Corporation, demonstrated that point in the 1981 operations of Bendix. After selling several profitable segments of Bendix and accumulating some $500 million in available cash, he invested it in the money market and earned 12 to 14% on the funds rather than buy other businesses which had been announced as the original intention. The result was a dramatic increase in Bendix's 1981 earnings over 1980 of 140%. Although the dividends were not increased nearly as much, the resulting increase in dividends satisfied stockholders. Mr. Agee wrote of this strategy in the April 25, 1982 Sunday *New York Times:* "Being 'cash-rich' is sometimes considered a negative for a business, somehow suggesting that management does not know how to put money to work. . . . In the future, most managers must have the skills to run a portfolio of assets whether they be cash, securities or investments in companies. . . . This strategy appears to be particularly timely right now, when most businesses have excess capacity and are nervous about their ability to earn a fair return on their existing businesses in the near term"[12]*

Inflation Is a Complex Problem

The complexity of the problem of inflation was indirectly illustrated by Professor David F. Hawkins in an article called *Thinking Real; Living with FASB 33.*[13] After discussing the challenge facing company managers, Professor Hawkins listed desirable company attributes, that is, those most suitable for coping with inflation. As we review them, keep in mind that every manager agrees with Professor Hawkins and wishes only that his company exhibited them all. Actually, about the only firms that do are professional services such as legal, public accounting, or medical firms.

Pricing flexibility: The ability to pass inflation on to others through price increases

High real margins: Firms with this advantage can absorb some of the inflation that cannot be passed on

New, technologically up-to-date equipment: Productivity in this case is higher than competitors, and profit margins should be higher

Low requirement for most rapidly inflating resources: Does not rely on labor or energy

Rapidly turning inventories: This frees capital and reduces carrying costs

Minimum dependence on inventories and low consumption of replaceable fixed assets: Only certain service industries

*Later in 1982, Mr. Agee achieved what might be the ultimate in the portfolio theory of management of a company as he entered into an acquisition battle for Martin Marietta Company which resulted in the liquidation of Bendix's stock at $75 to $85 per share, a figure considerably in excess of Bendix's book value.

Ability to avoid certain inflation risks: No need for long-term commitments or debt

Access to capital: If the firm has all the preceding, this will not be a problem

Competitors who cope well with inflation: Competitors too should not arbitrarily cut prices or create labor dissension

Low break-even point: Inflation tends to push break-even points up. The firm can at least continue to operate

Expanding market or share: An expansion of physical volume eases some of the pressure on prices

Higher productivity potential: Productivity gains offset some of inflation's effect

Low labor dependence: Automated facilities lessen pressure for cost-of-living allowances

Low exposure of monetary assets: A net monetary asset position is vulnerable to the loss of purchasing power

Ability and willingness to finance green-field projects: Dramatic market or product breakthroughs are thus possible

Unused borrowing capacity: Debt is a hedge against inflation and loss of purchasing power

Low future retirement benefits and pension obligations: These costs are quite sensitive to inflation

Current costs and revenues: No long-term assets with "old" (low) costs.

Ability to acquire: Buying technology is cheaper than R&D

Expenditures for future development currently tax deductible

Control over critical input resources and distribution system

Multinational conglomerates

Improved productivity

Competent managers

The point of the preceding is that business managers are aware of the problems enumerated by Drucker, Agee, and Hawkins. But few believe that the fault, or cure, is the basic accounting system.

Estimated Future Costs Included in Projections of Management

It was mentioned that, in our hypothetical company, we included the projected effect of inflation in future plans. However, all evaluation, modeling, and planning was done outside of the actual accounting system. Finance, economics, politics, engineering, marketing, and cost accounting were involved as well as management judgment. Once the long-term (five year) plan had been decided on, the short-term (one year) specific plan would be developed.

At this point, the accounting system is utilized. As the next year's budget is developed, it is based on the chart of accounts, so that the actual results can be compiled on a comparable basis. As discussed in Chapter 5, the system of internal accounting control now furnishes the discipline on which the results of the budget will be judged.

Little Distortion in Short Run

Since the annual budget included estimates of inflation's effect (e.g., labor and material increases as well as increased energy costs), the actual historical costs recorded through the year will permit a reasonable variance analysis. Put another way, for the short-term, there is little distortion due to inflation as long as the inflation rate is within a tolerable range, preferably in the lower single-digit range but certainly not at the rates experienced in many Latin American countries.

Inventories and Property Are Problems Areas

The only major areas where historical costs distort earnings over the longer term are inventories and property. The former can be corrected in a period of rising prices by the use of the Last-In First-Out method of costing sales. (This method does distort the balance sheet, but we will discuss this problem in Chapter 7.) Correcting cost of sales leaves depreciation of property as the only principal remaining area where costs are not appropriately matched with sales. Companies and governments have struggled with this problem for years and the Revenue Act of 1981, with its Accelerated Cost Recovery System, represented a major step toward resolving the inequities of income taxes based on unadjusted depreciation costs from earlier years. (This area too will be expanded upon in Chapter 7.)

Financial Statements Are Not Basis for Investment Internally

The point is that financial statements are not used internally as the basis for an investment decision, but the accounting system is an essential part of the ongoing control and appraisal of the investment decision. Professor McCosh, in a paper upon which his AAA speech was based, commented on this point:

> In his paper "The Two Cultures," C.P. Snow drew the world's attention to the problems of communication between the scientific and literary communities. . . . On a smaller scale, we have been led to wonder whether the same kind of

problem is present as between those in the accountancy and finance professions who are mainly concerned with annual reports and the financial markets, and those in the same professions whose concern is with keeping the industrial wheels in motion. The differences in attitude became very clear to us during the project. . . . Companies are very different from one another. Planning and control systems are very crucial elements of each firm, and the differences between the firms are reflected therein. Attempts to compare tend to lead to attempts to make comparable, which in turn tends to lead to standards of national or even multinational purview. . . . The debate about the usefulness of accounting standards for external reporting continues . . . but we are anxious that the steps being taken toward standardization for external reporting should not spill over into standardization of the planning and control systems from which some of the data for external reporting come. The dangers to the enterprise which may be caused by such distortions to the planning and control system are undefinable, but potentially serious . . . potentially more serious than the problems of external comparability.[14]

INFLATION NOT AN ACCOUNTING PROBLEM

It is essential that those who press for a change in the measurement base for accounting so that the "real income" can be reported to the stockholders understand that businessmen do not view inflation as an accounting problem. They understand the problem. They know that some of them can "cash out" and invest as Mr. Agee did; some can diversify into Professor Hawkins' "desirable" companies as General Electric has done; and some are "locked in" as is Chrysler. Furthermore, everyone would agree, I am sure, that cash is the ultimate goal. Except for philanthropic endeavors, no one invests in a business for any other reason than to receive back more cash than he put into the business, either through profits (dividends), interest, or appreciation in the market value of the investment. As Professor Hendriksen expresses it, "In the final analysis, cash flows into and out of a business enterprise are the most fundamental events upon which accounting measurements are based and upon which investors and creditors base their decisions. Cash attains its significance because it represents generalized purchasing power which can be transferred readily in an exchange economy to any individuals or organizations for their own specific needs in acquiring goods and services desired by them and available in the economy.

"Most accounting measurements are based upon past, present or expected flows of cash. Revenues are generally measured in terms of the net cash expected to be received from the sale of goods or services. Expenses are generally measured in terms of the cash paid or expected to be paid for goods and services used by the firm. Accruals represent the allocation to the current period of expected future receipts or disbursements for services. Deferrals represent the allocation to current and future periods of past receipts and disbursements for goods and services."[15]

Economists' View of Income

Why the argument over the measurement base then? For one thing, the advocates for a change from the historical cost base, both past and present, have concentrated on the data needed to make an investment decision in a given situation based on an economists' view of "income"* rather than on the data needed to judge the efforts of those involved in implementing the investment decision. As the American Accounting Association commented,

> Why did many of the prominent theorists advocate current costs or values? To a significant degree, they may have been influenced by the neoclassical economic theory of the firm, in which historical costs are ignored entirely. They may have observed the behavior of investors and other economic decision makers and concluded with a validated hypothesis that such decision makers seek current value, not historical cost, information. No findings from any formal hypothesis testing are reported; prior to the 1960s, it was not customary for accounting writers to conduct such research. Unlike the later group of normative writers who embraced a decision-usefulness approach, the early normative writers did not inquire deeply into the decisional framework of users. They posited the existence of specified users, and proceeded to argue that current values are a superior type of information to historical costs. . . . Only a relatively few universities awarded doctorates in business administration or commerce before the 1950s—and most of those appear to have required a strong dose of economic theory. Thus, many of the early doctorates awarded to accounting academics, to Hatfield and Paton, for example, were in economics. It should come as no surprise, therefore, that economic theory would influence to a considerable degree the deductive writings of those comparatively few academics who challenged doctrine with coherent accounting theories. Indeed, several of the most prominent writers, notably Canning and Alexander, were economists.[16]

Textbooks Emphasize Historical Cost

Thus, we have seen the paradox of accounting theorists, when writing of the conceptual nature of accounting, advocate some form of current cost or

---

*The noted American economist Irving Fisher was the first to attempt to rationalize accounting and economics. In 1906, he defined "income" as a flow of services through a period of time and capital as a "stock of wealth at an instant of time. . . ." (*The Nature of Capital and Income,* Reprints of Economic Classics, Augustus M. Kelley, Publisher, 1965, p. 52.)

value, while the accounting textbooks used to teach thousands of students over the past 50 years have held to the objective, transaction-oriented, historical cost model. Even William A. Paton, one of the most influential accounting theorists in the history of accounting, who still describes himself as a "value man,"* gained a great deal of his well-deserved reputation as an editor of the early editions of the very pragmatic "bible" of accountants— *Accountants' Handbook,* now in its sixth edition—and as coauthor, in 1940 with A. C. Littleton, of the definitive statement on the matching of costs and revenues—*An Introduction to Corporate Accounting Standards.*

As discussed earlier, the excesses of the 1920s—"watered stock," "hidden reserves," a blurring of the distinction between capital and income—changed the accounting field from a loose, subjective, poorly-oriented field toward the objective discipline of a historical-cost-based model with emphasis not on a balance sheet of "values" but tilted toward an income statement of matched costs and revenues. Thus, although the theorists continued to write of value-based accounting models, the profession, as practiced by the managerial accountants, generally ignored them, at least until 1973.

Inflation Not a Problem in United States Until 1973

Why were current-value advocates ignored for so long? Simply because, until 1973, inflation was not a problem in the United States; in fact, through the 1930s and 1950s (World War II being an obvious exception), the problem was one of sluggish growth. One of John F. Kennedy's major campaign issues in the 1960 election was a promise to "get this country moving again."

In the early 1960s, the economic policies of the Kennedy administration did just that, and for a five-year period, 1960 to 1965, economists thought they had mastered the art of "fine-tuning" our economy to achieve growth, high employment, and stable prices all at the same time. However, the expansion of the Vietnam War in 1965 without any corresponding tax increase brought the "fine tuning" to a halt. The inflation rate doubled (in retrospect, to a modest 6% in 1971), which led to price controls and the "freeing" of the U.S. dollar from gold in 1971. Then in 1973 OPEC brought the age of cheap, government-subsidized energy to an end, and inflation became a *real* problem in the United States.

---

*In the October 1980 *Accounting Review* of the AAA, Professor Paton comments on the 1940 monograph being reviewed by Yuji Ijiri: "Perhaps the main reason I am writing this statement is to make my personal stand clear. I have always been a *value* man. This is partly the result, no doubt, of my training in neo-classical economics, and several years of teaching in that area before wandering into accounting. My second article on accounting, published in 1918, is entitled "The Significance and Treatment of Appreciation in the Accounts."

Government Bears Basic Responsibility for Inflation

With regard to the role of government, it is important to keep in mind that accounting did not cause the problem of inflation, nor can it be cured by accountants changing their measurement base. In fact, many will argue that a change such as indexing would exacerbate the problem of inflation. Certainly the automatic indexing based on the Consumer Price Index of various government transfer payments, such as social security payments, has added to the task of bringing government spending under control. With regard to the basic responsibility for inflation, it is worthwhile to keep in mind the remarks of Dr. Arthur F. Burns before the U.S. Senate Committee on Banking, Housing and Urban Affairs, March 14, 1980:

> A nation that still remembers the Great Depression and the remarkable demonstration during World War II of our nation's capacity to produce both "guns and butter" naturally places a high value on continuing good times. It is not unreasonable for people to want the government to promote full employment. It is not unreasonable for an urbanized industrial society to expect some protection against the hazards of old age, unemployment, poor health and bad housing. It is not unreasonable for a compassionate people to expect the government to be responsive to the needs of the poor. It is not unreasonable for citizens to be concerned about the degradation of the environment and the hazards to health and safety of both workers and consumers. And it is not unreasonable in a democracy for particular groups to seek to advance their own economic interests by political means.
>
> However, these wide-ranging and insistent political demands and the *government's response* to them *are basically responsible* for the *present virulent inflation* [emphasis added]. Our government has promoted inflation in three ways: by persistently biasing economic policies towards stimulus; by continually interfering with the forces of market competition in order to benefit special groups; and by pursuing objectives for the environment and for the health and safety of our citizens in needlessly expensive ways.

It remains to be seen if the programs of the Reagan administration can resolve the problems of inflation *and* employment. In fact, the early success of the anti-inflation aspect of the programs (due in no small part to the temporary oversupply of world oil) has created another inconsistency in the question of accounting and inflation—disinflation! As the inflation rate in the United States actually dropped to a negative rate early in 1982, analysts were quick to point out that disinflation will require greater emphasis on tighter controls and better uses of resources to counter the effect of lower price increases in the face of costs that do not necessarily decrease at the same rate.*

Federal Income Taxes and Inflation

Of course, just as it is not correct to say that management has been oblivious to the need to cope with inflation, neither is it correct to imply that managerial accountants have completely ignored inflation's impact on accounting. Since the basic goal of business is to generate favorable cash flows, business has generally taken advantage of every opportunity offered by the government that afforded some relief from the impact of inflation.

Over the years, government has provided some means of relief through the income tax laws, the most notable policy being the use of the Last-in, First-out (LIFO) method of relieving inventories and costing sales, initiated in 1939. Other major income tax provisions initiated by Congress are the use of accelerated rates (as opposed to the then customary straight-line rate) for the depreciation of property (first passed in 1954[†] and liberalized over the years to the present Accelerated Cost Recovery System in the 1981 Revenue Act) and the investment tax credit (1962 and 1971).

Double Advantage of Depreciation for Tax Purposes

Of course the effect of these tax laws was to increase the deduction allowed for cost of sales (LIFO), depreciation, or direct tax reductions for expenditures (investment tax credit), all of which reduced the income tax payable to the government and thus favorably affected cash flows. In the depreciation option, management was able to "have their cake and eat it" since Congress did not require that the depreciation methods used for tax return purposes conform to the methods used for the books of account and audited published financial statements. Thus, depreciation for book purposes could be based on a true useful life of say 15 years for machinery or 40 years for a building on a straight-line basis, while the tax return method could be based on much shorter lives (now 5 years for machinery and 10 to 15 years for buildings). In addition, a double-declining balance rate could be used that greatly acceler-

---

*See "Inflation's Withdrawal Pains" by Karen W. Arenson, *The New York Times,* April 20, 1982. Also, "Disinflation—It's Not All Fun" by A. Gary Shilling, *Fortune,* May 3, 1982.

[†]During both World Wars and the Korean War, the government temporarily permitted greatly accelerated write-off of facilities, generally allowing a five year write-off of, for example, buildings constructed for the war effort. However, these write-offs were more of a special war condition in recognition of probable obsolescence rather than an attempt to offset the effect of inflation.

ated the tax deduction (and thus increased cash flows through lower income taxes) in the early years of the asset. Of course, the tax depreciation deduction would be used up much faster than the book depreciation and thus in the later years of the asset, the early cash savings in income taxes would be "paid back" to the government.

Why would managerial accountants want to use two different methods of depreciation? Because they are continually balancing the pressure of the stockholders and over-exuberant managers to maintain a good earnings pattern with the very real cash savings possible through lower income taxes in a company with major capital expenditures, particularly when those expenditures are growing.

LIFO Inventory Method Less Advantageous

This advantage of higher book earnings and lower income tax payments is not available to business under the LIFO (Last-in, First-out) tax regulations. Although typically the income tax laws do not follow GAAP, being oriented more toward settled transactions, the LIFO provision is a notable exception.

The LIFO concept evolved over a long period of time, beginning with what was termed the "base stock method"* before finally reaching full acceptance by the Treasury Department in 1961. The development of the matching of costs and revenues as the means of determining net income has been discussed earlier. However, many companies recognized the disadvantage, from an income tax standpoint in an inflationary environment, of using the strict physical flow of goods assumption for this matching process, particularly if the inventories were of a nature that turned over (sold) slowly.

During an inflationary period, inventories will generally cost more than when the goods were acquired or produced. However, under physical flow assumptions, goods produced the earliest in the production process are assumed to be sold first. Since these goods generally cost less than goods produced most recently, lower-priced goods are matched against higher revenues and additional income flows to the bottom line. (These are the so-called "inflation or inventory profits.") In order to minimize the inflated profits and also provide more meaningful income statements, reverse flow assumptions for inventory costing were developed.

As noted, LIFO was developed from earlier reverse flow assumptions such

---

*The base stock method used a minimum fixed level of inventory that was considered necessary to carry out a particular business. This base stock quantity was carried over from year to year at the original cost. In a manner of speaking, then, this base stock was considered a fixed asset. Only variations above the base quantity would be valued at current prices prevailing at acquisition or production of the goods.

as the base stock method. Use of LIFO reverses the normal assumed flow of goods, so that *last* goods purchased or the last production costs incurred are considered to be the first goods (or costs) sold.

Initially, the base stock method began to gather acceptance in the United States early in this century by several taxpayers because of its favorable impact on the business's tax liability. In 1930 a long dispute over this method reached the U.S. Supreme Court. In *Lucas vs. Kansas City Structural Steel Co.* the Court ruled in favor of the IRS and prohibited taxpayers from using base stock for tax purposes, effectively killing the base stock method. Congress would not yield to taxpayers since the Treasury argued that accounting theorists did not unanimously support the base stock concept.

Industry, however, differed with Congress. In August 1934 the Committee on Uniform Methods of Oil Accounting of the American Petroleum Institute (API) unanimously approved use of LIFO for financial reporting by petroleum producers. In May 1936, the Special Committee on Inventories of the American Institute of Accountants (now the AICPA) concluded that the API method of valuing inventories constituted an acceptable method in the petroleum industry. The committee, however, cautioned that it should be applied consistently and that full disclosure be made. It also pointed out that companies using LIFO would produce financial statements that were not comparable to those of companies using other inventory methods.

In 1938, pressure was put on Congress to approve the use of the base stock method in the tax act for that year. Although the original bill did not approve its use, the Senate adopted a floor amendment that would have approved use of the LIFO method.

Senator Lonergan argued in favor of the amendment stating that in certain industries (nonferrous metal melting and fabricating, and hide and leather tanning), the LIFO method is recognized by leading accounting authorities as most accurately reflecting income. He cited that it was used in reports to stockholders, the New York Stock Exchange and the SEC. The amendment he proposed would permit the use of LIFO for tax purposes, but it would be limited to industries that usually keep their books on a LIFO basis because that method is recognized as conforming to the best accounting practice. The use of LIFO was later restricted to use in only the nonferrous metals, brass, copper, and tanning industries.

Those industries that were not allowed to use LIFO began to pressure Congress in 1939. Congress acceded to these demands in the Revenue Act of 1939, which extended LIFO to all taxpayers regardless of the business in which they engaged. The Treasury, though, issued regulations for the implementation of LIFO that effectively made use of LIFO available only to taxpayers with a few basic tangible commodities that could be measured in terms of common units, such as tons, yards, barrels, and so on. This method, which became known as the "specified goods" LIFO method, could not be effectively used by taxpayers engaged in complex manufacturing operations.

For those businesses with many heterogeneous inventories, an effort was made to find a suitable LIFO valuation method. A method called dollar-value for retail inventories was suggested by H. T. McAnly, a partner of Ernst & Ernst, in 1941. This method involved conversion of items in a taxpayer's inventory to dollar of cost. Prices indices were used to deflate costs in inventory from different years to standard base dollars. By using dollars instead of items in inventory, it made no difference as to the inventory's degree of homogeneity.

After several court cases, notably the Hutzler Brothers case in 1947, the Treasury amended the LIFO rules in 1949 to allow all taxpayers to use this method of costing. However, no special rules were provided to deal with methods of pooling or classifying goods that should be employed by manufacturers. Consequently, there was a hesitancy on the part of manufacturers to use LIFO if their raw and finished goods would have required use of numerous pools. Those that did use LIFO generally used the dollar-value method with a different pool for each different raw material or product.

The service's intransigence on the pooling issue led it to litigate a pooling case involving a manufacturer. In *Kleine Chocolate Co.,* a manufacturer of chocolates adopted the dollar-value LIFO method in 1942. The taxpayer employed a single dollar-value LIFO pool for numerous raw materials, in-process, and finished goods inventories. The commissioner contended that a matching of specific goods was required and that a minimum of 10 pools must be maintained by the taxpayer. After clearing up initial confusion regarding whether the taxpayer had used the single-pool method consistently, the Tax Court ruled that the taxpayer could continue using its single dollar-value pool.

Finally, in January 1961, the Treasury promulgated final regulations under the dollar-value LIFO method that permitted manufacturers to use liberal pooling rules in grouping their raw materials, work-in-process, and finished goods inventories by natural business units. These rules are still in effect today, virtually unchanged.

However, as a result of the many disputes and legal cases, a company must use LIFO in the books of account for published financial statements if it wishes to gain the tax savings possible through the lower income the use of LIFO causes in a period of rising prices. This, of course, means that book income will also be lower than it would be under the First-in, First-out (FIFO) method of costing sales since the effect of increased inventory costs are costed out at once under the LIFO method.

The result is that the LIFO method, while used by about two-thirds of the companies in the United States, is not as widespread as the accelerated methods of depreciation used for income tax filing purposes by virtually everyone. Not all managers are willing to reduce their book income under LIFO just to obtain the tax savings. Of course, it should be noted that in high-technology companies, the effect of rapid technological improvements means that the "first costs" may be higher than the "last costs"; hence, the FIFO method may actually result in a lower taxable income (and cash savings) than LIFO.

Another point to keep in mind in considering the effect of inflation on accounting and the LIFO method is that in a period of declining volume and/or disinflation, the LIFO method will result in older costs being matched with current revenues and thus income will tend to be overstated (and some of the tax cash savings will be repaid to the government).

These situations where tax and book accounting policies are juxtaposed demonstrate the managerial accountants' and business managers' basic orientation toward cash flows as well as capital formation through the debt and equity markets. These goals have their roots in the pragmatic, transaction-oriented history of accounting rather than the abstract theories of income and profits still debated by economists today.*

Capital Maintenance Concept

After the excesses and fiascos of the 1920s, the accounting profession drew a clear distinction between capital and income (termed surplus in those days) and came down strongly for the hard, verifiable data of historical costs and the measurement of income by the matching of costs and revenues† Of course, today the FASB is reevaluating this strong income statement orientation in its conceptual framework project. This project, which we will discuss

---

*For example, Professor Paul A. Samuelson writes, "In addition to wages, interest, and rent, economists often talk about a fourth category of income: profit. Wages are the return to labor; interest is the return to capital; rent is the return to land. What is profit the return to? The answer that economists give is a complex one. This chapter will show that the word 'profits' has many different meanings in everyday usage. From these different possible meanings, the economist, after careful analysis, ends up relating the concept of profit to dynamic innovation and uncertainty-bearing, and to the problems of monopoly, incentives and exploitation." (Paul A. Samuelson with Peter Temin, *Economics,* tenth ed., McGraw-Hill Book Company, New York, 1976, p. 620.)

†See *A Tentative Statement of Accounting Principles* by the Executive Committee of the American Accounting Association (*The Accounting Review,* June 1936). This brief statement became the basis for the more complete monography by W. A. Paton and A. C. Littleton, published in 1940.

in more depth in Chapter 7, includes the possibility of the determination of income under a capital maintenance concept long proposed by economists.

This approach has been widely discussed but is best illustrated by an anecdote told by a FASB staff member at the University of Delaware symposium in April 1980 on inflation, in which I was also a participant. The almost legendary story attributed to W. A. Paton from his classroom lectures on the determination of income was recited:

"If I bought a dozen oranges for ten cents each, resold them for fifteen cents each, and then went back for more oranges only to find that their cost to me had risen to fifteen cents, what was my profit?"

Under the FIFO historical cost method of costing sales, my profit is sixty cents; under the LIFO historical cost method and the capital maintenance concept, my profit is zero. However, what is my profit if I decide against buying the second dozen oranges and put my $1.80 into a money market fund? If we exclude the income tax (and LIFO) considerations from the problem, then we can see that our profit was sixty cents, at which point we faced an investment decision, whether to buy more oranges or put the funds in the money market. At the very least, the story illustrates that the answer is not as simple as it might first appear.

Accounting and Economics

Professor R. J. Chambers expressed the frustration of the theorists quite well in his review in 1979 of John B. Canning's *The Economics of Accounting* after 50 years.[17] Citing the failure of the accounting profession to utilize Canning's pertinent criticism (made in 1929) as points of departure for what he believed should have been rigorous attempts to reconcile accounting and economics, Chambers writes, "Yet, 50 years later, the same criticisms may be made, notwithstanding the intervening experience of scores of reported cases of grossly misleading financial statements, and notwithstanding the expenditure of millions on the search for better standards and a better theory.

"That search has been befogged by confusion of the different but complementary roles of past information, present facts, and future prospects in the decision-making process. The linkage between accounting and economics cannot be properly established unless those roles are specified. Past values or prices and presently observed values or prices are necessary for the determination of past results and present position; presently observed values or prices and calculated net present values of future alternatives are necessary for the exploration of the feasibility and desirability of future alternatives. None of the three kinds of 'values' is a substitute for the other. Had the distinct functions of all three been identified by Canning (in 1929), as a prelude to 'the economics of accountancy,' there may have been, by now, a more disciplined attack on that part of accounting which concerns itself with statements of past results and present position from time to time."

A harsh criticism of accounting indeed, but, the law of supply and demand applies to accounting practice and theory too, and thus, in spite of over 50 years of value-based theories being in supply, the demand has been for the pragmatic, objective, historical cost-based system used during that period. Why?

VALUE-BASED THEORIES REJECTED

Basically, I believe that the rejection of current value theories by managerial accountants is due to two factors: first, its subjective, non-cash orientation, and second, the questionable value of inflation-adjusted data.

The first factor is probably the major reason public accountants have also shied away from advocating value-based or inflation-adjusted accounting—auditing objective, transaction-based data is a difficult enough job without adding the extra burden of evaluating the qualitative assessment of the value of assets by management. The creation of "paper profits or losses" through the subjective determination of the sales or liquidation value of a company's net assets at different points in time, unrelated to realized cash, would leave management with "profits" without perhaps the cash to pay dividends or to reinvest.

That is not to say that the determination of liquidation values is not pertinent at any time. Certainly, a creditor must make a similar evaluation in order to be assured of the collateral involved in a proposed loan. In addition, a similar evaluation would be essential when a company is considering purchasing another company (e.g., Dupont's acquisition of Conoco). Here again the purchaser would want to be assured of the reasonableness of the price of the assets being acquired in order to avoid paying so much that a satisfactory yield, commensurate with the risk, cannot be realized. However, neither of these conditions is compatible with the going-concern concept implicit in basic accounting theory. These types of evaluations do illustrate the need to understand the goal of the user of the data so that the appropriate analysis can be prepared.

We will explore this last point in more depth in Chapter 7, but for now let me observe that this is a fundamental point of dispute between the theorists and managerial accountants. The latter view the goal of financial statements to be basically attestory in nature. They are a permanent historical record of transactions that form the objective base against which the expectations of both management and investors and creditors are measured.

Financial Statements a By-Product

Furthermore, and perhaps more significantly, the managerial accountant views the published financial statements to be only a by-product of his primary responsibility—which as we explained earlier is the daily, weekly, and monthly accumulation, analysis, and reporting of the results of operations so that management can measure the effectiveness of its current programs and make changes if necessary (and possible).

Earlier in this chapter, from the report on *Sunset Review of Accounting Principles,* eleven standards of GAAP were cited from which the committee believed private companies should be excluded. It should come as no surprise that most companies, large, medium, or small, would agree with the committee's conclusion. Many of the standards and rules issued by the FASB (and the APB) and the SEC are implemented only at the final consolidated level, that is, they are not integrated into the divisional accounting and reporting systems simply because they are not pertinent to the maintenance of budgetary control nor to the success of the investment programs. Instead, they are viewed as legal reporting requirements established to make companies more comparable for external review.

Thus, for example, the top management committee of a large company may not even see nor even need to see a monthly balance sheet or even a formal income statement. Instead they will review monthly comparisons of the budgeted sales, costs, and expenses by function (i.e., volume, product mix, direct labor, indirect labor, material, scrap, utilities, etc.) with the actual results for the current month. In addition, they may see forecasts (revised budgets) for the coming few months or year and projections of liquidity, based on anticipated future capital expenditures and sales and related receivables, inventory, and payable levels.

This type of analysis points up again the need to distinguish between the uses of financial data by the decision makers (management) and the judges of the results of those decisions (investors and creditors).

What Benefits Would a Value-Based System Provide?

Let us turn now to the second reason given for the rejection of value-based theories by practicing accountants—What benefits would be gained in exchange for the sacrifice of the discipline of a historical-cost based accounting system?

The major problems that a manager faces that are exacerbated by inflation are:

Selling a product in a competitive market

Dealing with labor and suppliers who themselves are struggling with inflation

Replacing or expanding productive capacity with more efficient plants and facilities

Satisfying stockholders through the payment of dividends and/or appreciation in the value of the common stock

Maintaining appropriate debt-to-equity ratios and adequate liquidity to obtain the best credit rating (and lowest interest cost)

Struggling with a national income tax policy that only gives partial recognition to inflation

A review of each of those areas reveals that inflation-adjusted data* are not as much help as might appear at first glance.

Selling a Product in a Competitive Market

On the surface, this appears to be an obvious area where some type of inflation-adjusted data would be of great benefit. After all, depreciation is a significant portion of the cost in a manufacturing firm and the price of a product must cover all costs with a little to spare if a firm is to stay in business. Thus, if inflation is forcing up the replacement price of the asset (machinery and equipment or buildings), then the selling price of the product should be such so as to recover the eventual replacement price of the asset less any technological improvements that improve productivity. And there is a great deal of truth to this. As Gordon Shillinglaw points out,

> Cost figures can enter into product pricing decisions in two ways: (1) in conjunction with price/volume estimates, to identify the most profitable sales volume; and (2) in conjunction with estimates of desired profit margins, to identify normal or target prices.

---

*It should be noted that the restatement of historical cost in terms of a general purchasing power (GPP) index, also called a "constant dollar" adjustment, is not a change in the measurement base as some form of current value adjustment (exit value, replacement value, etc.) would be. In the words of the FASB, "Some persons contend that the expression of financial information in units of general purchasing power is a departure from the historical-cost basis of accounting. The Board does not believe that to be a valid contention. . . . Restatement represents only a change in the unit in which accounts are stated and *not* in any accounting principle by which information is prepared." (Exposure Draft of December 1974 pp. iv, 7.) Nevertheless, most preparers and users of accounting data group GPP with current value since the amounts do change from the traditional data. Thus I have referred to inflation-adjusted data so as to include all such adjustments.

Price/Volume Pricing. *If satisfactory estimates of the price sensitivity* of a product's sales can be obtained, a profit-maximizing price can be selected . . . [emphasis added].

Cost Formula Pricing. Difficulties in estimating the price/volume relationship limit the direct application of profit/volume pricing. Another limiting factor in many cases is the dependence of sales in one period on price in previous periods. Price may be kept deliberately below the short-term optimum so as to achieve a greater penetration of the market and impede the entry and growth of competitors during the early stages of the product's life cycle. In either of these circumstances, company price setters often rely heavily on cost-plus pricing formulas. The justification for the widespread use of such formulas is that they help the decision maker to predict either the competitor's costs or a competitive price. . . . This kind of thinking is particularly valid in oligopolistic industries. Recognizing that price competition is likely to be self-defeating, the prices may set a price that is expected not to attract competitors unduly and then focus competitive efforts on other factors such as delivery, credit terms, and so forth. . . .

The amount of fixed cost (e.g., depreciation) included in product cost will depend on the operating volume over which the fixed costs are to be spread. . . . A good starting point is "designated capacity." For factory costs this is the average operating level assumed by the designers when they were deciding how big a plant to build.[18]

While it is extremely important for a company to have an excellent cost accounting system, the rules of economics, not accounting, will ultimately more likely govern the pricing of a product or a service. (Note the references to price sensitivity and oligopolies by Shillinglaw in the excerpt just quoted.) Thus in a market economy, as Paul Samuelson states it, a basic rule of pricing is, "The equilibrium price, i.e., the only price that can last, is that at which the amount *willingly* supplied and amount *willingly* demanded are equal. Competitive equilibrium must be at the intersection point of supply and demand curves. . . . Our curves of supply and demand strictly apply only to a *perfectly competitive* market where some kind of *standardized* commodity such as wheat is being auctioned by an organized exchange that registers transactions of *numerous* buyers and sellers."[19]

Imperfections in the market structure can and usually do distort this basic economic rule, which nevertheless is still the driving force behind the optimum price. As a result, the cost of a product is significant, not because it forms the basis for the price, but rather because its relationship to price will determine whether or not the product can be sold at a profit. Thus, while a business should try to recover the replacement value of its facilities over their useful life, a change in the depreciation base from historical cost to replacement cost, an indexed-adjusted cost, or some other value-adjusted base, will not necessarily change the selling price of the product, just the determination of the profit.

The complexity of the pricing decision was illustrated in a research study done by the National Association of Accountants and The Society of Management Accountants of Canada, "The study results indicated that both costs and market conditions were important ingredients to the determination of specific prices for product lines. . . . Although the firms seemed to use both costs and competitive prices . . . differences did emerge. . . . The larger firms in the study indicated a stronger preference than their smaller counterparts for the use of competitive or market conditions in setting prices. . . . Companies that vigorously competed on the basis of product quality tended to rely more heavily on costs. . . ."[20]

Dealing with Labor and Suppliers Who Themselves Are Struggling with Inflation

The problem of inflation-adjusted data and their effectiveness in this area seems self-evident. Both labor and suppliers are facing the same problem of "cost recovery" in order to at least hold even, as the company that employs them or buys from them faces. Neither group is inclined to be sympathetic to the problems of others, particularly if such concern causes considerable sacrifice on their part. Experience has shown that a company must be losing money or at best only breaking even, even on a historical-cost based system, before any relief is gained.

The drastic state that must be reached before recognition of the problem of inflation and cost control is given by labor was demonstrated in the first quarter of 1982. Of the 66 major contract settlements in that period, 61 included wage gains in spite of the depressed state of the economy at that time. However, the three largest contracts settled then stabilized wages where they were. Outright wage cuts were incorporated in the two other contracts. As expected, those three major contracts were in industries where labor force reductions had been the largest (the UAW agreements with Ford and GM) and the Teamsters' new National Master Freight Agreement.[21]

Replacing or Expanding Productive Capacity with More Efficient Plants and Facilities

As we discussed earlier in this chapter, in the analysis of our hypothetical company, the evaluation presently being done of projected capital expenditures takes into account future prices, future costs, markets, and projected returns. There would be no benefit then, after the basic decisions have been made, the funds expended, and production started, to continually revalue or adjust the original expenditures unless it were possible to "pass through" such estimated costs to customers in the form of price increases or the government were to base tax-allowable depreciation on such adjusted costs.

Satisfying Stockholders Through the Payment of Dividends and/or Appreciation in the Value of Common Stock

This is probably the most difficult problem with inflation that management faces. The stockholders invested their money with the intent to protect their savings from the loss of purchasing power caused by inflation and to build a base of wealth. Thus, they want a return higher than the inflation rate.

Except for the higher-growth companies, particularly low capital-intensive ones, where the appreciation of the stock can meet this desire, it is impossible to raise the dividend faster than the rate of inflation and still maintain the productivity of the facilities as well as a high credit rating (which determines the borrowing cost of money). The dividend is always the first expenditure to be frozen or cut when a company faces the necessity of balancing those factors. And no amount of adjusting the historical dollars for inflation will allay the ire of the stockholder.

As we will see later in this chapter, when we consider the short- versus long-term goals of management and capital formation, the American tradition of equity financing rather than debt capital, and thus the pressure for a dividend, versus the Japanese emphasis on low interest rate debt over equity as a source of capital, may be one of the key factors in the success of the Japanese in long-term capital formation.

Maintaining Appropriate Debt-to-Equity Ratios and Adequate Liquidity to Obtain the Best Credit Rating (and Lowest Interest Cost)

As discussed in Chapter 3, the income statement gained preeminence over the balance sheet in financial reporting in the late thirties. However, inflation developed into a serious problem in the United States in the 1970s. With it we saw such problems as the "liquidity crunch" of 1974 and the decline in the productivity of an aging American industry, which, although reporting record profits, was reluctant or unable to replace plants and equipment. As a result, the economists' view of capital maintenance and a new focus on the balance sheet and cash flows developed. As we shall discuss, in the final chapter, this view is the heart of the FASB's conceptual framework project.

Today, the treasurer's staffs of all companies work continually on the bond and note ratings assigned to their companies by such services as

Moody's or Standard & Poor's. Such ratings are critical to a company since they will directly affect not only the interest rate charged for a new offering but may well even be the final factor in whether or not an offering is attempted at all.

The analysis done by the rating agencies is quite comprehensive, encompassing all the factors discussed earlier in this chapter with regard to our hypothetical company's evaluation of future investments. However, the rating agencies will concentrate on three major areas—short-term liquidity, long-term debt and equity capital, and long-term cash flow prospects from earnings.

Interestingly enough, the adjustment of such data for inflation is of no direct significance. The last factor, long-term cash flow, of course, will be greatly influenced by the pricing considerations mentioned earlier as well as the future markets for the company's products. The other factors cited by Professor Hawkins will also obviously influence future earnings and cash flows. Nevertheless, the analysis of liquidity deals more with monetary items, such as cash, securities, receivables, and accounts payable, which are of such a short-term nature that the inflation effect is ignored. Inventories are considered in relation to the utilization of LIFO. Of course, debt is monetary and in inflationary times is a hedge and thus is not adjusted for inflation.

This leaves for consideration the long-term assets, the land, buildings, machinery and equipment, purchased to produce income for a long period of time. Implicit in the generation of income is the ability to produce enough profits not only to pay a reasonable return to the investors but to maintain the productivity of the long-term assets. In an inflationary economy this is an almost insurmountable problem for a high capital-intensive business as the cost of new plants, machinery, and equipment outstrip the price increases the company's market will accept either because of the elasticity of demand for the product (many capital goods purchases can be postponed) or because of lower-cost, foreign competition.

This, then, is the crux of the value-adjusted data argument. Management, so the value advocates argue, is "eating their seed corn," that is, paying dividends because of apparent earnings when, in fact, the earnings based on the historical cost model have not adequately provided for the maintenance of the productive capacity of the company. This is a valid concern, but, as pointed out earlier, it is more a problem of evaluating a new investment decision than one of restating earnings.

Here again, we can see that the emphasis in the United States on equity capital and thus dividend-paying ability affects the value-adjusted data argument. As we shall see, this emphasis also dramatically influences the emphasis on the short term for which American managers are so often criticized.

Struggling with a National Income Tax Policy That Only Gives Partial Recognition to Inflation

Where does all the preceding leave us? Inflation-adjusted data certainly have a place as a part of the analyses done regarding future products, and so forth, but their great value may be in focusing attention on the need for a coherent national fiscal and monetary policy designed to bring inflation and unemployment under control. It would be virtually impossible to verify, but the greatest value of the FASB Statement No. 33, covering the disclosure as supplemental data of the effects of changing prices (inflation) on published financial data may be the passage of the 1981 Tax Reform Act. Certainly the attention given by the business press to the deflated profit figures reinforced the position of those in Congress who argued for the need for income tax reform.

What the question of inflation and accounting comes down to then is that businessmen and managerial accountants are not only quite cognizant of the effect of inflation on their operations and plans but that they make wide use of inflation-adjusted data in their planning *outside* of the formal accounting system.*

The General Electric COIN program mentioned earlier is an example of this. Inflation-adjusted data are prepared for use by management in evaluating investment opportunities as well as for judging the performance of divisional managers. These data supplement rather than replace the more conventional financial data.

U.S. ECONOMIC SYSTEM EMPHASIZES SHORT TERM

Nevertheless, the most popular criticism today of the American management system is its emphasis on the short term. Financial papers and journals regularly carry articles sharply critical of management's emphasis on short-term results at the expense of long-term growth and of compensation programs geared to "quick" results. A typical quote (from *The New York Times*) is, "But like other European executives, particularly the West Germans, the French fault the American emphasis on maintaining quarterly increases in profits. The pressure for continuous earnings gains,† they say, has shifted the focus of American managers from long-term objectives that would help secure the company's place in the future. Indeed, the reasoning goes, rapid

---

*The investing public seems to be quite aware of the effect of inflation on financial data; otherwise the Dow-Jones index would be in excess of 3000!

†Also see the discussion regarding Datapoint in Chapter 5.

turnover of managers who fail to achieve short-run profit goals makes it more unlikely that investments will be made in long-range programs."[22] Professor Alfred Rappaport has written extensively of what he has termed "a fatal fascination with the short run."[23]

But are the managers really to blame for what admittedly is an American preoccupation with short-term results? Others are not so sure. In an interview given to *Forbes,* Professor Peter Drucker commented, "We have a real problem in American business in that the pension funds, our way of capital intermediation, push companies into short-term thinking. And we have the takeover pressure, which may be greater. I know a number of high-technology companies that should plow back money long-term, and know it, and don't do it because the pension funds are their source of capital. The companies have to maintain those 40 times price/earnings ratios. The moment they show one quarter with disappointing results, the pension funds unload and they are being snapped up by . . . whichever piranha is out there. So we have to find a way to balance a great achievement—the pension fund—with some way of managing for the long term. And I don't know the way."[24]

Others criticize our basic use of equity capital as opposed to long-term debt. James Fallows, Washington editor of *The Atlantic*, wrote,

> Ultimately, the villain in this piece is the same system of equity capital—that is, the stock exchanges—whose flexibility and refinement are the envy of most of the world. It has long been a truism in American business that "equity"—selling shares of stock—is a good way to raise money, and "debt"—loans from a bank—is bad. Now businessmen have begun denouncing, as if it were a devious Oriental trick, the Japanese practice of heavy debt financing for crucial industries such as computers and steel.
>
> The central difference between debt and equity, at least for mature businesses, is what the lenders can ask. If a bank gives a loan, what it wants is to have the money repaid. An equity share entitles the owner to something less—if the company goes down, he's left with nothing—but also something more: *the right to demand that the management maximize profits now* [emphasis added]. In the stockholder's name, corporate directors know they have a fiduciary duty to keep the dividends up, and to protect the value of their shares (and bond rating) on the stock exchange. There are quarterly earnings reports to be filed, price/earnings ratios to maintain. "The American steel companies were prisoners of Wall Street," David Ignatius wrote in an excellent analysis of the steel industry in *The Washington Monthly.* "Unlike Japanese steelmakers, which are financed mostly by bank debt and thus don't have to worry about stock market expectations, the stockholder-owned U.S. makers were expected by Wall Street to present neat, quarter-to-quarter increases in earnings. . . . It's an unhappy truth that sometimes what is best for a company or an industry—for example, a long period of forgone earnings while the profits are plowed back into new facilities—is not always what keeps the stockholders happy."[25]

Even our business schools, once the envy of the business world, have come under criticism. Two Harvard professors, Robert H. Hayes and William J. Abernathy, have done considerable work critical of the management techniques taught by most "B-schools." Their thesis is that American management doctrine has drifted too far from basics—the factory floor and the assembly line—and concentrated on an excessive concern for short-term profits at the expense of a long-term emphasis on growth and technology.[26] This thesis is contrary to the "portfolio theory" of management so prevalent in business schools' teachings, that is, that a company should be managed the same as an investment portfolio with the various divisions competing for investment funds. Certainly there is overemphasis placed on one figure—earnings per share. And, as we saw in the Datapoint experience discussed in Chapter 5, the pressure on managers to perform is quite strong.

The need to improve the relevancy of accounting data while maintaining its reliability will be considered in the next and final chapters as we draw all of these needs together.

REFERENCES

1. Ann M. Morrison, "How DeLorean Dashed His Dream," *Fortune,* May 3, 1982, p. 150.

2. H. Thomas Johnson, *System and Profits: Early Management Accounting at DuPont and General Motors,* Arno Press, New York, 1980, p. 2.

3. Ibid., p. 203.

4. A. Thompson Montgomery, *Managerial Accounting Information,* Addison-Wesley Publishing Company, Inc., Reading, Mass., 1979, p. 15.

5. Ibid., p. 4.

6. Kathy Williams, ed., "Small Business," *Management Accounting,* NAA, New York, May 1981, p. 20.

7. Technical Issues Committee Report, Private Companies Practice Section, AICPA Division For CPA Firms, *Sunset Review of Accounting Principles,* AICPA, 1982, p. 1.

8. Ibid., p. 2.

9. Ibid., pp. 3-10.

10. William H. Beaver, *Financial Reporting: An Accounting Revolution,* Prentice-Hall, Englewood Cliffs, N.J., 1981, p. 143 and p. 147.

11. Peter F. Drucker, abridged specified material from *Managing in Turbulent Times,* pp. 10–11. Copyright © 1980 by Peter F. Drucker. Reprinted by permission of Harper & Row, New York.

12. William M. Agee, "How Companies Should Use Their Cash," *The New York Times,* April 25, 1982, p. 2F.

13. David F. Hawkins, "Thinking Real: Living With FASB 33," *Harvard Business Review,* Sept.–Oct. 1980, p. 119.

14. Andrew McCosh, Edwin Whiting, and Sidney Howell, *Planning and Control Systems and Their Evolution During Inflation,* Manchester Business School, Manchester, England, 1981, pp. 101–102.

15. Eldon S. Hendriksen, *Accounting Theory*, 3d ed., Richard D. Irwin, Inc., Homewood, Ill., 1977, p. 241.

16. *Statement on Accounting Theory and Theory Acceptance*, American Accounting Association, Sarasota, Fla., 1977, p. 6.

17. R. J. Chambers, "Canning's The Economics of Accounting—After 50 Years," *The Accounting Review,"* October 1979.

18. Gordon Shillinglaw, *Handbook of Modern Accounting*, 2d ed., Sidney Davidson and Roman L. Weil, eds., McGraw-Hill, New York, 1977, Chap. 39, pp. 13–14. Reproduced with permission.

19. Paul A. Samuelson, *Economics*, 10th ed., McGraw-Hill, New York, 1976, pp. 63 and 68.

20. Lawrence A. Gordon, Robert Cooper, Haim Folk, and Donny Miller, *The Pricing Decision*, National Association of Accountants and The Society of Management Accountants of Canada, 1981, pp. 9–10.

21. *Detroit Free Press*, May 9, 1982.

22. Thomas C. Hayes, "Europe's Management Approach," *The New York Times International Economic Survey*, February 8, 1981.

23. *Business Week*, May 4, 1981.

24. James Flanigan, "The wrong bottom line," *Forbes*, May 25, 1981.

25. James Fallows, "The American Industry, What Ails It, How to Save It," *The Atlantic*, September 1980. Copyright © 1980, by The Atlantic Monthly Company, Boston, Mass. Reprinted with permission.

26. R. H. Hayes and W. J. Abernathy, "Managing Our Way to Economic Decline," *Harvard Business Review*, July–Oct. 1980.

seven

THE FASB AND THE CONCEPTUAL FRAMEWORK

FASB's SEARCH FOR A CONCEPTUAL FRAMEWORK

With the preceding chapters as background, let us return to the question posed at the end of Chapter 1—How can the accounting profession, which includes managerial as well as public accountants, meet the broad, sophisticated needs of the users of accounting data, including management, investors, and creditors, as well as the regulators?

Some believe the answer is the FASB's project on a conceptual framework of accounting. Speaking to the Houston chapter of the Texas Society of CPAs, Michael O. Alexander, then director of Research and Technical Activities for the FASB concluded, "The real impact of a conceptual framework will be measured in the standards issued by the FASB on the difficult accounting problems of the day. How the conceptual framework is used to resolve these problems will be the test.

"Education in universities will have to move in the direction of a conceptual approach. New students—a new generation of accountants—may be the first to start out by learning the conceptual framework as a way to resolving accounting issues and to guiding judgment.

"Practitioners and preparers, through interpreting standards, may start to use the conceptual framework to resolve problems.

"But all of this will take time. Possibly a generation. Certainly more than eight more years [the time already devoted to the project through 1982]."[1]

However, even this conservative evaluation may be overoptimistic. Before expanding on this viewpoint, let us review the conceptual framework project in more detail.

In earlier chapters, we discussed how accounting evolved from a tool used exclusively by owner-managers to one used not only by managers (no longer themselves significant owners) but by absentee-owners to judge managers, prospective investors and creditors, and government regulators including tax authorities. We reviewed how the varying needs of these groups, coupled with the public accountant's (auditor's) need for protection from the unreasonable expectations of the many users of accounting data, have slowly led to a preoccupation with uniformity, comparability, and specific rules, and, at the same time, a change in emphasis from "hard," transaction-based data to subjective, economic evaluations.

Donald J. Kirk, chairman of the FASB, spoke of this at the AICPA's Seventh Annual National Conference of CPAs in Industry, "We live in an uncertain world; the realities of this uncertain economic world are such that an accountant's (and many investors') craving for certainty may be a major roadblock to *making financial reporting a reflection of economic activity* [emphasis added]. In multinational, long-cycle businesses, the certainty of income measurement is an illusion. In my judgment, income must chart progress during the long cycles by recognizing the progress that has been made, even though it is not realized in cash. At the same time, the funds statement must be more useful so that it more clearly distinguishes the cash and non-cash parts of income."[2]

Trueblood Report

The conceptual framework project is supposed to be the means by which these goals will be accomplished. Although, as is apparent from the history already discussed, the genesis for the conceptual framework can be traced all the way back to the excesses and abuses of the 1920s, the current project really got started with the 1971 study of the AICPA's *Objective of Financial Statements,* termed the Trueblood report after the committee chairman, Robert M. Trueblood, who was the managing partner of Touche, Ross & Co.

This study, published by the AICPA in October 1973, was made in response to the pressures that caused the demise of the AICPA's Accounting Principles Board (see Chapter 4). The study group consisted of nine members—three from academia, three from public accounting, two from business, and one from the securities investment field, as follows:

Richard M. Cyert	Carnegie-Mellon University
Sidney Davidson	University of Chicago
James Don Edwards	University of Georgia
Oscar S. Gellein	Haskins & Sells
Robert M. Trueblood	Touche, Ross & Co.

Frank T. Weston	Arthur Young & Company
Andrew J. Reinhart	The Singer Company
Howard O. Wagner	Jewel Companies, Inc.
C. Reed Parker	Duff, Anderson & Clark, Inc.

The staff of six and a group of seven members termed "consultants and observers" were drawn entirely from public accounting and academia.

Trueblood Report Quite Revolutionary

Not surprising, the study group's conclusions were totally oriented toward the use of accounting data by those not involved in the operations of a business. Also, not surprising, the conclusions included the recommendation that the financial statements contain forecast data, current value data, and social responsibility data. The report was at least as radical as Accounting Research Study No. 1, written in 1961 by Professor Maurice Moonitz and Accounting Research Study No. 3, by Professors Moonitz and Robert Sprouse in 1962, which, as noted in Chapter 4, the Accounting Principles Board had disavowed as "too radically different."

But the 1970s were a different time than the early 1960s. Government agencies were pressing for more and more regulation and for more and more "relevant" data for the public. And how could anyone not choose the route which implied that his work was critical to the survival of the American system of free enterprise by the way in which his product aided capital formation? That certainly is more dynamic than being a historian who compiles the actual results of a firm's actions and tells it how it fell short or excelled.

As noted earlier, the Wheat committee report resulted in the formation in 1973 of the FASB as a full-time, fully funded organization. The Trueblood report became its major concern. In 1974, a Discussion Memorandum covering the Trueblood report was issued and public hearings held by the FASB on the objectives of financial statements.

1976 Discussion Memorandums Formed Basis for Continuing Debate

In December 1976, the FASB published three landmark documents that have formed the basis for the extensive work done since then by the FASB on the specifics of a conceptual framework. The documents were: *Tentative Conclusions on Objectives of Financial Statements of Business Enterprises; Scope and Implications of the Conceptual Framework Project FASB Discussion Memorandum*; and *Conceptual Framework for Financial Accounting and Reporting: Elements of Financial Statements and their Measurement.*

In the first document, the FASB accepted 3 of the 12 objectives of financial statements stated in the Trueblood report as "tentative conclusions." The 3 clearly illustrate the emphasis on external reporting and its use by external parties:

1. Financial *statements* of business enterprises should provide information, within the limits of financial accounting, that is useful to present and potential investors and creditors in making rational investment and credit decisions. Financial statements should be comprehensible to investors and creditors who have a reasonable understanding of business and economic activities and financial accounting and who are willing to spend the time and effort needed to study financial statements.

2. Financial *statements* of business enterprises should provide information that helps investors and creditors *assess the prospects* of receiving cash from dividends or interest and from the proceeds of the sale, redemption, or maturity of securities or loans. Those prospects are affected by (1) an enterprise's ability to obtain enough cash through its earning and financing activities to meet its obligations when due and its other cash operating needs, to reinvest in earning resources and activities, and to pay cash dividends and interest, and (2) by perceptions of investors and creditors generally about that ability, which affects market prices of the enterprise's securities relative to those of other enterprises. Thus, financial accounting and financial *statements* should provide information that helps investors and creditors *assess* the enterprise's *prospects* of *obtaining net cash inflows* through its earning and financing activities.

3. Financial *statements* of a business enterprise *should* provide information about the *economic resources* of an enterprise, which are *sources of prospective cash inflows* to the enterprise; its obligations to transfer economic resources to others, which are *causes* of *prospective cash inflows* from the enterprise; and its earnings, which are the financial results of its operations and other events and conditions that affect the enterprise. Since that information is useful to investors and creditors in *assessing an enterprise's ability to pay* cash dividends and interest and to settle obligations when they mature, it *should* be the *focus* of financial *accounting* and *financial statements*[3] [emphasis added].

Emphasis on Prospective Analysis

Note the emphasis throughout on prospective analysis and the use of financial *statements*, audited by independent public accountants, and in accordance with Generally Accepted Accounting Principles as well as auditing standards, to present this prospective analysis to the external users.

No one really disputes the reasonableness of these needs of external users. As noted earlier, investors (including management) or creditors only enter into profit-oriented activities with one goal—to receive back more cash than was invested. The basic point of difference is whether or not financial accounting and audited financial statements should be the means by which these data are furnished; that is, should this be how usefulness of accounting data is defined?

Tentative Conclusions then states that "the Board has not attempted to reach conclusions on certain matters that are comprehended in the 12 objectives in the Report of the Study Group [the Trueblood report]—for example, reporting current value and changes in current value, providing a statement of financial activities, providing financial forecasts, determining the objectives of financial statements for governmental and not-for-profit organizations, and reporting enterprise activities affecting society."[4] Nevertheless, although "tentative conclusions" on these matters were not stated, a definite trend certainly was indicated. For example, in paragraph 165 the *Tentative Conclusions* continues, "In the purest or ideal form of accrual accounting, sometimes called *direct valuation,** each non-cash asset represents expected future cash receipts, each liability represents expected future cash outlays, and each revenue and expense represents a change in an asset or liability or a current cash receipt or outlay."[5]

Clear Trend Toward Economist's View of Income

This trend toward an economic view of income is not surprising when one recalls that throughout the twentieth century, theorists with an economics background have written much of the basic conceptual basis for the accounting that was evolving since the fifteenth century in stewardship books of account. This "purists' " approach, coupled with the acceptance by the AICPA (driven by the SEC) that the external user must be served, made the conclusions of the Trueblood report and then its executor—the FASB— inevitable.

The theme continues, of course, through both the second and third documents published by the FASB in 1976. In the second document, a relatively brief 24-page summary titled *Scope and Implications of the Conceptual Framework Project,* the main discussion points of the third document are summarized. It is in the discussion concerning the elements of financial statements that the major point of contention was introduced; that is, what are earnings? The following is the key passage from the *Scope and Implications* document:

> Part 1 [of the Discussion Memorandum] begins with a discussion of a matter that is prerequisite to considering specific definitions of the elements of financial statements (assets, liabilities, revenues, expenses, etc.): Which, if any of

*The term is usually attributed to John B. Canning, *The Economics of Accountancy: A Critical Analysis of Accounting Theory,* The Ronald Press Company, New York, 1929.

those elements are the most fundamental and, therefore, control the definitions of the other elements?

The answer to that question depends on one's conceptual view of earnings. Two principal conceptual views of earnings are advanced in the Discussion Memorandum: (1) the *asset and liability view,* under which earnings are determined as a measure of change (but not necessarily as the entire change) in net economic resources of a business entrprise for a period and (2) the *revenue and expense view,* under which earnings are a direct measure of the effectiveness of an enterprise in using its inputs to obtain and sell outputs and are necessarily limited to changes in net economic resources.

Under the asset and liability view, those two elements are the most fundamental, and their definitions are critical. Definitions of the components of earnings—revenues, expenses, gains, and losses—are derived from the definitions of assets and liabilities.

Although the asset and liability view does not require that *all* enterprise resources and obligations be recorded as assets and liabilities or that *all* changes in assets and liabilities be included in earnings, it limits the population from which elements of financial statements can be selected to the underlying economic resources and obligations of the enterprise and to the transactions and events that change measurable attributes of those resources and obligations.

The revenue and expense view depends on definitions of those two elements to define earnings. Under that view, careful timing of recognition of revenues and expenses by appropriate matching is essential to avoid distortion. Thus, to obtain a good or appropriate matching of costs with revenues for a period, proponents of the revenue and expense view are normally willing to introduce into the statement of financial position or balance sheet certain items that proponents of the asset and liability view reject. Those items are often called "deferred charges," "deferred credits," and "reserves."

The first basic issue raised in the Discussion Memorandum, therefore, is which of those two views about earnings should be adopted as the basis underlying a conceptual framework for financial accounting and reporting?

The next six basic issues relate to definitions of the elements of financial statements, starting with assets. How one defines an asset depends, in turn, on one's overall conceptual view of earnings.

Under the asset and liability view, assets are defined in terms of resources: An asset of an enterprise is an economic resource that represents a potential benefit to the particular enterprise. The potential benefit is an eventual direct or indirect net cash inflow to the enterprise. There are aspects of the definition of assets about which proponents of the asset and liability view disagree, in particular, the extent to which legal concepts (for example, ownership or physical possession) should affect the accounting definition, whether exchangeability is an essential asset characteristic, and whether assets arise from wholly executory contracts (no performance by either party). The pros and cons are examined in the Discussion Memorandum.

Proponents of the revenue and expense view are less concerned with whether assets are economic resources than with whether costs (historical or other) are appropriately matched with revenues. Many believe that the nature of an asset is determined primarily by the needs of earnings measurement. Thus, proponents of the revenue and expense view would probably include in an enterprise's balance sheet all items that would be included under the asset and liability view, plus deferred charges and other costs waiting to be matched with revenues in future accounting periods even though those deferred charges and other costs do not represent economic resources.

The definition of a liability, like that of an asset, depends on one's conceptual formulation of earnings. Proponents of the asset and liability view restrict liabilities to an enterprise's obligations to transfer economic resources to other entities in the future. Proponents of the revenue and expense view accept that concept but also recognize certain deferred credits and reserves perceived as necessary to match costs with revenues to measure earnings properly. Among the related matters considered in the Discussion Memorandum are whether the accounting definition of liabilities should be restricted to include only legally binding obligations (legal debt) and whether liabilities include potential obligations resulting from wholly executory contracts.

Earnings under the asset and liability view are defined in terms of certain changes in net assets, and the definition thus depends on the definitions of assets and liabilities. Under that view, definitions of revenues, expenses, gains, and losses, while useful for constructing earnings statements to show how earnings are obtained, are not needed to define earnings. They are matters of presentation rather than definition.

Earnings are defined in the revenue and expense view by explicitly defining revenues, expenses, gains, and losses. The definition of earnings does not depend on definitions of assets and liabilities. Enterprise flows are the central concern of the revenue and expense view, and earnings measurement depends on matching the flows of expenses with the flows of revenues properly and without distortion. Thus, the meaning of "matching" and "distortion" are critical to this view.

The Discussion Memorandum sets forth several definitions of revenues, expenses, gains, and losses, some consistent with the asset and liability view of earnings, some with the revenue and expense view, some that separate gains and losses from revenues and expenses, and some that combine gains with revenues and losses with expenses. Respondents are asked to choose from among them or to propose additional definitions, and to provide supporting reasoning.

Earnings result only after capital has been maintained or costs have been recovered. The concept of capital chosen, therefore, divides an enterprise's returns on investment (earnings) from its returns of investment (costs recovered). The Discussion Memorandum describes two major concepts of capital—financial capital and physical capital—and raises as a basic issue the question of whether accounting earnings should be defined in terms of maintenance of financial capital or maintenance of physical capital.

The major difference between the two concepts is the way they account for changes in values of assets held. The financial capital concept views capital maintenance in *money value* terms and recognizes increases or decreases in values of assets held as gains or losses, which may be separated from "operating" earnings by describing them as "holding gains or losses." The other concept views capital maintenance in terms of the *physical properties* of assets and, therefore, recognizes no gains or losses from changes in value of the "same productive capacity" of an enterprise. Thus, changes in values of assets held, such as inventory, property, plant, equipment, and some intangibles, are included in earnings in the financial capital maintenance view but are excluded from earnings and taken directly to capital in the physical capital maintenance view.

Proponents of a financial capital maintenance view disagree about the timing of recognition of increases or decreases in values of assets held and about whether they should be included in operating earnings or disclosed separately as holding gains or losses. Proponents of a physical capital maintenance view disagree about the definition of "same productive capacity." Some favor replacement of physical assets *in kind.* Others regard productive capacity either as the capacity to produce the same volume of goods or services or the capacity to produce the *same* value of goods and services.

It should be recognized, of course, that maintenance of capital is an abstraction needed to measure earnings—to divide return of capital from return on capital. The abstraction does not assume that assets are actually replaced when used or that they will necessarily be replaced in the future.[6]

1930s Debate Reopened

Shades of the 1930s, for here we have the basic issues of that period reintroduced. The "matching concept" expounded so well in the 1940 Paton and Littleton monograph,* which supposedly ended the 1930s debate, is questioned as being too subjective. It was not the "conceptual anchor, a base about which few would argue . . ." that former FASB member Oscar S. Gellein wrote about.[7]

An Introduction to Corporate Accounting Standards (see Chapter 3).

The third document* published by the FASB in 1976 then expanded on the points and conclusions of the first two. A long (360 pages), complex, rather vague paper, it contained many generalities that critics and proponents alike could agree on and also many they could wonder about. However, the reintroduction of the asset/liability view and the question of what constitutes earnings created a storm of controversy within the accounting field.

Ernst & Ernst Led Opposition

The opposition was spearheaded by Ernst & Ernst (now Ernst & Whinney), specifically two partners, Robert K. Mautz (later director of the Paton Research Center, chairman of accounting at the University of Michigan, and a member of the AICPA's Public Oversight Board) and Albert A. Koch (later partner-in-charge of the firm's Detroit office). These two men presented a series of seminars in early 1977 that were sharply critical of the basic thrust of the conceptual framework project. Their presentation was published by Ernst & Ernst, and the objections are summarized as follows:

"The proposed objectives of financial statements are narrowly directed to benefit investors, a single, special interest, with inadequate consideration of the effect this might have on the total economy or on other interests in financial reporting.

"The bias toward substantive change in generally accepted financial reporting practice is so overwhelming as to negate the asserted neutrality of the Discussion Memorandum.

"The positive emphasis on current value accounting and the negative treatment of traditional accounting tend to lead the reader to a predetermined conclusion, a conclusion that we are convinced would not be in the best interests of the free enterprise system.

"No consideration is given to the influence of inflation on the determination of taxable income, a problem which we consider to be of first importance to the economic welfare of our country."[8]

These concerns were widely supported by the business community, and the long debate over the conceptual framework began. This controversy and debate has continued into the 1980s as the FASB splintered the original project into seven subprojects (elements, recognition, measurement, financial statements and other means of financial reporting, income, funds flow and liquidity, and qualitative characteristics), issued several more Discussion

---

*FASB Discussion Memorandum, *Conceptual Framework for Financial Accounting and Reporting: Elements of Financial Statements and Their Measurement,* FASB, Stamford, Conn., 1976.

Memorandums, held several hearings, and began issuing a new series—Statements of Financial Accounting Concepts—which they plan will ultimately be the "conceptual framework of accounting," that is, become the accounting field's "constitution."

Basic Issue of Usefulness (Relevance) of Accounting Data

The basic reason for this controversy, once again, stems from the different points of view as to the usefulness of accounting data held by internal users (management) and external users (potential investors or creditors), *as perceived by the FASB* rather than as expressed by the external users themselves. Of course, the other "external" user—the government—clouds the picture with periodic arbitrary rules such as we saw in the case of LIFO accounting, the investment tax credit, and, notably, the Foreign Corrupt Practices Act.

FASB Focuses on Perceived Needs of External Users

Following the tradition established by the SEC's delegation of its rule-making capability to the AICPA in 1938, the FASB has viewed its own role as protecting the interests of the external users of financial data, which, in turn, should assist in the maintenance of orderly, efficient capital markets for our nation's economic health. Statement of Financial Accounting Concepts No. 1, issued in November 1980, clearly spells this out:

> Since management accounting is internal to an enterprise, it can usually be tailored to meet management's informational needs *and is beyond the scope of this Statement.* . . . The objectives in this Statement are those of general purpose external financial reporting by business enterprises. The objectives stem primarily from the informational needs of external users *who lack the authority to prescribe the financial information they want* from an enterprise and, therefore, must use the information that management communicates to them. . . . The role of financial reporting in the economy is to provide information that is useful in making business and economic decisions, not to determine what those decisions should be. For example, saving and investing in productive resources (capital formation) are generally considered to be prerequisite to increasing the standard of living in an economy. *To the extent that financial reporting provides information that helps identify relatively efficient and inefficient users of resources, aids in assessing relative returns and risks of investment opportunities, or* otherwise assists in promoting efficient functioning of capital and other markets, *it helps to create a favorable environment for capital formation decisions*[9] [emphasis added].

Must Accounting Base Change?

Lofty goals? Yes. And it is impossible to disagree with the need to achieve such goals. The controversy over the conceptual framework does not stem from disagreement as to the goals but, rather, from the question of whether we must change the very foundations of accounting in an attempt to achieve them? Particularly when managerial accountants were not having any problem with the existing framework for accounting (see Chapter 3).

In order to achieve the stated goals, the investor or creditor must have the type of data about a company that we discussed in Chapter 6—future product plans, market research data, capital spending programs, sensitivity of a company's revenue sources to national and international economic conditions, and so on. If accounting and financial statements were to even attempt to supply these needs, it would be necessary to change to a future-oriented, inflation-adjusted, capital maintenance concept of measuring and reporting results. This is the ultimate goal of the conceptual framework project just as it was of the Trueblood study group. At the Houston seminar (mentioned earlier), Michael O. Alexander said, "I find it hard to conceive of a conceptual framework that does not address the effects of changing prices. To ignore the effects of changing prices in accounting can produce an absurd result. Accounting cannot go on producing absurd results for long unless it is indeed an end in itself."[10]

We noted in the preceding chapter that businessmen and managerial accountants understand the need to take the effects of inflation (changing prices) into account in evaluating their performance, plans, and investment choices, but most* believe the usefulness of accounting itself would be destroyed if such adjustments were made a basic part of the measurement system.

SPECULATORS AND FINANCIAL STATEMENTS

Moreover, even more to the point, many question the use of financial statements to satisfy the perceived needs of a specific group—the investor or creditor—particularly when the primary emphasis of the former group is on short-run speculation rather than long-term returns, as described so well by Lord Keynes (see Chapter 4).

*Although no specific research is available that would give the positions of the majority of managerial accountants, based on the position papers filed by the representative organizations—the Committee on Corporate Reporting of the Financial Executive Institute and the Management Accounting Practices Committee of the National Association of Accountants— the deduction appears logical.

The attitude of the short-term investor is also described quite well by Ralph E. Bailey, formerly chairman of Conoco, Inc. and later vice chairman of E. I. du Pont de Nemours & Company following their 1981 merger. He is quoted in *The Corporate Raiders,* an article by Leslie Wayne written for *The New York Times Magazine.* Mr. Wayne writes of forced mergers and stockholders' interests: "Corporations are owned by their shareholders. But rarely is the vast majority of the shares in the hands of small individual investors who may be sympathetic to the pleas of management. Most typically, the critical blocks are owned by institutional investors—large pension funds or insurance companies—and arbitragers, big investors who amass large blocks of shares in a target company the moment it is tendered for in the hopes of turning a quick profit. 'These are not shareholders in the traditional sense,' said Ralph E. Bailey. . . . When Conoco's Canadian assets were being sought by Dome Petroleum Ltd. . . . Mr. Bailey personally visited some leading institutional investors and pleaded to no avail that they stick with Conoco. 'They don't pay taxes, so they are interested in short-term profits,' he said; 'You can't rely on that class of shareholder to take the long-term view.' "[11]

Although Mr. Bailey was understandably dismayed at such an attitude, it is, after all, quite reasonable and understandable. No one invests for any reason but to receive back more cash than was invested, either as dividends or interest or in appreciation in the market price of a security. Although management may be "locked-in" because of such factors as length of service or position, and must stay with the present investment, nothing binds absentee owners, nor should anything so constrain them.

Financial Statements Must Be Objective

It is futile, however, to attempt to construct an accounting system and accompanying financial statements that can indicate the best course of future action to this type of absentee owners. Instead, such statements should be concentrated upon objective reporting of results. They should be the "rock" against which expectations are tested.

An Example of the Sophistication and Goals of Investors

The sophistication and intent of investors can be demonstrated again and again by regular reviews of financial journals such as *Barrons, The Wall Street Journal, The New York Times, Forbes, Business Week, Fortune,* and so forth. However, the following simple analysis clearly displays both the investors' short-term views as well as the fact that they are already discounting inflation.

The 30 stocks in the Dow-Jones Industrial Average are displayed in Table 7.1, along with certain data per share:[12]

Table 7.1 Thirty Stocks of the Dow-Jones Industrial Average

The 30 DJIA Stocks	Book Value[a] 12-31-81	Market Price July 1982	Replacement Cost 12-31-81	Replacement Cost as a Percentage of Mkt. Price
Alcoa	41	24⅝	89	361
Allied Corp.	56	29⅜	104	354
American Brands	33	40⅝	46	113
American Can	54	28⅝	96	335
AT&T	68	50⅞	147	289
Bethlehem Steel	63	15⅜	138	898
DuPont	37	33⅜	65	195
Eastman Kodak	42	72¾	68	93
Exxon	54	26⅝	121	454
General Electric	40	64¾	62	96
General Foods	32	37⅜	45	120
General Motors	57	44¼	34	77
Goodyear	33	24¼	62	256
IBM	31	61½	33	54
INCO	17	8⅝	41	475
Int'l Harvester	40	3¾	61	1627
Int'l Paper	65	37⅛	94	253
Merck & Co.	26	67⅜	34	50
Manville Corp.	40	10¾	43	400
3M	29	52⅛	37	71
Owens Illinois	47	22⅞	89	389
Proctor & Gamble	47	82⅝	76	92
Sears Roebuck	24	18½	24	130
Standard Oil of California	37	28	93	332
Texaco	53	28⅜	102	359
Union Carbide	77	43	113	263
U.S. Steel	69	18½	178	962
United Technologies	62	37⅝	83	221
Westinghouse	33	16	54	338
F. W. Woolworth	44	18⅜	76	414

Actual DJI average: [July 11, 1982]. 804.98
DJI average calculated by replacement cost: 1756

[a]Book value is the value of a company's assets, based on its historical price. Replacement cost is the estimated cost to replace those assets at current prices.

In analyzing Table 7.1, keep in mind that the book value per share is based on historical costs which in each case is an accumulation of dollars over the years. Each book value thus has a combination of different purchasing power values. As you can see, 22 of the 30 companies have a book value per share of stock in excess of the market price of their stock at the time the table's data were current (July 1982). The reason for this is evident in the case of International Harvester, which was struggling with severe financial problems, but in most of the other companies the only conclusion that can be drawn is a preoccupation of the market with short-term yields instead of underlying values and long-term potential. The other figures in Table 7.1 also illustrate this point; for instance, the replacement cost per share is higher than the market price for 23 of the 30 companies. The author of the article[13] in which the table appeared reported that on this basis, John M. Templeton, a very successful mutual fund manager, was predicting a Dow of 3000 before 1990, arguing that the company's stocks were overdeflated; that is, short-term pessimism had resulted in an "oversold" condition.

Was historical cost data to blame for this "oversold" condition? Obviously not, since even the market value per share was under the historical cost book value per share. What then caused this condition if not cost, rather than value-oriented, data? The answer illustrates the complexity of the problem of meeting the needs of investors and the need to move slowly in holding financial accounting responsible for these needs.

At the point of the preceding analysis (July 1982) in the United States and in the world generally, future economic forecasts could best be described as "uncertain." The Reagan administration had instituted drastic cuts in economic programs in 1981 designed to halt inflation in the U.S. and revitalize our economy, but in mid-1982 the nation was still mired in a recession. Inflation had slowed, but unemployment had reached pre-World War II levels and the government was facing the largest budget deficits in history. Meanwhile, the Mideast was in more turmoil than usual following Israel's invasion of Lebanon, and Iran had invaded Iraq following its successful repulsion of Iraq's own invasion of two years earlier. This open warfare placed the world's supply of oil, always on a knife-edge following the 1973 OPEC embargo, in jeopardy again. In addition, the discord among Western allies, such as our government's embargo of the U.S. technology and equipment needed by Western European firms working with Russia on the Siberian gas pipeline, added to the uncertainty of the future.

As a result of the preceding factors (and many, many others, such as the state of U.S.-Russia relations and its effect on world peace), the *risk factor* involved in the evaluation of any investment rose significantly, and as a result, interest rates in the U.S. stayed abnormally high in relation to the inflation rate, resulting in a further "stalling" of the hoped-for economic recovery.

Since in a time of uncertainty, investors tend to attempt to stay liquid so as to keep their options open, Mr. Templeton was apparently betting that following the likely resolution of most of the problems mentioned, investors would feel confident in the long-term prospects of the economy and rush to convert their short-term, high-yield money market funds to stocks. (He proved to be an excellent prophet as demonstrated by the surge of the stock market to record highs in the following months.)

Common stocks, of course, can appreciate faster than any fixed-rate debt-type investment if the companies are able to expand and develop and sell new products and services in a growth economy. The capital for this expansion comes from loans or new stock issues; hence, the lower the interest rates, the better the opportunity for a return rate in excess of the cost of capital.

What Place Does Accounting Have?

Where does financial accounting and reporting fit in all of this? Professor Homer Kripke, for one, believes that they do not fit at all. In his critique of the SEC and accountants, *The SEC and Corporate Disclosure,* he writes, "I submit that an organization (the FASB) dominated by (public) accountants is not the vehicle to determine broad questions of financial reporting including emphasis on the future rather than the past, possibilities of useful disclosure of sensitivities to elements of the macroeconomy. . . . The most valuable recent developments in financial disclosure necessarily involve judgment, and, therefore, *do not involve* the public accountants, e.g., the management discussion of the earnings statements and the move toward inflation disclosure through replacement cost. We may be building up to an overall absurdity in which certified financial statements remain firmly anchored in objective but largely irrelevant historical costs, while the relevant financial disclosure is judgmental, not covered by the [public] accountants' opinion, and found only outside the financial statements or in uncertified footnotes."[14]

This loss of relevancy is what the Trueblood committee and the FASB are the most concerned about. After all, who wants to be involved in a reporting process that no one deems of significance—just a "police action." Thus, the thrust of the conceptual framework has been toward future-oriented, value-based data—data to be used in making the decision to buy or sell the company's stock or to loan it money. However, this assumes that the preparation of such data is the proper goal of accounting. The needs of the managers are ignored, as we have seen.

FASB STATEMENTS OF CONCEPTS

Thus, the conceptual framework project has unfolded slowly but steadily on a course that could not help but lead to a collision with managerial accounting. Since the 1976 Discussion Memorandum and related papers, the FASB has issued four Statements of Financial Accounting Concepts (SFAC):

November 1978 — SFAC No. 1 — *Objectives of Financial Reporting by Business Enterprises*

May 1980   — SFAC No. 2 — *Qualitative Characteristics of Accounting Information*

December 1980 — SFAC No. 3 — *Elements of Financial Statements of Business Enterprises*

December 1980 — SFAC No. 4 — *Objectives of Financial Reporting by Nonbusiness Organizations*

Distinction Made Between Reporting and Statements

Statement No. 1 is so broad and general that little quarrel can be taken with its general comments and conclusions. It does, however, draw the distinction between financial *reporting* and financial *statements.* Thus, while the area of financial reporting *includes* audited financial statements and footnotes, it also comprehends a much broader area of so-called "soft" unaudited data, including textual descriptions, analyses, press releases, trade journal articles, interviews with management, and so forth.[15]

This distinction between the broad area of financial reporting and the narrower area of financial statements is of major importance. It marks a sharp departure from the AICPA's (and Trueblood committee's) rigid adherence to the notion that if a matter has financial significance, then, by definition, a "fair presentation" of the company's financial position requires that it be included in the financial statements or footnotes. By recognizing that the audited financial statements and footnotes were only a part (albeit the major part) of the financial reporting spectrum, the FASB laid the groundwork for accommodating the reporting of highly relevant but subjective data, such as the impact of inflation on a company, while retaining the highly desirable objectivity of the historic-cost-based financial statements. Unfortunately, the FASB has not explored the full potential of supplemental analysis as a means of balancing the needs of all users for reliable and relevant financial data.

Concepts Statement No. 2, dealing with qualitative characteristics, is another broad, general statement that leaves little room for dispute. Written by

Professor David Solomons of the Wharton School, it covers the subjective qualities of financial data—understandability, decision usefulness, relevance, reliability, predictive value, feedback value, timeliness, verifiability, representational faithfulness, comparability (including consistency), neutrality, and materiality—and concludes that relevancy *and* reliability are the two most important qualities.[16] Unfortunately, these two qualities are often not complementary. For example, an analysis of the trend in the nation's economy over the next 12 months, including such matters as the government's fiscal and monetary policy and the supply of oil, would certainly be highly relevant to any evaluation of a particular company's expectations over that period but would probably be quite low in reliability.

Although these first two statements were not controversial, the FASB began to encounter some resistance to the conceptual framework project in Concepts Statement No. 3 and broad opposition in the exposure draft for what would have been Statement No. 5* covering *Reporting Earnings, Cash Flows, and Financial Position of Business Enterprises.*[17]

Comprehensive Income Introduced

In Concepts Statement No. 3, the FASB began to be more specific as it defined the elements of financial statements. The definitions of assets and liabilities disclosed a shift away from income determination through the application of the concept of matching of costs and revenues (the income statement emphasis) to the change in assets and liabilities more rigidly defined. In addition, the concept of *comprehensive income* was introduced in the 1980 publication of Concepts Statement No. 3: "Comprehensive income is the change in equity (net assets) of an entity during a period from transactions and other events and circumstances from nonowner sources. It includes all changes in equity during a period except those resulting from investments by owners and distributions to owners. . . . The Statement does not define the term *earnings,* which is reserved for possible use to designate a significant intermediate measure or component that is part of comprehensive income."[18]

This careful distinction between *earnings* and something called *comprehensive income* raised a great deal of concern among managerial accountants and businessmen. The business world is complex enough without introducing several types of earnings or net income or some new type of income, particularly when viewed from the standpoint of the dividend that a

---

*Concepts Statement No. 4 dealt with nonbusiness organizations, and although the governmental and charitable organizations may have some concern in this area, we will exclude them from this book.

stockholder could expect or the distribution an employee could expect under some form of incentive or profit-sharing plan. Considerable dissension could result from the payment (or nonpayment) of dividends or profit sharing out of one pool of "earnings" while a larger pool of comprehensive income was ignored. This is particularly true when the latter pool could conceivably include "earnings" quite far removed from the cash realization needed for dividends, reinvestment, or payment of amounts due under profit-sharing plans.

These concerns, plus others having to do with the apparent detailed reporting requirements, had crystallized by the time the exposure draft covering Reporting Income, and so forth was published in November 1981, and, as a result, the FASB held up any publication of a standard pending completion of the recognition of income and measurement phases of the conceptual framework. If the past is any guide, resolving these issues may take years.

However, the FASB faces a dilemma. If the conceptual framework is to truly be the "constitution" for accounting, then it should encompass all present and future needs and uses. This means that it should include at least a provision for all the measurement bases possible, for instance, historical cost, current cost, replacement cost, and so on. Of course, the introduction of "comprehensive income" would accomplish this. Thus, the FASB is faced with the problem of maintaining the support of a significant portion of its constituency—the business world represented by the Financial Executives Institute and the National Association of Accountants—which is strongly in favor of a historical cost measurement base, while developing a conceptual framework that comprehends all measurement bases.

WHY DOES FASB WANT A CONCEPTUAL FRAMEWORK?

Why does the FASB press so hard for a broad conceptual framework?* Is it because the real practitioners of accounting—the managerial accountants who prepare and analyze the budgets, make forecasts, oversee the maintenance and control of the books of account, and interpret the actual results—are badly in need of such a conceptual framework in order to perform their work? Hardly. If all regulatory agencies, both governmental and

---

*Various members of the FASB staff have indicated in public comments that as much as 40% of staff time was devoted to the project, which means that several millions of dollars have been spent on the project over the past five years. (The FASB's annual budget was $8.5 million in 1982).

private, were to cease operations at once, managerial accountants would continue to practice their profession. The basic accounting theory discussed in Chapter 3 would continue to serve the managerial accountants quite well in the execution of their primary responsibility, namely, assisting in the planning and control of the operations of a company. Instead, the need, as perceived by the FASB, was explained by Michael O. Alexander in the Houston speech cited earlier in which he spoke of the need for a conceptual framework "to guide standard setters by providing a cohesive, consistent set of underlying concepts that form the basis for conclusions of all standards. The framework is intended to provide guidance to preparers, practitioners [public accountants in this case], and others in the interpretation of standards and the resolution of issues where standards are not available. The framework is intended to aid users by making it easier to understand the basis underlying the preparation of all financial statements as well as *providing comparability among enterprises*"[19] [emphasis added].

It should be clear that the conceptual framework being developed is not for managing and controlling a company but rather to support external reporting of results and future expectations for use in external investment decisions. To the exent these reporting concepts conflict with good internal management and control, managerial accountants and financial executives will oppose them. Such a conflict would be a change from a historical cost, "hard" data base to a subjective, value-oriented base. The result would be a loss of relevancy since the transaction base that forecast and budgets are measured against would be lost.

Public accountants who have to deal with smaller companies, many of them privately owned, are upset by the trend in financial reporting also. Their disaffection has led to the growth of alternatives to GAAP, such as tax basis accounting, that is, books maintained in accordance with the Internal Revenue Code, or modified or complete cash basis.[20]

ACCOUNTING—ATTESTORY OR PREDICTIVE?

The heart of the controversy is, What is the objective of financial accounting? Is it attestory or predictive? The answer to this depends on whether or not investors use financial statements as the basis for their investment decision. If they do, then it would be appropriate to include in those statements highly relevant, if subjective, predictive data as to the future cash flows of a company. If, on the other hand, the investor, whether for the short or long term, bases his decision on a host of data dealing with a wide range of factors such as population trends, international monetary markets, the status of the world's oil supply, the federal budget, interest rates, comparative yields and risks, and the like, then he has a need for some objective, relatively independent data base against which his expectations can be measured—the same as the manager of a company has.

FASB Would Say Predictive

From the viewpoint of the FASB, the answer to the purpose of financial statements is apparently the first, that is, to be predictive. This view is understandable since it enhances the role of both the public accountant and the FASB. If, however, the objective of financial statements is to be attestory, as many believe, then the role of the public accountant and the FASB is diminished somewhat since the statements are relegated to a less vital position in capital formation.

Although no in-depth research has ever been done as to whether investors use financial statements to make their basic investment decisions (predictive) or to judge the reasonableness of past investment decisions (attestory), empirical evidence such as the analysis of the Dow-Jones cited in Table 7.1 would lead one to strongly suspect the latter use takes precedence over the former.

A classic illustration of the subjective nature of the evaluations, the sensitivity to yield and risk factors, and investor ability (and inclination) to move billions of dollars from one investment to another without new financial statement data, was given by the action of the stock market in the closing months of 1982 referred to earlier. Other examples include the highly subjective analyses of the vast mergers in the early 1980s of DuPont and Conoco, or U.S. Steel and Marathon. In these mergers, the key was the future value of the large oil reserves* held by Conoco and Marathon particularly if considered in conjunction with the needs and goals of the acquiring company. DuPont, a chemical company, sought more reliable sources of raw materials while U.S. Steel, a mature company facing intense foreign competition, sought diversification into a potentially more lucrative business.

Interestingly enough, considerable second guessing has followed the decisions of DuPont and U.S. Steel to pursue the mergers. Although it is far

---

*Although the SEC had experimented with Reserve Recognition Accounting in the late 1970s and the entire subject of accounting for oil and gas exploration costs and values had been a major point of dispute among the SEC, the FASB, Congress, and business, the conclusion by the SEC was that it was not practical to attempt to quantify the dollar value of such reserves because of the complex and subjective evaluations involved. Instead, the dollar value was left to the marketplace to determine.

too early to determine the long-run effect of the mergers, the companies involved have been criticized for the short-run impact of the significant increase in their debt as a result of the mergers and of the choice of oil as a potential revenue producer since the world oil market has shown definite signs of stabilizing and even decreasing as an energy source.

Accounting Should Be Attestory

The point is that while the financial statements are an integral part of any financial analysis of a company, their value lies more in the objective basis they provide on which to build (plan) than in the predictive quality of any values they might contain. In debating the usefulness of accounting, we should keep in mind that it is quite probable that we will lose relevancy (the goal espoused by many in support of value-oriented accounting) if we attempt to develop a measurement base that depends on several different levels of income starting with a "comprehensive income" determined by the differences in values between balance sheets at different points in time.

An Illustration of Attestory Nature

The irrelevance of financial statements as a key factor in an investment decision is best illustrated by what transpires when an entirely new venture is begun. No financial statements are available since all there is is one or more persons who have pooled their resources and raised some capital. With this first move (which really constitutes a demonstration of the seriousness of their intentions to other prospective investors and creditors), the group approaches either a banker (for a loan) or an underwriter (for equity capital), or both. If the group is able to convince the banker or underwriter of the viability of their venture through the presentation of market research that indicates a demand for their product or service coupled with their assembly of the sales, manufacturing, engineering, and financial talent to capitalize on the demand, the banker and/or underwriter will back them. This process, of course, involves projections of expected sales and profits and cash needs, but more than anything else, it revolves around the subjective evaluation of the group's combined managerial abilities. Ultimately, that is the most significant factor on which every investor/creditor bets.

Later, the wisdom of the investment must be evaluated. The key to this evaluation is the preparation of financial statements prepared in a reasonable, objective, consistent manner so as to give an independent, reasonable basis for the evaluation. It is the need for independence, consistency, and objectivity in the present world of absentee owners that has created the need for public accountants and for standard setters as well.

DO WE NEED A CONCEPTUAL FRAMEWORK?

All of this brings us back to the question of whether or not we need a "conceptual framework" for reporting. The FASB has its own perception of the "usefulness" of accounting data and places its highest priority on maintaining an orderly capital market through an attempt to guide investment decisions rather than through supplying attestory data. However, another major factor behind its conceptual framework project is the desire for uniformity. Ostensibly, this is to permit comparisons of data among companies, as discussed in Chapter 4, but it also narrows the legal liability of the public accountants, as well as to diminish the competitive "auction" of accounting practices by public accounting firms.

An example of the competitive nature of public accounting arose in the summer of 1982, when the issue of defeasance of debt sprang up when a major company removed $515 billion in long-term debt from its balance sheet through the establishment of what was, in effect, an irrevocable trust in which government securities were deposited sufficient to retire the debt.

Speaking at the American Accounting Association 1982 annual meeting, a member of the FASB staff noted that seven of the Big Eight firms had called and asked the FASB to take action prohibiting such an offset, commenting that although they (each firm) opposed the practice, they understood other firms would permit it and thus create pressure on their firm by a client ready to change auditors to suit the client's desires. Only seven firms called, presumably because the remaining firm had been the one concerned with the company—its client.

Elimination of Alternatives—"Managed Earnings"

However, the question of earnings management, particularly through accounting alternatives, is vastly overrated by the government, the media, and the public. Earnings, in any significant amount, rest on two basic factors *and only two*—the volume of revenues and the ability to produce those revenues at a cost less than the sales price.

What is being overlooked or misunderstood by those who comment on "earnings management" is the basic subjectivity of accounting itself. The precision of bookkeeping (once the subjective accounting evaluations have been made) has led the majority of nonaccountants to believe that an exact answer is possible. Many over-precise accountants contribute to this myth with such comments as "true cost" or "real net income."

Three Types of Alternatives

Professor Dean E. Graber and Bill D. Jarvazin wrote in the *Financial Analysts Journal* of both this misunderstanding and of the futility of such a goal. They defined three types of earnings management alternatives:

> Type 1 alternatives comprise the accounting principles that are both generally accepted and equally available to all managements for application to their financial reports. Since they must be disclosed in footnotes to the financial statements, these alternatives are visible to external users [e.g. the use of LIFO vs. FIFO for costing inventories].
>
> Type 2 alternatives, on the other hand, constitute the behind-the-scenes accounting judgments required in the implementation of a single accounting principle. The reader of financial statements may well remain ignorant of these judgments on reported income [e.g., adequacy of the provision for bad debts].
>
> Type 3 alternatives also involve judgments not fully disclosed to outsiders. But Type 3 alternatives encompass business—as opposed to accounting—choices, such as those regarding the timing of asset purchases, retirements, or the nature of retirements.[21]

In their conclusion, Professors Graber and Jarvazin noted that "while the FASB has certainly narrowed the range of acceptable, Type 1, alternatives . . . no standard-setting body, whether private or public, can prevent or eliminate Type 2 and Type 3 alternatives unless it restricts business enterprises and accountants to such an extent that all accounting and managerial judgments are removed. The wisdom of this degree of restriction is clearly questionable."[22]

Again, it should be clearly understood that all three types of alternatives cannot have any truly major impact on earnings. Sales and efficient operations are an absolute must for significant earnings.

Subjectivity of Accounting

Another illustration of the subjectivity of accounting (and the futility of "uniformity" as a goal) was given by the FASB staff themselves at a special meeting in 1978 with selected theoreticians and practitioners (including the author) concerning the conceptual framework project.* An example was

---

*This public meeting, held July 26, 1978 at FASB headquarters, included the entire board; M. E. Alexander, director of Research for the FASB; Reed K. Storey, director of the Conceptual Framework Project for the FASB; Professors Robert Anthony and Robert K. Mautz; Phillip Defliese, retired chairman of Coopers & Lybrand; Robert Espie, vice president of Aetna Life Insurance Co.; Robert Mays, former board member; Arthur Wyatt of Arthur Andersen & Co., and the author.

given of the accounting for costs of a development stage company. The basic facts were as follows:

E Company was formed at the beginning of the year to develop, manufacture, and sell a new product. During the year, it spent $400 on developing the product, $250 on manufacturing units ready for sale, $100 on advertising of the product, and $200 on general and administrative activities. It is ready to begin selling the product during the first month of the next year, and all indications are that the market will exceed the company's manufacturing capacity, at least in the beginning. The company prepared four sets of financial statements:

	Set 1	Set 2	Set 3	Set 4
	$	$	$	$
Balance sheet:				
Inventory	250	250	250	250
Deferred development cost	400	400		
Prepaid advertising	100	100	100	
Deferred general and administrative cost	200			
	950	750	350	250
Capital stock	950	950	950	950
Deficit	0	(200)	(600)	(700)
	950	750	350	250
Income statement:				
Revenues	0	0	0	0
Development expense			400	400
Advertising expense				100
General and administrative expense		200	200	200
Net loss	0	(200)	(600)	(700)

During the discussion it became evident that depending on the degree of conservatism of the discussant, any of the four financial positions could be defended on a theoretical basis and that probably the least conservative position (Set 1) was the fairest presentation, even though it would not be permitted under present accounting rules.

FASB Persists

Nevertheless, uniformity and comparability remain as prime goals of the FASB.* This is viewed as the primary purpose of a standards board and certainly, as we have seen, the actions of Congress as far back as 1933 have from time to time reinforced this view. But this view is based on the misconception of accounting as a precise science amenable to the establishment of absolute rules. As a result of this emphasis on uniformity, coupled with the subtle shift toward economic valuations, we have seen a steady drift of accounting theory as espoused by the FASB away from cash-oriented, transaction-based data with a sharp increase in over-specific standards. Thus, we have standards such as those requiring the deferral and allocation of income taxes among years without regard to the movement of cash involved, or those standards covering accounting for leases, which attempt to specify by fiat when the agreement has resulted in a purchase. Those of us among the managerial accountants in industry have attempted, usually in vain, to convince engineers, salesmen, and other nonaccountants in management positions of the logic behind such standards. As noted earlier, the private companies' Practice Section of the AICPA has gone so far as to recommend that private companies be exempted from such abstract, impractical rules.[23]

Henry P. Hill, editor-in-chief of the *Journal of Accounting, Auditing and Finance* commented on the growing gap between the expectations of businessmen and the abstract concepts being developed by the FASB.[24] Mr. Hill writes of the poor relationship of accounting standards to business purposes. He cites, as an example, a hypothetical acquisition of a company with an unused income tax loss carryforward. After brilliantly planning a successful merger and utilizing the loss carryforward (and realizing a significant increase in cash and retained earnings), the management finds that the ap-

---

*Although we have generally limited our review in this book to the U.S. practice of accounting, it should be noted that this issue of uniformity (termed "harmonization" in many foreign countries) is being pressed by public accountants (through the International Accounting Standards Committee) and governments (through such groups as the European Economic Community or the United Nations's "Group of Experts") for much the same reasons as it is pressed in the United States.

In response to these groups, in 1976, the Organization for Economic Cooperation and Development, an informal organization representing 24 "Westernized" nations, published a voluntary Code of Conduct for Multinational Enterprises with general guidelines for disclosure of financial data. However, all these groups face the question of enforcement or sanction powers. With the exception of the EEC, none have any such power; hence their efforts are only advisory.

plicable accounting standards (Nos. 11 and 16 of the Accounting Principles Board) would not permit any recognition of their efforts in the current year's operating results. Instead the obvious gain had to be recorded as a retroactive adjustment and excluded from the current year's net income. Other examples including leases and translation of foreign currency financial statements are cited. Mr. Hill concludes, "The actions of most intelligent people make sense when you know what is in their minds. To ignore the collective wisdom of the business community in favor of a structure of abstract thought interesting only to the accounting community would be to give the lie to the idea of accounting's being a useful discipline, yet that is what is in danger of happening if the present trend of developments in accounting principles continues. If we do not pay more attention to the language of the business community, we shall end up talking to ourselves."[25]

Of course, there has to be some basic comparability—uniformity—of accounting theory. It would be useless to attempt to compare the financial results of two companies—one prepared on a cash basis and the other on an accrual basis. However, the broad concepts discussed in Chapter 3 provide much of this basic foundation. It is the proliferation of over-specific rules and abstract concepts, personified by the pronouncements on leasing and income tax allocation, that managerial accountants and private practice firms of the AICPA alike object to.

Moreover, the concern for this trend goes beyond business and private practice firms. In 1979, Stephen Zeff, then editor of *The Accounting Review,* wrote an editorial expressing his concern about the way in which the intermediate accounting course has been changed "from a mixture of theory and practice to an undiluted indoctrination in the practices recommended" by the various standard-setting bodies.[26] He went on, "I do not propose that so-called 'legal accounting' should not be taught in university accounting curricula. I do, however, insist that instruction in 'legal accounting' should not drive out instruction in the theory of one's field. . . . Are students to be encouraged to believe that accounting has no theory worth learning or that the only 'theory' is an amalgam of authoritatively recommended practices (as of a given moment)?"[27]

In 1982, Maurice Moonitz, professor emeritus, University of California, Berkeley, also commented on this situation. "Widely used textbooks contribute greatly to this deplorable state of affairs. They are larded with references to and discussions of the voluminous output of the standard setters. . . . The practices followed drive out the underpinning of accounting, the 'theory' of the field. . . . Rules, practices, and procedures can be learned more quickly . . . on the job (after the student has learned the 'theory')."[28]

SUMMARY OF BASIC POINTS

What can be done? First, let us sum up several basic points and then attempt to find a solution that can accommodate them all:

1. Accounting is not a branch of economics* but rather has its origins in the beginning of civilization as a cash/transaction-oriented discipline.

2. Accounting is not one of the physical sciences in that its practice is not based on discoverable, absolute truths that, once discovered through observation of phenomena or analytic reasoning, can never change. Instead, it is a behavioral science for which only subjective evaluations (including the author's) can be made. Thus, it is impossible to ever establish immutable rules, even though the FASB tries; indeed, as the board's composition changes, the rules change.

3. The basic use of accounting is by business as a structured discipline by which controls over assets, liabilities, revenues, costs, and expenses can be established and maintained and through which budgets and standards can be prepared according to a business plan. This will ultimately furnish reasonably objective results against which the success or failure of the plan can be measured (and altered as need be).

4. The growth of our complex, highly integrated industrialized society and of the ensuing separation of owners and managers of businesses and the growth of capital markets led to a need for an independent attestation of manager's reports of results of operations and financial position and a degree of uniformity and consistency in accounting conventions among companies.

5. The basic confusion among many accountants as well as nonaccountants of the preciseness of bookkeeping with the subjectivity of accounting theory, along with the non-auditor's misunderstanding of the real goal of the audit itself (i.e., satisfaction as to the overall general reasonableness of management's representations rather than a verification of the exactness of all data) has repeatedly led to broad dissatisfaction with the auditing and accounting profession. The result has been more and more needless (and futile) regulation. This confusion and misunderstanding has also led to a great increase in litigation involving public accountants, particularly large firms, which, in turn, gave them an understandable incentive to seek more and more specific rules.

6. The amazing growth of public accounting led to increased pressure to

---

*Some economists have even said that economics might be viewed as an extension of accounting necessitated by the complex societal relationships arising from the Industrial Revolution and the subsequent urbanization of the Western World.

maintain that growth and thus to competition among firms. This growth also led to the desire for more specific rules by public accountants since this would tend to lessen the "shopping" for favorable accounting practices by companies.

7.   There is a clear difference between the type of data concerning future operating plans a decision maker needs (management) and the type of data a judge of the wisdom of management's decisions (the potential investor/ creditor) needs.

8.   The significant increase in inflation in recent years increased the pressure (long sought with little success by academicians) for some form of recognition of its effect in financial data and statements.

With these points in mind, the following is offered for consideration:

FASB Should Be Reviewed

The orientation of the FASB should be given a full review. The review should start with the conceptual framework project. While it is not practical to suggest the abandonment of the entire project into which so much money has been sunk, its basic thrust towards a value-based system should be stopped.*
As we have seen, this debate about "value" versus "cost" was carried on through the 1930s, and the income statement orientation that resulted has served accounting and business too well to be abandoned now. There is no demonstrated demand for value-oriented data or the determination of income based on a comparison of balance sheets at the beginning and end of a given period. The revolutionary concepts implicit in the conceptual framework project are the product of a staff too strongly influenced by abstract theory and lacking in the practical application of managerial accounting.

Business is not alone in expressing this concern through such organizations as the Financial Executives Institute's Committee on Corporate Reporting. See, for example, "Accounting For 'What Might Have Been' " in the *Financial Executive,* September 1982. In this article, William J. Schrader and Robert E. Malcom, professors of Accounting at Pennsylvania State University, and John J. Willingham, a partner with Peat, Marwick, Mitchell & Co., note that "practicing accountants may wake up some not-too-distant morning to find their everyday livelihood revolutionized by the new accounting—accounting for 'what might have been'." They go on, "as a result

---

*Not all FASB members favor the trend toward a value-based system. Speaking at the 1982 International Conference of the Financial Executives Institute, John March voiced his opposition and concern.

of the FASB's Conceptual Framework project, historical accounting has been charged with lacking the key element of representational faithfulness. The authors believe the Concepts Statements issued to date are biased toward a shift away from historical costs, a view they feel is unjustified."

In considering a resolution to this issue, keep in mind that the balance sheet, in its customary public reporting format, is not widely used internally.* Instead, management will typically review only the portions related to every-day operations. Thus, the working capital position and debt-to-equity position will be monitored in conjunction with projections of future needs for funds both for working capital, capital expenditures, and dividends, all in light of the debt-to-equity position. The replacement cost or sales value of property, plant, and equipment are of little immediate concern except, when a liquidation or desirable merger appears to be preferable to continuing the present business. Of course, as we have pointed out, in many cases, the company's investors are "locked in" to their investment because neither the business nor the assets are able to give the prospect of a desirable return.

Need for Attestation Exists

The FASB should recognize that its basic reason for being is the very real need for the objective attestation of the results of operations reported by management to an absentee owner group and potential investor/creditor group. There can be no question that this need exists. The basic integrity of management is implicit in all financial reporting and in auditing itself; nevertheless, the natural exuberance of management can be carried to the extreme, as it was in the case of Datapoint Corporation. A sense of balance, needed in all things, is furnished by the independent public accountant in financial reporting. This need for balance should be reaffirmed by the FASB, rather than displaced by the emphasis on predictive data for investment decisions, which if pursued to an extreme could well lead to the loss of objectivity and relevance so badly needed in financial reporting.

The board's apparent rejection of the position that annual earnings per share be determined through the matching of costs and revenues with the balance sheet a repository for unallocated costs, seems rooted in a belief that management is able to (and does) manipulate earnings. In addition, they evidently view the balance sheet, with its collection of unallocated costs, as irrelevant, and wish to change this. Finally, they seem to desire to remove the board from political pressures by changing standards setting from a "rules of

---

*It should be noted that although income statements are universally used by management, the format is more likely to be by function (labor, material, scrap, etc.) than in a public reporting format.

conduct" approach to a "rules of measurement" approach that would conceptually be beyond the political process.*

The desire to avoid political pressure is futile, of course, and, with the exception of a major management fraud such as McKesson-Robbins, the "management of earnings" by accountants is a myth. Also, what is construed by many observers as "management of earnings" is usually simply an illustration of the subjectivity rather than the exactness of accounting. It is important to keep in mind that responsible management, including managerial accountants, has no quarrel with the FASB in this area, to the extent that there is an attempt by some managers to unfairly represent earnings. What we do object to is the wide use of the "managed earnings" label to describe all the subjective evaluations present in accounting and the apparent acceptance by the FASB of the pervasiveness of the "management of earnings" with the result that the basic accounting concept of the matching of costs and revenues is discredited.

The Balance Sheet

There is a much broader disagreement between managerial accountants and the FASB over the question of the relevance of the balance sheet, however. It should be clear by now that, in the author's opinion, most[†] managerial accountants believe that the *primary* function of accounting is to provide information for management pertinent to the daily operation of the business rather than to provide potential investors and creditors with data with which to make their investment choices.

The question of the significance of the balance sheet is also closely related to the value-based thrust of the board implicit in the conceptual framework project. As the board searches for Oscar Gellein's "anchor," it also seeks an investor-oriented, future-value statement.

There is no question that at least in the capital intensive industries, where

---

*David Mosso, a member of the FASB, expounded on this area of concern in a May 1979 speech before the University of California, Los Angeles, Conference on Regulation and the Accounting Profession: An Exploration of the Issues. After discussing three views of accounting standards—rules of measurement, rules of conduct, and economic incentives to promote national goals—he rejected the last, out-of-hand, but concluded that "the first view of accounting standards, as guides to accurate measurement, must be paramount. But it must be tempered by the second view, as restraints on unfair economic behavioral tendencies."

[†]As noted earlier, although no specific research is available that would give the positions of the majority of managerial accountants, based on the position papers filed by the representative organizations—the Committee on Corporate Reporting of the Financial Executive Institute and the Management Accounting Practices Committee of the National Association of Accountants—the deduction appears logical.

costs are accumulated over long periods of time in property, plant, and equipment, the balance sheets do not represent the "value" of those assets in today's dollars. Nor were they intended to do so under the matching of cost and revenues concept prevalent in financial reporting for the past 50 years or so.

Historical Cost Should Be Retained

Certainly there is a need for more comprehensive reporting beyond that possible in the audited financial statements. But before we consider the broader area, one point should be clear—historical cost is the proper base for audited financial statements. Professor Yuji Ijiri best expounded the position of the majority of managerial accountants (and perhaps many accountants in academia and public acccounting) in his 1981 monograph on the subject: "The key point in historical cost accounting is that prices are generated internally, based on accumulation of accountants' judgment on each of numerous exchanges that the entity actually participated in, whereas other valuation methods require accountants to go outside the entity and select prices from a global viewpoint of the economy. There is nothing wrong with taking the global viewpoint, except that it is very difficult to do so. That is why a decentralized system is widely adopted in business operations; it is, in fact, efficient even if theoretically a global optimum can be attained only by a centralized system.

"This process of constructing a cosmos of business operations from atomic exchanges is what is at the heart of historical cost accounting, and this is why it deserves Goethe's praise as one of the finest inventions of the human mind."[29]

Not only is historical cost the appropriate base, but there is a need for the FASB to return to a stronger orientation toward cash- and transaction-based data. The abstractions of interperiod tax allocation, leasing, foreign exchange, capitalization of interest and others objected to by the Small Practice Division of the AICPA bothers most of those practicing accounting.

Inventories and Property Are Problem Areas

This is not to say that accounting should not change. But the question is what needs to be changed? The fundamental quarrel with historical cost in an inflationary environment is essentially limited to inventory costs and depreciation expense in all material respects. This is true because the other assets such as cash, receivables, prepaid expenses, investments in securities (adjusted to the lower of cost or market) are of a short-term monetary nature and thus are always quite close to current value. The payables and accruals are also of the same nature. Of course, depending on the variability of interest rates, long-term debt can have implicit gains or losses that will be recognized as the debt is liquidated. Some would have this change reflected in income regularly rather than when realized, if it is realized, but this is not a major issue in reporting results of an enterprise.

The major issues being debated in the accounting profession are:

1 Is income overstated to the extent there is a mismatch of costs and revenues due to prior years' "old" costs, in the form of depreciation and inventory costs, being matched against current year's revenues, which are higher in part solely because of inflation, that is, changing prices?

2 Since the nonmonetary assets of a balance sheet are a collection of "old" costs from several years and only accidentally bear any relationship to their "values" the balance sheet has less significance than either the income statement or the funds statement. Should its significance be improved?

3 Does the mismatch of costs and revenues and the resultant over-statement of income result in management decisions that do not pre-serve the physical capital (the production capacity) of the enterprise? In short, are dividends paid out of "earnings" without regard to the failure of those earnings to reflect the cost of maintaining productive capacity?

Furthermore, this mismatch of costs and revenues and subsequent over-statement of income does result in higher income taxes being paid. These are valid questions and the accounting profession (including managerial ac-countants) must address them. Of course, the wide acceptance of the LIFO method of allocating inventory costs, particularly in the 1970s as inflation became the major economic issue in the United States, represented management's recognition of the inventory costing problem and the adverse effect it had on a company's cash flows.*

The government attempted to recognize the unfavorable effect on the nation's economy of taxing profits overstated by the mismatch of deprecia-tion costs and revenues in the 1981 tax law changes, notably the Accelerated Cost Recovery System (ACRS). Under this approach (nicknamed the "10-5-3 rule" because of the greatly shortened years over which the cost of buildings [10 years], machinery and equipment [5 years], and cars and trucks [3 years] could be recovered), the "useful life" concept of the applicable asset

---

*Keep in mind that for some companies, notably high-technology industries where costs decrease faster than the applicable inflation rates because of rapid technological changes in production, the FIFO method resulted in *lower* income tax payments, and these companies remained on the FIFO method.

was abandoned. Instead, recognition was given to the need to recover quickly the costs of longer-lived assets in an inflationary economy.*

However, the 1981 tax law changes were not nearly enough. The net income reported for financial statement purposes still is higher because of the mismatch of costs and revenues in an inflationary economy. Thus, pressure for higher dividends and wages remains. Although the use of LIFO corrects the inventory effect to a large degree, the accounting profession should study the entire concept of depreciation once again.

Depreciation Concept Needs Review

In a field where exactness and comparability are overemphasized, it is ironic that depreciation, which is one of the major costs of operation (and a major factor influencing the determination of income and comparability among companies), is determined by a variety of arbitrary† allocation methods subject to several greatly different definitions. In Statement No. 3 of Financial Accounting Concepts, the FASB reaffirmed the view of the old Accounting Principles Board that depreciation is defined as the systematic and rational allocation of costs to the periods in which benefits are received. No suggestion is given as to what would be "systematic and rational," however. In practice, this has been construed as "useful life" with the allocation of costs for a given year varying from the simple straight-line method to more complex methods such as decreasing charge (double-declining balance and the sum-of-the-years' digits), the activity methods (machine hours or use and units of production) or other special methods (group-life or composite method and the compound interest method). All of these approaches are based on the acquisition or historical cost of the asset. The assumption implicit in the allocation of that cost is that the revenue produced by the asset should be matched with a proportionate share of its cost.

Furthermore, although, as discussed, the pricing of a product or service is often independent of the cost, one of the factors used to test the reasonableness of the price should be the replacement cost of the asset used to produce

---

*In 1982, Congress backed away from the progressiveness of the 1981 changes as the economy failed to respond immediately to the impetus of the 1981 changes. Of course, this was a classic illustration of "short-term" thinking since the effect of the 1981 changes would take several years to appear. In all fairness, the proponents of the 1981 changes oversold its short-term impact.

†Eldon S. Hendriksen notes that "as pointed out by Thomas [Arthur L.], "The Allocation Problem: Part Two," *Studies in Accounting Research No. 9,* The American Accounting Association, Sarasota, Florida, 1974], the most serious difficulty with depreciation is that no allocation method is fully defensible." *Accounting Theory,* 3d ed., p. 388.

the product or service rather than the historical cost since ultimately the asset will have to be replaced out of the profits it earns.*

Finally, as we have noted, the depreciation allowed by the government as a deduction for purposes of calculating the federal income tax may vary widely from the annual depreciation expense used in the financial statements reported to the public (termed "book" as opposed to "tax" by most accountants). This is because the income tax laws are used by the government as an instrument to achieve what are deemed to be desirable national goals rather than a "systematic and rational" allocation. Since the government and U.S. accounting practice limits the total depreciation claimed for an asset to its original acquisition (historical) cost the differences between "tax" and "books" is only a matter of timing; that is, ultimately only the assets' acquisition cost will be used to reduce the income taxes payable. It is only a question of what year the tax will be paid.

This "timing difference" between depreciation allowable for income tax returns and that allocated for "book" purposes was the major reason the concept of interperiod allocation of income taxes was conceived. Theorists believed that "book" income should be charged with income taxes (defined as an "expense") normalized for these timing differences. As noted earlier, this was a classic illustration of the matching of costs and revenues concept. However, in issuing Opinion No. 11 (which required this "normalization") the Accounting Principles Board chose to ignore the concept of realization. The result was the creation of large amounts of deferred credits (or deferred charges in some cases) deemed to be income taxes payable or receivable eventually. No clear liability or receivable existed, however, and, as companies expanded and invested more money in property at higher costs, and thus were allowed more depreciation for tax purposes, it became evident that the cumulative deferrals would remain on the balance sheet indefinitely. Following the 1981 tax law changes, the FASB formed a task force to study the entire concept of income tax allocation, particularly since the FASB was

---

*Not everyone agrees with this conclusion, however. The *Accountant's Handbook*, 6th ed., vol. 1, noted that "depreciation is a factor in business planning because it is a deductible expense when computing income subject to taxation. For many business decisions, however, depreciation expense is considered irrelevant." Meigs, Mosich and Johnson's *Intermediate Accounting* is then cited: "Except to the extent that an existing asset can be sold and some portion of the past investment recovered, no present decision can change the amount of cost that has been sunk into that facility." Bierman's *Financial Accounting Theory* is then cited with regard to pricing: "The solution to the problem of output and price is solved without reference to any fixed cost. Because depreciation is generally considered to be a fixed cost, it is also excluded." (*Accountant's Handbook*, 6th ed., vol. 1, ed. Lee J. Seidler and D. R. Carmichael, John Wiley & Sons, New York, 1981, p. 22.4).

moving toward a more definitive balance sheet which would prohibit vague assets and liabilities.

The very concept of depreciation is also widely misunderstood by many analysts. Two of the most common errors are that "net income plus depreciation is the cash flow from operations" or that depreciation expense is a "source of cash."

In the former case, net income determined under the accrual method of accounting must be adjusted for *all* current noncash charges or revenues in order to arrive at the current year's cash from operations rather than just depreciation. This can be illustrated by the oversimplified example which follows, in which depreciation is eliminated from consideration through the substitution of rental expense.

Net income is the cash a company can reasonably expect to receive *ultimately* as the result of the transactions and activities it has engaged in over a period of time. Conceivably, it could sell shares in an enterprise, receive cash, incur debt, receive more cash, hire employees and buy materials, rent a building and equipment, manufacture a product, spend all its cash, make sales *all* on open accounts receivable, collect nothing on account, and report a profit for the period even though its net cash "flow" was zero. To carry this further, the company could cease manufacturing operations at the start of the next period, only collecting all its accounts receivable, and thus report *no* profit or loss for the second period even though its cash flow in that period equaled all of its original sale of shares, its debt, plus its profit for the first period. (I might add that this example is also representative of how many business managers define "income" rather than the net change in the estimated "value" of assets they do not plan to sell.)

In the case of "depreciation as a source of cash," the depreciation expense *allowed* for income tax purposes reduces a company's tax payment and thus 46% (the federal income tax rate) of the expense *will reduce* the cash outflow—to that extent cash will be higher than it would have been without the depreciation deduction.

Irrelevancy of Physical Capital

This raises the question of the preservation of physical capital (productive capacity). First of all, it should be stressed that the best interests of the stockholders, creditors, and management *may not* be served by some form of accounting that attempts to maintain the present productive capacity. Instead, it may be more appropriate to "harvest" the profits (and dividends) from a mature (i.e., no growth) product line and not replace its productive capacity. As we have seen earlier, many companies, such as General Electric, are doing just that. As Professor Eldon S. Hendriksen points out, "It is not the responsibility of the accountant to see that invested capital is preserved."[30] Instead, it is the responsibility of the managerial accountant to reasonably match the costs and revenues so as to be able to report the results of earlier business decisions in financial terms.*

The irrelevance of maintaining physical (productive) capacity with regard to the payment of dividends is also true in the question of the "value" of the nonmonetary assets (principally, property and equipment) in the balance sheet. It is a separate decision as to what product lines hold the best growth potential and which should be phased out or at least minimized, based on the evaluations of markets, competition, national and international economic conditions, and so forth (Chapter 6); the amounts carried in the balance sheet are irrelevant. Management can include in any evaluation the possibility of selling all or some of the company's assets without incorporating any "value"-based data in the accounting system.

However, if the combination of the concept of "useful life" and inflation results in a mismatch of "old" costs and "new" revenues, then perhaps the useful life concept should be abandoned. Certainly the 1981 "10-5-3" tax changes did just that. Instead, the changes in depreciable lives were termed an Accelerated Cost Recovery System (ACRS). Robert K. Mautz and Albert Koch proposed something along these lines in 1977 as a part of their lecture series on the conceptual framework referred to earlier. Under their approach, the depreciation expense would be indexed based on a given national index and thus be greater in periods of increased inflation.

LIFO and ACRS Would Correct Matching of Costs and Revenues

Of course, while the LIFO method and an ACRS depreciation method would correct much of the problem of matching costs and revenues in the income statement, the balance sheet would appear to suffer badly since it would become a presentation of nothing more than the monetary assets and liabilities (cash, receivables, and payables) and a collection of unallocated costs.

But this may not be a bad result. After all, it is the way that many businessmen view the balance sheet. In Chapter 6 we discussed the emphasis businessmen and managerial accountants place on projecting revenues, costs, and expenses, budgeting the projected income, and controlling the costs and expenses—all expressed basically through the operating (income statement) accounts.

---

*Professor Yuji Ijiri even argues that the two capital maintenance concepts converge in the ultimate theoretical world. See *Historical Accounting And Its Rationality,* Research Monograph No. 1, The Canadian Certified General Accountants' Research Foundation, Vancouver, British Columbia, 1981, chap. 7, p. 63.

Balance Sheet Would Have Two Parts

The balance sheet, on the other hand, is basically viewed in two parts—liquidity or cash sources and needs and unallocated costs. There is no consideration given to the balance sheet as a statement of values per se. (Of course, many businessmen in search of an acquisition, will analyze the stated book value, which is really the net unrecovered costs, in comparison to the market price of the company's stock, which reflects a host of factors real and imagined, and the businessmen's own evaluation of the future cash flow potential of the company, particularly if it holds physical assets such as oil reserves.)

The businessman is interested in cash flows just as the investor/creditor is. His management of the business reflects this. Thus, the great majority of businessmen use some form of cash flow analysis to evaluate the desirability of a capital project, be it the elementary "payback period" or the more sophisticated discounted cash flow rate of return.

Therefore, a balance sheet with property amortized under a form of write-off a great deal shorter than its probable "useful life," such as occurs under the ACRS, would fit into the concept of a capital project evaluation based on cash flows used by most businessmen.*

The transformation of the balance sheet to a basis more meaningful to businessmen would be further improved if the allowance for the LIFO deduction were shown on the right-hand side as a noncurrent deferred credit. Inventories would then be reflected at the most recent acquisition cost and the elements of working capital—cash, receivables, inventories, payables, and accruals—would then reflect the short-term effect on liquidity.

The third financial statement—the funds statement—would then correlate the net income and working capital (liquidity) needs with the flow of cash (and short-term securities).

All of the preceding would be further improved if the correlation of near-term cash flows to financial accounting were increased by the modification of those accounting standards that bear little relation to cash flows, an example of this is the aforementioned APB Opinion No. 11, "Accounting For Income Taxes," which requires complete normalization of the book (reported) income tax expense regardless of what the actual taxes paid might be.

What the author is striving for is to have the financial reporting reflect the manner in which businessmen manage their operations. If the accounting

---

*Professor Yuji Ijiri includes a discussion of the discrepancy between the way businessmen evaluate capital projects (cash flows) and the way accountants measure the project's actual performance (earnings under accrual accounting) in his monograph on historical cost.[31]

THE FASB AND THE CONCEPTUAL FRAMEWORK

"profession" (public and managerial) does not return to this approach, we will, as noted earlier in the words of Professor Henry Hill, "end up talking to ourselves." The emphasis in financial accounting and reporting should be on the income statement and the matching of costs and revenues, coupled with a return to a more basic cash/transaction orientation. The funds statement should gain recognition as being equal in importance to the income statement, whereas the balance sheet would rank lower.

EARNINGS PER SHARE AND RETURN ON INVESTMENT

A few comments are in order at this point concerning the widespread use of "earnings per share" (EPS) as the measure of an enterprise's performance. The FASB has been concerned with what they have perceived to be an overemphasis on one number. This is implicit throughout the conceptual framework project as it has reflected a trend away from an emphasis on EPS by the FASB. This is apparent in the change to the asset/liability view of income determination from the matching of costs and revenues view, discussed earlier. The introduction of "comprehensive income" in Statement of Financial Concepts No. 3, *Elements of Financial Statements of Business Enterprises,* reflects this trend also.

It seems apparent that if the comprehensive income definition were applied in full, we would be measuring comparative changes in the market value of net assets in order to determine net income—much as an economist might. Such an approach, which ignores cash flows and the concept of a "going concern" in favor of a measure of liquidation or "exit values," has no place in the financial accounting and reporting of an enterprise.

"Earnings per share" as the summary indicator became popular in financial reporting following World War II when the accounting profession settled on the matching of costs and revenues concept, expounded on in the 1940 Paton and Littleton monograph, as the appropriate goal of financial accounting.

Businessmen still use "return on investment" (ROI)* quite widely as a measure of performance. However, it is subject to many interpretations such as the "discounted cash flow method" used in analyzing investment alternatives or the "accounting method" or "mercantile rate of return" used to evaluate an enterprise's performance. Even the latter is subject to various applications. The ROI can be based on stockholders' equity or total capital,

---

*Much of this discussion on EPS and ROI is based on a piece written by A. M. Long, then comptroller of General Motors Corporation, "Return on Investment as a Measure of Financial Responsibility."[32]

including either long-term debt or all debt and even, in some cases, deferred credits such as unamortized investment tax credits. Finally, the base can be total assets. This is referred to as the "DuPont method" because of its originator. The DuPont method is widely used to evaluate divisional performance simply because most divisional managers cannot control their debt or equity capital but can, to a degree, control their total assets. The use of stockholders' equity as the base is usually preferred for overall enterprise performance because it comprehends a factor for leverage, that is, to the extent that debt is used in place of equity capital to finance the business, the return on equity will be higher.

However, partly because of the various interpretations of ROI, the use of EPS as a quick summary indicator of performance was popularized. Of course, the EPS is an integral part of the more complex ROI; thus a company's ability to show a steady growth rate in its EPS is considered to be an indication of management's ability to maintain a steady rate of return on the stockholders' equity. From this the investor can evaluate the degree of risk and the possibility of either a satisfactory (to him) return through dividends or an appreciation in the market price of the stock over the long term.

Of course, these are broad generalizations. The EPS can be affected by many factors including the dividend payout, the use of interest-bearing debt instead of equity capital, changes in the number of shares of common stock outstanding, the effect of a merger accomplished by a pooling-of-interests, and, of course, by inflation or disinflation. Nevertheless, the most common factor contributing to an increase in the EPS is the reinvestment of earnings, with the subsequent increase in the asset base, coupled with management's ability to continue to earn at least the same rate of return on the increased investment base. In short, the EPS is a fairly good overall summary indicator.

SUPPLEMENTAL DATA

However, although the preceding should be the basis for the reporting of results of operations and financial position by management, such reporting should not preclude management's furnishing supplementary data to be used for various purposes *if the need can be demonstrated.**

---

*After preparing the research report, *Reporting of Summary Indicators: An Investigation of Research and Practice* for the FASB in 1981, Paul Frishkoff concluded, "In general, there is little pressure for standard-setting action by the FASB. Nevertheless, education of users away from dependence on a single summary indicator (the earnings per share) is suggested. This research may also illustrate that users don't depend on accounting data for their future projection."

Professor Eldon S. Hendriksen has summarized the appropriate valuation concepts which might be used in an analysis of future cash flows.[33] However, a review of the "conditions where applicable" points up the basic problem of the reliability of all the concepts except the one related to actual transactions, that is, historical costs.

Valuation Concept	Conditions Where Applicable*
Exchange output values:	When reliable evidence of output values is available as an indication of future cash receipts.
1. Discounted future expected cash receipts or service potentials	1. When expected cash receipts or the equivalent are known or can be estimated with a high degree of certainty and when the waiting period is relatively long
2. Current output values	2. When current sales prices represent the future output price
3. Current cash equivalents	3. When the best alternative is orderly liquidation
4. Liquidation values	4. When the firm is not likely to be able to sell its product in the usual marketing channels or it is not likely to be able to utilize normal expected service values
Exchange input values:	When reliable evidence of output values is not available or as an indication of future cash requirements:
5. Historical cost	5. As a measure of current input value when acquired recently
6. Current input costs	6. When verifiable evidence of current input values can be obtained

*Assuming an objective of the prediction of future cash receipts or future cash requirements.

7. Discounted future costs	7. When future services of known or estimated costs are purchased in advance instead of being acquired when needed
8. Standard costs	8. When they represent current costs under normal conditions of efficiency and capacity utilization
9. Direct costing	9. When the asset could be produced in a future period without causing any increment in total fixed costs of the future period, or when the use of current fixed facilities will not increase future revenues
Eclectic concepts:	
10. The lower of cost or market	10. Inferior to all of the above concepts

Moreover, an even more fundamental question relative to the usefulness of these valuations must be, Who uses them? For unless there is a real need for the data, the preparation and distribution of the data are both needlessly costly and irrelevant. This was illustrated by the requirement of the SEC in 1976 for replacement cost data. Millions of dollars were expended by companies to comply with that rule, and no one has ever demonstrated that any constructive use was ever made of the data.*

We commented previously on the revolutionary aspect of Statement No. 33 of the FASB concerning the effect of inflation on financial data. The statement represented an innovative step by the FASB in that the data were supplementary rather than a part of the audited financial statements. However, from the standpoint of usefulness, it may have been as irrelevant as the SEC's replacement cost data.† Thus, in considering how financial reporting can be improved, the need must be demonstrated before the product is supplied.

---

*Paul Frishkoff reported that "securities prices and volume do not appear to have been affected by the release of the data required by (the SEC)." *Financial Reporting and Changing Prices: A Review of Empirical Research,* FASB, Stamford, Conn., 1982.
†Paul Frishkoff reported "that the market *may* have reacted to the *prospect* of (the standard)." Frishkoff, *Financial Reporting.*

Financial Reporting Versus Financial Statements

With this in mind then, the key to accomplishing the goal of improved reporting while maintaining the objective pragmatism of traditional accounting lies in the distinction between financial *statements* and financial *reporting.*

The reader may have noted that initially the studies done by the AICPA as far back as the 1932–1934 *Audits of Corporate Accounts* up to the Trueblood report in 1973 dealt with audited financial *statements.* Certainly the AICPA seemed locked in to the concept that all relevant financial data had to be included in the audited financial statements and accompanying footnotes. And until Statement No. 33, which may or may not have been relevant, the FASB too seemed to be bound to this idea.

SEC's Integrated Disclosure Program

However, the basic data needed to make an intelligent investment decision do not lend themselves to the format of the financial statement or an accounting presentation. The SEC recognized this in 1980 when it initiated its "Integrated Disclosure Program."

This program, a continuation of the commission's broad disclosure theme of the 1970s, represented a major shift in financial reporting. Up to then, companies prepared their financial statements in accordance with customary accounting practice and specific rules (GAAP), and then modified the reports as necessary to meet the technical filing requirements of the SEC. Then the companies had to be certain that the statements also conformed to GAAP. The result has been virtually the complete integration of companies' annual report to stockholders (usually a journalistic-style document) and the Form 10K (the legal document filed annually with the SEC).

However, even more far-reaching than this change was the introduction of the requirement for a "Management's Discussion and Analysis of Financial Condition and Results of Operations." Under this, a company's management is required to discuss in narrative form, rather than financial-statement-style, such matters as capital resources, liquidity, and future-oriented data such as "any known trends or any known demands, commitments, events or uncertainties which will result in or are reasonably likely to result in the registrant's liquidity increasing or decreasing in any material way."[34]

Although a review of the initial reports filed under this requirement would indicate a tendency toward generalities, the existence of such a requirement, which will evolve as time goes on, is revolutionary in the financial reporting field. The FASB may well have been "scooped" by the SEC.

The FASB made a feeble attempt to enter the "soft" data field with their

Invitation to Comment under the conceptual framework termed *Financial Statements and Other Means of Financial Reporting* issued in May 1980. This document was a tentative step toward recognizing that the really significant data relative to future cash flows (and thus highly relevant to the prospective investor/creditor) lay beyond the formal financial statements and footnotes. Such matters as population growth, mix, and trends, government fiscal and monetary policy, international tensions, energy supplies, and so on, could best be considered in a qualitative, narrative format and certainly were not subject to audit by independent public accountants simply because they were beyond their area of expertise.

Few of those in business would advocate specific forecasts of earnings simply because they cannot do such projections with anywhere near the accuracy that would be assumed by the outsider. However, many companies do discuss future plans regarding products and markets, capital spending programs, and research and development, and comment in general terms as to their ability to meet the various challenges of the future.

This area of "soft" data has apparently proven to be too soft for the FASB, and the subproject has become simply an exercise in what is called big GAAP versus little GAAP, that is, a debate as to whether private and/or small companies should be exempted from the more complex standards, such as leasing or interperiod tax allocation.

SHOULD THE FASB SERVE AS AN APPEALS BOARD?

However, let us consider a possible solution·to what some believe is the major point of contention between preparers of financial data and the standards-setters (and even the smaller public accounting firms)—the proliferation of over-specific as well as abstract rules. Public accountants have a very real problem with legal liability, which creates pressure for uniformity and specificity in standards.

As noted earlier, in a 1977 speech, David Mosso, an FASB member, described the present method of standards setting (rules of conduct) and compared this to the more desirable (in the board's view) method of viewing standards as rules of measurement:

> Rules of conduct call for a political process. Bargaining, horsetrading, log-rolling, clout—describe it as you will, it is a power game. The stake in the game is business income and the object is to report it when you want it. The stan-dards-setters in this environment try to write rules only when rules can't be avoided, and then to write them so the power is balanced. Balancing the power forces may lead to rules that favor a single interest group or it may lead to rules that create or preserve a stalemate. Logical consistency and economic reality

cannot be overriding objectives. Income determination is the image, political power is the reality.

Rules of measurement, on the other hand, call for a research process of observation and experimentation—a trial and error search for the dimensions of business income. The object is to report it when it is. The standards-setter tries to write rules that link the reporting of income to the period in which it arises. It doesn't matter whether the business is large or small, rich or poor, volatile or stable—if the income is there, report it, if not, don't.

Intellectually the case is compelling for viewing accounting as a measurement process and all accounting training in the English-speaking countries is geared to that view. But the history of accounting standards-setting has been dominated by the other view—that accounting standards are rules of conduct. The FASB was created out of the ashes of predecessors burned up in the fires of the resulting political process.

The clinker in the research approach is, of course, that income reporting is tied to objectively determinable events and measures. Debate is certain whenever the linkage between income creation and objective events is uncertain. The 'loser' of such a debate is always tempted to turn to the government for sustenance.[35]

Another "clinker" in the research approach is that there is a tendency to become too abstract and theoretical; the technocrats take over, and, in the absence of any real-world pressure, they establish more and more esoteric standards with little practical application.

In Chapter 3, we noted that Charles G. Steele, managing partner of Deloitte Haskins & Sells, commented on Mr. Mosso's last point and noted that companies will shop for what they want; hence, we are headed for more rules. Perhaps the best compromise between the prospect of more and more rules and "shopping for auditors"* would be to have the FASB function as an Accounting Appeals Court. In practice, any dispute between a company and its independent public accountant could be presented to the FASB, by either party, for a ruling. The ruling would be published and become a "case" under GAAP. No broad, mandated statement requiring everyone to comply whether there was any disagreement or not would need to be issued. If a company or an independent public accountant believed that they had a situation that conformed to the one covered by the ruling, they could consult with their auditor/client and follow the ruling if in agreement. This procedure is very similar to that of the judicial procedure and case law. Such

*The SEC recognized the undesirable qualities of such "shopping" and, in 1974, issued Accounting Series Release No. 165 which requires disclosure of the reasons for any change in auditors. This has not eliminated the problem, however.

a procedure could result in swifter action by the FASB since only a single specific problem would be ruled upon. The improvement in response time could well forestall the preemptive actions taken by the SEC from time to time.

Under this approach, a specific problem or dispute could be resolved without disturbing the accounting practices of thousands of companies that were not involved in the dispute. A corollary to this procedure would be disclosure of the accounting practices followed where alternatives exist.

Take, for example, the question of capitalization of interest. Some companies, notably those in the real estate field, argued that the interest costs associated with a longer-term construction project should be capitalized and amortized over the life of the project at completion. This, of course, would result in an appropriate matching of the revenues from, for example, a shopping center with the cost of constructing the center. Other companies, notably in the manufacturing field where the construction of an asset (building) is not the primary revenue producer itself, argued to the FASB that much of the construction involved the use of reinvested earnings and thus the related interest cost should be accounted for as a period cost. The FASB listened to the various parties and then voted (4–3) to require everyone to capitalize such interest, implicit or explicit.

The result has been an increase in record keeping with a negative benefit for most companies involved. This stems from the deterioration of the "quality of earnings" in the minds of the readers and analysts, as well as the seizure by the Internal Revenue Service (in 1982) of the concept of capitalization so as to increase taxable income.

Had this whole episode been handled as an appeal to an Accounting Court, the real estate people could have been granted their favorable ruling while the rest could have ignored the ruling as not applicable in their circumstances. Of course, the policy followed would have been disclosed in the footnotes.

Another major improvement that would alleviate the proliferation of rules is the specific identification of a perceived problem by the FASB. If, for example, before placing a subject on its agenda, the FASB would publish in a monthly (or quarterly) report the specific questions and/or problems that it had been requested to review, everyone concerned would be better able to focus on the issues. In such a report the FASB could identify the company, auditor, or other party who had raised the question as well as summarize the basic points involved, thus placing the problem in the specific rather than abstract form. Such a procedure would be in keeping with the FASB's "sunshine" rules and might even result in fewer questions being raised.

To sum up, there is no need for a conceptual framework of accounting beyond what has served the profession for nearly 50 years. Such a goal is illusory at best and would still fail to resolve the subjectivity of accounting even after such a framework as the FASB proposes is in place. Instead the FASB should return to the more traditional transaction-oriented determination of income through the matching of costs and revenues coupled with a more flexible approach to the establishment of accounting standards, which would result in better financial reporting of results of operations while keeping the cost of regulation within bounds. In the final chapter we will consider how this might happen and the role *all* accountants must play in accomplishing these goals.

REFERENCES

1. Michael O. Alexander, "The FASB's Conceptual Framework Project—After Eight Years, Is The End In Sight?" *FASB Viewpoints*, June 2, 1982.

2. *Journal of Accountancy*, July 1982, p. 14.

3. *Tentative Conclusions on Objectives of Financial Statements of Business Enterprises*, FASB, Stamford, Conn., 1976, paragraphs 8, 14, and 16. Copyright by Financial Accounting Standards Board, Stamford, Conn. Reprinted with permission. Copies of the completed document are available from the FASB.

4. Ibid., paragraph 2.

5. Ibid., paragraph 165.

6. *Scope and Implications of the Conceptual Framework Project*, FASB, Stamford, Conn., 1976, pp. 12–15. Copyright by Financial Accounting Standards Board, Stamford, Conn. Reprinted with permission. Copies of the completed document are available from the FASB.

7. Burton, Palmer, and Kay, *Handbook of Accounting and Auditing*, p. 8.

8. *FASB Conceptual Framework Issues and Implications*, Ernst & Ernst, Cleveland, 1977, pp. 3 and 4.

9. *Objectives of Financial Reporting by Business Enterprises*, Statement of Financial Accounting Concepts No. 1, FASB, Stamford, Conn., November 1978, paragraphs 27, 28, and 33. Copyright by Financial Accounting Standards Board, Stamford, Conn. Reprinted with permission. Copies of the completed document are available from the FASB.

10. Alexander, *After Eight Years, Is The End in Sight?*

11. Leslie Wayne, "The Corporate Raiders," *The New York Times Magazine*, July 18, 1982.

12. *Detroit Free Press*, July 11, 1982.

13. Bernie Shellum, "Stocks' Replacement Value Dictates a Surge, Some Say," *Detroit Free Press*, July 11, 1982.

14. Kripke, *The SEC and Corporate Disclosure*, pp. 330–331.

15. Statement of Financial Accounting Concepts No. 1, November 1978, pp. 3–4.

16. Statement of Financial Accounting Concepts No. 2, Financial Accounting Standards Board, Stamford, Conn., May 1980, p. 15. Copyright by Financial Accounting Standards Board, Stamford, Conn. Reprinted with permission. Copies of the completed document are available from the FASB.

17. Exposure Draft, Financial Accounting Standards Board, Stamford, Conn., November 16, 1981. Copyright by Financial Accounting Standards Board, Stamford, Conn. Reprinted with permission. Copies of the completed document are available from the FASB.

18. Statement of Financial Accounting Concepts No. 3, Financial Accounting Standards Board, Stamford, Conn., December 1980, pp. 12 and 13. Copyright by Financial Accounting Standards Board, Stamford, Conn. Reprinted with permission. Copies of the completed document are available from the FASB.

19. Alexander, *After Eight Years, Is The End in Sight?*

20. C. Wayne Alderman, Dan M. Guy, and Dennis R. Meals, "Other Comprehensive Bases of Accounting: Alternatives to GAAP?" *Journal of Accountancy,* August 1982, pp. 52–62.

21. Dean E. Graber and Bill D. Jarvazin, "The FASB–Eliminator of 'Managed Earnings'?" *The Financial Analysts Journal,* March/April 1979, p. 73.

22. Ibid., pp. 25 and 26.

23. *Sunset Review of Accounting Principles,* Technical Issues Committee Report, Private Companies Practice Section, AICPA Division for CPA Firms, 1982.

24. Henry P. Hill, "Rational Expectations and Accounting Principles," *Journal of Accounting, Auditing & Finance,* vol. 5, No. 2, winter 1982. V. C. Ross Institute of Accounting Research. New York University, New York, pp. 99–109. Reprinted by permission. Copyright © 1982, Warren, Gorham and Lamont, Boston, Mass. All right reserved.

25. Ibid., p. 99.

26. Stephen Zeff, Editorial, *The Accounting Review,* American Accounting Association, Sarasota, Florida, July 1979, p. 592.

27. Ibid., p. 593.

28. Maurice Mooritz, "The Intermediate and Advanced Financial Accounting Courses: A Suggestion to Authors and Publishers of Textbooks," *Accounting Education News,* American Accounting Association, Sarasota, Florida, May 1982.

29. Yuji Ijiri, *Historical Cost Accounting and Its Rationality,* Research Monograph No. 1, The Canadian Certified General Accountants Research Foundation, Vancouver, British Columbia, Price Printing Limited, 1981, pp. 83–84.

30. Hendriksen, *Accounting Theory,* p. 145.

31. Ijiri, *Historical Cost Accounting and Its Rationality,* pp. 69–75.

32. A. M. Long, "Return on Investment as a Measure of Financial Responsibility," in *The Corporate Accountants' Handbook,* edited by James Don Edwards. Dow-Jones Irwin, Homewood, Ill., 1976.

33. Hendriksen, *Accounting Theory,* p. 282.

34. Securities and Exchange Commission, Release No. 33-6349 and 34-18120, Washington, D. C., September 1980.

35. David Mosso, speech before the South Texas Chapter, FEI and San Antonio Chapter, Texas Society of CPAs, *Viewpoint,* FASB, Stamford, Conn., January 26, 1978. Copyright by Financial Accounting Standards Board, Stamford, Conn. Reprinted with permission. Copies of the completed document are available from the FASB.

eight

THE FUTURE OF ACCOUNTING

SUMMARY

Looking back over the seven chapters, what can we conclude? First, and perhaps most importantly, is that the "profession" is far broader than just the public accounting (auditing) sector so generally identified as the "accounting profession."

Second, we have observed that accounting's origins are ancient, dating back to the beginning of civilization. Implicit in this tradition are the concepts of discipline and transaction-orientation. However, as business and society became more complex, the need for more subjective, qualitative analysis arose. Furthermore, this need has never been met satisfactorily by accountants since they have tended to attempt to incorporate all such data into the basic discipline rather than expand the forms of reporting.

Third, we noted that the basic concepts underlying accounting evolved out of centuries of practice and that no comprehensive set of accounting principles covering all accounting practice exists. We have, however, seen that the discipline of accounting has proved to be a two-edge sword in that it has resulted in unreasonable expectations on the part of many users as to the absolute precision of all accounting data.

Fourth, we have seen that accounting theoreticians and economists have struggled with the concept of income and value as applied to the corporate entity form of business for all of this century. We have, however, observed that these questions were of no more than academic interest until the past decade when the U.S. inflation rate rose well above its historical rate. We have also observed that the relevance the theoreticians profess to seek for financial statements, through a value-based measurement system, may actually result in the loss of the true relevance of those statements, that is, their basic reliability which gives them the attestory quality. Nevertheless, we suggested that the problem of the differences between "economic values" and historical cost-based earnings and balance sheets could be resolved by some relatively slight changes in the concept of depreciation along with the expansion of reporting into qualitative analysis in a supplemental data sector.

Finally, we have concluded that, although the accounting and reporting system rests on the basic integrity of management, there is a need for a third-party attestation and some form of overall regulation of the reporting process.

FASB Should Continue to Function

Implicit in the discussion to date is that the Financial Accounting Standards Board will and should continue to function. From time to time the FASB and its governing body have sponsored or conducted surveys as to the effectiveness and acceptance of the FASB by the users and preparers of accounting data. These surveys have always been overwhelmingly positive. And yet criticism of the board continues. This paradox stems from the basic understanding by all concerned that the field of public financial reporting *will* be regulated either by the government directly or by a quasigovernmental group in the private sector. Overwhelmingly, those concerned with accounting prefer the latter; hence, the FASB has broad-based, fundamental support.

That is not to say that this basic support could not be lost. From time-to-time one hears the comment that the Securities and Exchange Commission is one of the most reasonable of government agencies, and it might be better to deal with them direct with regard to accounting and reporting standards. This feeling is, naturally enough, more common during the administration of a commissioner such as John Shad, who is concerned with regulation overload, than it is during the tenure of a commissioner such as Harold Williams, who was an activist, frequently providing answers before the questions were asked.

Regardless, there is no question that our nation does need some form of regulation of financial accounting and reporting. The basic question is, how can this be accomplished efficiently?

We discussed some fundamental changes that we believe could improve the credibility and quality of financial reporting. But how can the orientation of accounting as directed by the FASB be redirected?

MANAGERIAL ACCOUNTANTS AND BUSINESSMEN SHOULD BE MORE ACTIVE

The answer it seems is that the preparers and primary users of accounting data—the managerial accountants and businessmen—must take a more active leadership role in both improving the quality of the public financial reports and in communicating their goals and needs to their public accountants, educators, and the FASB. Typically, only a few score of letters are received by the FASB on an issue published for comment out of the thousands of businesses that will ultimately be affected by the proposed standards. If public hearings are held by the FASB, business will typically be represented by only a few companies. In many cases, the number of individual educators alone will exceed the companies' representatives, even though the representation from the education sector is relatively small. On the other hand, representatives of all of the major public accounting firms will usually appear. In all fairness, the Financial Executives Institute's Committee on Corporate Reporting, as well as the National Association of Accountants' Management Accounting Practices Committee, are represented at the hearings, as are a few trade councils.

Nevertheless, much more needs to be done by managerial accountants. No longer can we accept the FASB's apparent disclaimer regarding management accounting as being "beyond the scope of this Statement [Objectives of Financial Reporting by Business Enterprises].* Their actions *are* affecting management accounting, and although we certainly do not want them to begin issuing specific cost accounting standards, for example, we do want them to recognize the need to correlate the needs of management accounting and public accounting and reporting. As noted, the accounting profession is far broader than public accounting (auditing). In fact, most of the nearly 59,000 people who received undergraduate degrees in accounting in 1982 entered private industry, government, or education rather than public accounting which traditionally recruits about 30% of the graduates. About 6700 of the graduates will receive master's degrees, and over half of this group will be hired by public accounting firms.[1] In addition, just under half of the membership of the American Institute of Certified Public Accountants is no longer in public accounting.

The broader definition of the accounting profession is important because traditional accounting (i.e., for planning and control) is practiced by those in industry, not public accounting. This perspective is essential in considering

---

*Statement of Financial Accounting Concepts No. 1, p. 13.

the question of the regulation of accounting and the relevancy of the data being developed by accountants.

Dean John C. Burton of Columbia University (and former chief accountant of the SEC) wrote of the need to develop broad-based accountants. Although the thrust of his comments was directed to public accounting and his perception of the need for social activists, his comments concerning the education of accountants fit the entire profession.

> But both the reality and the image of accounting have had serious effects on the ability of the accounting profession to recruit young talent. Most of the outstanding students in our universities seek careers that promise an impact on society as well as a comfortable living. They tend to be attracted to the legal profession, which promises both. Within business schools, the best students seem to find consulting and investment banking more innovative. This is a tendency that must be reversed if accounting is to maintain and increase its role in society and ultimately its economic success as well. . . . the potential breadth of accounting must be recognized in the literature and in practice. Accounting should be seen as measurement and communication of results as related to goals. While accounting will probably remain quantitative, it need not stay tied to one dimensional measurement in financial units. It should include the talents of many disciplines and should be applied to many sectors of society.[2]

Public Accountants and Academia Should Join in Effort

Public accountants and those in academia should join in the effort to make financial accounting and reporting more relevant while maintaining its great tradition of discipline and objectivity. The Commission on Auditors' Responsibilities (The Cohen commission) noted in its 1978 report that "the ability of a learned profession* to fulfill its responsibilities is inextricably tied to the strength of its educational base." The commission went on to note, however, "the research effort of academic accounting has become almost totally devoted to matters other than auditing and the concerns of accounting practice; practitioners find themselves unable to relate to most published accounting research. At the same time, many academics view themselves as virtually excluded by the practitioners from the processes that determine the direction of financial accounting and auditing practice."[3]

*The commission was using the commonly accepted definition of the "profession," i.e., those certified public accountants in public practice, but the comments are even more appropos for those certified public accountants in private practice as well as the certified management accountants and others with advanced accounting degrees, i.e., the full "profession."

Professional Schools May Not Help

About the time of the commission's report (1978), the development of expanded professional schools and programs of accountancy began. The
American Assembly of Collegiate Schools of Business (AACSB) appointed
an Accreditation Planning Committee in 1978 to draft proposed accreditation standards for expanded accounting programs. The standards developed
provide for three accounting degree programs: baccalaureate, with a concentration in accounting; master's in business administration with a concentration in accounting; and a master's degree in accounting, this being part of
an integrated five-year program. Accreditation of an initial group of 18
schools was announced by the AACSB at its April 1982 meeting.[4] (A total of
231 schools presently hold AACSB accreditation at one or more levels under
the old standards.)

Although such a program would appear to be a major step toward resolving some of the problems we have outlined, some of us are skeptical that
the result might be to widen the gap between the practice of accounting in
industry and the development of reporting standards. Although it is far too
early to be sure, some people fear that the new professional schools will
primarily serve the auditing sector (public accounting) while the managerial
accounting ranks will be drawn more strongly from the graduate business
schools rather than accounting schools, thus exacerbating the gap between
managerial accounting (practice) and public accounting (auditing).

MAJOR ISSUES LIE AHEAD

Major issues face the accounting professional in the 1980s: At the FASB, the
conceptual framework project has progressed to the point where the major
issues as to recognition (of "earnings" and of "values") as well as the measurement base (historical cost or something else) must be faced. In addition,
the FASB will be struggling with the explosive issues of accounting for
pension costs, particularly, unfunded costs based on an employee's past
service, and also accounting for postretirement costs such as health and
insurance plans; consolidation theory (specifically the question of reporting
joint ventures and financing subsidiaries of a manufacturing company);
interperiod income tax allocation; and, of course, accounting for the translation of foreign currency financial statements.

Thus far, the FASB has operated in a relatively insulated manner with
little day-to-day interface with practicing managerial accountants. This approach has perhaps led to a more abstract, technical approach to standards-

setting. Managerial accountants must become more active in relating the everyday problems they face to the FASB. Managerial accountants are in a particularly good position to help resolve the challenges the profession faces. For the key to improving the relevancy of financial data while maintaining the objectivity of the audited financial statements is in the unaudited supplemental financial reporting mentioned earlier. Along with this type of data must go the recognition that one set of financial statements cannot possibly serve all the needs our sophisticated society has for financial data. The needs of a lending institution are far different from that of the speculative investor searching for a high-growth stock.

Supplemental Qualitative Analysis Is Needed

As noted in the previous chapter, the Securities and Exchange Commission recognized the need for qualitative analysis of operations, liquidity, future plans, and so on, in its requirements for management's discussion and analysis in 1981. Also, Statement No. 33 of the FASB concerning the effects of inflation was a significant step (though a too complex one) toward supplying relevant "soft" data by the FASB.

But business and managerial accountants must strive to expand and improve on this type of reporting. Without expanding into the area of quantitative forecasts of earnings, companies can furnish qualitative analyses of future capital programs, market analysis, and uncertainties in various economic assumptions, to name a few areas that would assist the potential investor or creditor in estimating the future earnings (cash flow) potential.

If the accounting profession—public, managerial, and academia—can retain the fundamental discipline and objectivity of traditional, cash/transaction-oriented accounting while building on a qualitative, analytic supplemental data sector, we can meet the challenges of relevancy and regulation.

REFERENCES

1. *Management Accounting,* August 1982, p. 20 and *The CPA Letter,* June 28, 1982.
2. John C. Burton, "Where Are the Angry Young C.P.A.'s?" *The New York Times,* April 13, 1980.
3. The Commission On Auditors' Responsibilities, *Report Conclusions and Recommendations,* New York, 1978, p. 85.
4. Keith Bryant, Jr., "Accounting Education," *Management Accounting,* New York, August 1982, p. 64.

NAME INDEX